In Search of the Whole

In Search of the Whole

Twelve Essays on Faith and Academic Life

John C. Haughey EDITOR

GEORGETOWN UNIVERSITY PRESS / WASHINGTON, D.C.

Library of Congress Cataloging-in-Publication Data

In search of the whole : twelve essays on faith and academic life /
    John C. Haughey, editor.
        p.   cm.
    Includes bibliographical references and index.
    ISBN 978-1-58901-781-8 (pbk. : alk. paper)
    1. Catholics—Intellectual life. 2. Christian college teachers—
Religious life. I. Haughey, John C.
    BX1795.I57I52 2011
    378'.0712—dc22   2011004080

∞ This book is printed on acid-free paper meeting the requirements of
the American National Standard for Permanence in Paper for Printed
Library Materials.

15 14 13 12 11   9 8 7 6 5 4 3 2 First printing

Printed in the United States of America

In memory of Peter Winter, friend and benefactor

Contents

Preface

Like clouds, no two of us human beings are exactly alike. This volume bears eloquent witness to this. As one reads the different chapters in this volume, one will marvel at the distinctiveness of each consciousness, at how subjectivities are even more sui generis than our unique sizes and shapes and other physical characteristics. Although not everyone is gifted at plumbing interiorities and putting them on paper, the twelve writers here certainly are. The result is a coming together of twelve highly defined individuals whose rich self-disclosures address the same question, one that had not been posed to them before I asked it: What is the *whole* you are seeking to name, confect, be?

This question had its genesis in a discovery I made and articulated in *Where Is Knowing Going? The Horizons of the Knowing Subject*.[1] Data for that study came from deeply listening to some two hundred academics address a prior question about the good they are seeking to do with their growing academic competence. I discovered that the common note in their work was making wholes.

The two hundred people were taking pieces and putting them together to make meaning, connect dots, get incoherences to cohere. The point goes beyond Aristotle's primary insight that human action is generated by a good to be done. The good when aggregated by behavior makes a virtue, when articulated by minds makes a whole. Whole-seeking, whole-making, is what the twelve authors in this volume do with what otherwise is left disassembled. Seven of them were members of the team I brought together to help me think through that first volume. The other five are equally entrepreneurial, so I invited their entries.

Subjectivity, consciousness, interiority—whatever you want to call it—tends to be all over the place most of the time in most of us. But it is also always questing. Readers who are aware of this in themselves—that is, that their consciousness functions in anticipation of wholes—will be enriched by learning their similarity to these authors. We are wired to be unidirectional.

I like the way the twentieth-century genius Bernard Lonergan often put this: There is an anticipation of an entirety in our seeking, thinking, choosing.[2] Three strands are woven together in our subjectivities: One looks for being, the second for value, and the third for meaning. Together these three strands get very particular in this volume, as each author produces a unique determination of a sought-for "entirety."

Readers will see immediately that none of the twelve authors here repeats anyone else. But after reading any selection readers will see how this pattern of anticipating an entirety emerges from each author. This similarity alone was justification enough for putting this book together. But each chapter is also a stand-alone essay, a mini-education worthy of attention in and of itself. One of the sad consequences of our information age seems to be an inability to be attentive to the wealth of subjectivity we are in the midst of but seldom come to relish.

Peter Steele has a more picturesque way of saying what I have said above. He speaks of his attraction to "finished things" or to "the manifestly coherent," in contrast to unfinished, incoherent things. He further observes Catholic Christianity's "propensity for divining and discerning coherences, its stress on the way in which this answers to that, within this world and between this and another world."

Each of these twelve chapters is a finished thing. Each author makes a whole where there wasn't one, displaying how "this answers to that." Each is an autobiographical account of an intellectual conversion. For some it is an account of a personal identity; for others it is an account of the whole they are trying to birth for the sake of others, for society at large.

Patrick Byrne is a philosopher whose essay weaves his personal narrative around an idea that has transformed his view of the universe and his philosophical work. Lonergan's theory of emergent probability has been key to Byrne's work. It is an idea quite different from Charles Darwin's insights into evolution. Byrne weaves together his three passions for science, justice, and religion into a synthesis that is remarkably whole.

Cynthia Crysdale has a tale to tell about Catholicism that is more interesting because she tells it as an observer from her perch within two Catholic institutions, first with St. Michael's University in Toronto, Ontario, and then with The Catholic University of America in Washington, DC. It is the more insightful because she is an *amicus curiae* rather than a member of the Roman Catholic Church. Influenced by Lonergan and by Sharon Welch's ethic of risk, Crysdale's wisdom describes the difference between a religion that seems to have it all together and one that is attentive to the process of the self-appropriation of the learner.

Robert Deahl's chapter has one foot in his own interiority and the other in his vocation as an administrator of an educational culture where personal transformation is emphasized. He covers the main personalities and insights that have enabled him to come to understand what is entailed in wholeness in education, both his own and the education of others that he is responsible for overseeing. Combining Lonergan's method with a "central integrating thought" of a Buddhist master, he spells out his wholistic philosophy of education.

William George has been gnawing on a bone, the Law of the Sea, for some time, and we are all the wiser for his labors on the subject. He elaborates on how that subject matter first hit him in the Regensburg Library at the University of Chicago and where it has taken his insights since that day. The faculty and administration at Dominican University and many of us who have known him and read his work can testify to the value of his ponderings about this way of anticipating the possibilities of international law.

Richard Liddy's personal narrative takes note of how the classics of Catholicism have shaped him. He compares the similarities and differences between these earlier classicist works and the later historically conscious, more symbol-sensitive ones. An understanding of the wisdom of the Catholic intellectual tradition emerges from his analysis. His piece ends with how he conveys his appreciation of this tradition to faculty at Seton Hall.

Michael Stebbins did his doctoral work in systematic theology, a specialization that tries to make a whole out of the different mysteries of Christian faith. How he gets from these to assisting businesses in their efforts to develop patterns of cooperation and an ethics of achievement is a page-turner. He elaborates specific steps that those who are in business might take, but the chapter can be a delight for a nonbusiness person to read.

Michael Amaladoss is dealing not with an academic subject in his chapter but rather with his own contextualized self-understanding as a Hindu-Christian. How he developed this sense of his own religious identity leads to an autobiographical essay that I believe could become a classic in interreligious understanding. This Jesuit director of the Institute of Dialogue with Cultures and Religions in Chennai, India, gives one a sense of the deeply personal character of the wholes we are able to become.

Ilia Delio, a Franciscan nun, discusses two authors who have helped her find her own voice. Her immersion in St. Bonaventure and Teilhard de Chardin has led her to go where they did not go, because she is not they. She exhibits the dynamism of the Catholic intellectual tradition, especially when it speaks to the heart and with prayer is sufficiently schooled in the old to produce a credible new Christology.

Patrick Heelan encapsules the quality of inimitability for those of us who have come to know him. He has been under the tutelage of some of the twentieth century's giants in the fields of science and mathematics for much of his life. One of his interests within his field, which is the philosophy of science, has focused on perception. How he understands Van Gogh's painting *Bedroom at Arles* is a tantalizing example of how the wholes we confect have both our own subjectivity and the object to thank for the resulting perception.

Michael McCarthy elaborates his personal journey beginning with the *aggiornamento* of John XXIII and the Second Vatican Council. Having been an undergraduate at Notre Dame, a doctoral student at Yale, and finally a professor of philosophy and an administrator at Vassar, McCarthy shows concretely how both Lonergan and Charles Taylor enabled him to understand both himself and Catholicism in terms of the challenge of the intellectual conversions that are entailed.

Peter Steele despairs of describing himself in life-sized terms and chooses instead to speak of himself through a few poems that "are the holy spaces of my life." His gift for poetry and for the right word, conveyed with joy and simplicity, makes his words a holy space, indeed an "affair of the Spirit." He describes himself as having been "a congenital scribbler" even before he went to college. He also confesses that all his life he has been "God-haunted" and a "God-hunter."

Finally, Cristina Vanin is a devotee of the recently deceased Thomas Berry. She is a worthy successor of Berry in how she carries on his sense of "the great work" of the present generation of human beings: to be present to the planet and its multiple life-forms in a mutually beneficial manner. She does this through her writings and retreat work and through the witness of her own lifestyle for all who know her.

Notes

1. John C. Haughey, *Where Is Knowing Going? The Horizons of the Knowing Subject* (Washington, DC: Georgetown University Press, 2009).

2. Bernard Lonergan, *Insight: A Study of Human Understanding*, ed. Frederick E. Crowe and Robert M. Doran, Collected Works of Bernard Lonergan 3 (Toronto: University of Toronto Press, 1992), 396.

PART ONE

Whole as Task

CHAPTER I

Wholeness through Science, Justice, and Love

Patrick H. Byrne

A Passion for Science

For as long as I can remember, I have loved science. Even before I knew that science was the category, I loved learning about the universe and just about everything within it. I think I was probably born with this love, but I was also fortunate to come of age in the late 1950s and 1960s, when science permeated the cultural atmosphere around me. The United States was then engaged in a great romance with science, and there was a rich and steady flow of scientific writing to stimulate my passion for learning about the natural world. Scientists were constantly making discoveries and breakthroughs, and I read about them with eagerness and excitement.

One of my first memories of scientific wonder came in elementary school. A relative of one of my classmates loaned a collection of stuffed birds to our class. There must have been fifty or more species of birds represented in that collection—a male and a female of each species. If we finished our assignments early, we were allowed to examine the collection, even to carefully handle the individual birds. I spent hours enraptured by these wonderful creatures. I marveled at the differences in colorings and feather types, and I wondered why the males were so different from the females in most species but quite similar in a few cases. I was fascinated by their legs, claws, beaks, breasts, and wings.

Soon I began to check out library books about science. I remember one book in particular about the then deepest descent into the ocean in a bathysphere. The author described very strange creatures that lived at such depths. My imagination went to work trying to put shape and color to the descriptions in that book. Some of my images were close to, and some quite far from, what I later saw in photographs of these creatures. But my imaginative exercise took me into the realm of the unknown, and I found it tremendously enticing.

I was not yet asking why there were so many different kinds of birds or sea creatures or why they had the features they did. Nor was I yet asking what made all those birds be *birds*, despite their being so dramatically different from each other. My wonder had not yet developed into scientific wonder. But my scientific wonder grew from this intoxicating dialogue with the marvels of nature.

It was in this context that I discovered my vocation to be a teacher. In one of my elementary school classes I had been assigned a presentation on one of the science units. After I finished my presentation, my teacher said, "That was very good. You should think about becoming a teacher." With barely a moment's hesitation I said, "I think I will." I had never considered being a teacher before. I have no idea why I responded so spontaneously. Somehow, what my teacher said just seemed to fit. I have been blessed throughout my education with a great many inspiring teachers who continually nourished that initial decision. What I would teach, to whom, how, and where—these were further questions that I had to answer. My answers have changed several times since then. But from that moment on, I never wanted to pursue any other profession.

Although my earliest memories of being drawn toward science pertained to the wonders of animals, the world opened up by the science of physics eventually became the more powerful attraction. I had a very talented physics teacher who communicated his love for the subject with examples and humor. He also drew upon recent educational innovations that made it possible for us to be creative in the investigation of scientific phenomena. We were encouraged to use very ordinary objects such as wooden blocks, roller skates, doorbells, and balloons in creative combinations to study such phenomena as accelerated motion, free fall, temperature, and gas laws.

At about the same time I was also becoming intrigued by rockets. I thought about where they might take me and what might be there to discover. I read about what scientists knew of the planets in our solar system and the stars in the universe, and about the many questions they still pondered. As I was growing up, it seemed that astronomers almost daily were discovering different kinds of galaxies, stars, and quasi-stellar objects. They were making discoveries that they did not know how to explain, and it amazed me that scientists could make observations that defied any explanation yet devised.

Some of these phenomena did have explanations—such as the redshifts of the spectral lines from distant stars. I learned from my teachers and my reading that redshifts happened because space itself was expanding. "Expanding into what?" I wondered. I read books that provided imaginative analogies, such as the movement of spots painted on the surface of an expanding balloon. I could understand how these spots moved apart as the two-dimensional balloon's surface expanded into three-dimensional space. But how could space itself expand? I could not picture this, but I wanted to be able to do so.

I also came to wonder about the smallest things in the universe—elementary particles. I learned about the structure of atomic nuclei, how they are composed entirely of either neutral or positively charged particles (neutrons and protons). These particles are packed so unimaginably close to one another in a nucleus that the mutual repulsions among them would have to be immensely powerful. I could not figure out why they do not fly apart. Further reading informed me that the secret had something to do with other elementary particles, and that new ones were being discovered constantly. One of them, the positron, was predicted before it was discovered. It was originally conceived as an electron with negative kinetic energy. How could there be an actual concentration of negative energy in a tiny bit of space? Taken together, these strange elementary particles were almost as numerous as the different atomic nuclei they were supposed to explain. And they disintegrated into one another! What did "elementary" really mean after all?

These and many other images and questions percolated in my mind during my school years. I set off for college to study physics and learn the answers. In addition to courses in physics and mathematics during my first year of undergraduate studies, I also had my first encounter with philosophy. Here were thinkers who were wondering about the same things I wondered about—the largest and the smallest realities. Not surprisingly, Plato and Socrates made the first big impression on me. I was amazed to discover that they had thought about these questions and had profoundly intelligent answers—and that they lived thousands of years ago. (Like most adolescents I assumed that the dawn of human intelligence occurred somewhere around the time of my birth.) I would go to the dorm rooms of my classmates and say, "Can you believe these guys were thinking all this way back then? This is incredible!" They looked at me as a droll fellow, wondering how anyone could get excited about philosophy.

Undaunted, I looked forward to the day when I could take the course on the philosophy of science offered at the university. But when I finally did, I was sorely disappointed. Although a great transformation was about to occur in that field, most of the course was dedicated to the approach of logical positivism (advanced by the Vienna Circle, the Berlin Circle, and their successors). To greatly oversimplify, in this approach science was taken to be a matter of empirical observation, formal logic, and rigorous deduction. The heart of science was taken to be abstract universal laws and theories. Scientists deduced individual observational statements from the theoretical statements. They then set out to determine if these observational statements were true by making sensory observations. Really good theories yielded true deductions covering large ranges of observed phenomena. Less noble theories explained fewer observations or, worse yet, were contradicted by observations.

Hans Reichenbach, founder of the Berlin Circle, was one of the leading figures in this approach to the philosophy of science. He articulated a famous and highly influential distinction between "the context of discovery" and "the context of justification."[1] The context of justification is the context of observation, logic, and truth. Real scientists and real philosophers, so this approach claimed, are dedicated to the logical pursuit of truth. They are dedicated to fiercely testing and justifying (or discrediting) any hypothesis that cannot compete in the survival of the fittest ideas. The context of discovery is "left to psychological analysis."[2] According to this view real scientists and real philosophers leave it to psychologists and historians to determine plausible explanations of why famous people come up with their ideas. Those ideas might be caused by what they had for breakfast, their genes, their family psychodynamics, the deeply entrenched beliefs of their cultures, and so on. But no amount of study in the context of discovery could tell whether the idea itself is true. That was considered the work of the real scientist and the real philosopher. They have their sleeves rolled up and go to work where the action is.

The picture of science presented in this approach had very little to do with the adventures in inquiry and discovery that had drawn me into science and that provided recurring epiphanies during my advanced classes in physics, mathematics, or philosophy. Of course, I was well aware of the fact that observation and logic played roles in science; but in my experience these roles were always secondary. Logic helped to clarify and refine bright ideas and to reveal flaws in them. But how logic was put to use depended upon discoveries. Without discoveries, logic was just a lifeless engine awaiting a spark that would set it in motion. The deterministic universe envisioned by this logical edifice was just as lifeless. Subtly and not so subtly, I was being taught that the discoveries I had read about and experienced myself were to be ignored as irrelevant to the philosophy of science. (Later I would learn from Bernard Lonergan that discovery versus justification is a false dichotomy. As he put it, we need "a flow of insights [discoveries] to have a single judgment [justification].")[3]

It was against this background that I first encountered Lonergan's work *Insight*. It spoke to my own experiences of science as nothing else had. The opening page made it clear that Lonergan was intimately familiar with the passion for scientific discovery: "Our first instance of insight will be the story of Archimedes rushing naked from the baths of Syracuse with the cryptic cry, 'Eureka!'"[4] This philosopher was on to something, and I really wanted to find out what that something was. Lonergan's initial descriptions of insight struck familiar chords: Insight comes "suddenly and unexpectedly" and "as a release to the tension of inquiry."[5] The tension of inquiry had been my constant companion, if not a friend. Many times I had walked around for days, nagged by a problem from my physics or mathematics homework. I would try every technique I could think of, but nothing led to the solution. Then, usually when I thought I had shoved the problem out of my mind, "suddenly and unexpectedly" something would leap out, and I would understand how to solve the problem.

Lonergan also showed me how to pay attention to what that "something" was: "The image is necessary for the insight."[6] I hadn't noticed that, but now

I realized that Lonergan was right. The keys to solving problems and making discoveries in science have to do with imagination. Sensory observations and data are indispensable in science, but they are not the whole story. Novel observations present new problems and puzzles for explanation; but breakthroughs to those explanations almost always require novelties of imagination that go even beyond novel observations. Scientists frequently tell of such episodes of creative imagination. One of the best-known accounts comes from the chemist Friedrich August Kekulé, who discovered the structure of the benzene molecule:

> I was sitting writing on my textbook, but the work did not progress; my thoughts were elsewhere. I turned my chair to the fire and dozed. Again the atoms were gamboling before my eyes. This time the smaller groups kept modestly in the background. My mental eye, rendered more acute by the repeated visions of the kind, could now distinguish larger structures of manifold conformation; long rows sometimes more closely fitted together all twining and twisting in snake-like motion. But look! What was that? One of the snakes had seized hold of its own tail, and the form whirled mockingly before my eyes. As if by a flash of lightning I awoke; and this time also I spent the rest of the night in working out the consequences of the hypothesis.[7]

Though my insights were less momentous than Kekulé's, I realized that I similarly made discoveries when novel images led to insights that released my tensions of inquiry.

So Lonergan's initial descriptions fit experiences with which I was already familiar; but his expanded descriptions made me aware of ways in which I had been thinking without paying much attention. Something else was also happening: I was beginning to notice that the familiar experiences (the tension of inquiry and the occurrences of insights) were more frequent than I realized. They were occurring at times and in contexts that I had not previously noticed. I was initially drawn to Lonergan's philosophy because it resonated with my prior experiences. Soon, however, Lonergan's philosophy was leading me to discover new and unexpected things about myself.

The fact that Lonergan's philosophy leads into unfamiliar territory is the source of a common complaint about his book *Insight*. Many times I have heard it said that it is a book written for scientific minds, not for ordinary minds. Nevertheless, I have also spoken with a great many readers of *Insight* who came to it with scientific backgrounds. They are just as bewildered. Even though the early chapters abound with topics from mathematics and natural science, Lonergan speaks about these topics in ways that are just as unfamiliar to those with scientific training as they are to those without that training. The reason for this, I believe, is that in order to understand what he is saying about science, the scientist has to venture into the unfamiliar territory of the scientist's own mind. What makes this especially difficult is that the scientist will eventually be faced with the fact that, according to Lonergan, he or she is driven by an intellectual inquiry that knows no bounds. Scientific inquiry desires to know everything about everything, but this radical openness at the heart of all real science is easily overlooked. To actually know something about something, scientists have to specialize—as I myself had begun to specialize in physics. Still, that specializing can lose its claim to being truly scientific, if it loses touch with the deep, unrestricted, inquiring spirit that is the foundation of science. Although I initially understood very little else of what Lonergan had written, I did understand these fundamental points, because they spoke so profoundly to my own experiences of involvement in science.

There was one other idea, however, that I also comprehended in my first reading of *Insight*, and it has paid rich dividends over many years. Lonergan's idea of emergent probability struck me as an ingenious philosophical theory, one that transformed my vision of the universe. In a sense, emergent probability is a kind of evolutionary theory, but one dramatically different from the mainstream legacy of Charles Darwin (although Lonergan had great respect for Darwin). Where most evolutionary theories focus upon the emergence of new things—whether stars, planets, plants or animals—Lonergan focuses upon the emergence of whole environments. The "plant or animal is only a component. The whole schematic circle of events does not occur [only] within the living thing, but goes beyond it into the environment."[8] These circles of events emerge and function regularly only when the right conditions occur, just as insights emerge only once the right images arise. For example, protons and neutrons emerge only after the conditions present in the initial plasma of the earliest phase of the universe change to a cooler state. Again, elementary metabolic pathways could emerge only after many sets of conditions were fulfilled; stars, for example, had to undergo supernova explosions that fused the nuclei of elements such as carbon, nitrogen, and oxygen. Further conditions had to occur that favored the coalescence of these nova remnants into planets. At least one such planet, the Earth, had to cool and to revolve just close enough to and yet far enough from the sun. For oxygen-breathing life circles (like our own) to emerge, ancient anaerobic organisms had to expire oxygen into the atmosphere as a by-product of their living.

Two thoughts most struck me about Lonergan's theory of emergent probability. First, it was a radically nondeterministic view of the universe. For Lonergan the universe is "upwardly yet indeterminately directed."[9] The universe does not follow any systematic metanarrative in its unfolding. It is a universe with a real future. There is real emergence, true fertility, genuine novelty. This is a theory of the universe as not yet whole but nevertheless as dynamically headed toward an undetermined wholeness. That wholeness is presently being worked out by the dynamics of the universe itself, but it is presently beyond human prediction or comprehension. The second thing that struck me was that Lonergan had fashioned his theory of emergent probability from the very sciences that had for centuries been regarded dogmatically as proof of a materialistic and closed, deterministic universe. He accomplished this by noticing an "oversight of insight" and by meticulously following the implications of restoring these lost insights.[10] Lonergan was able to make this argument in an unprecedented way by paying careful attention to the ways scientists have introduced statistical methods and made them so pervasive a feature of their work. His deep intellectual curiosity about this development, and his relentless search for its meaning, led him to articulate his unique vision of the dynamic wholeness of the natural universe.

Lonergan extended his analysis to a vision in which the upward dynamism of the very universe itself emerges into human beings as "a conscious tension," the tension of unrestricted wonder about everything.[11] In short Lonergan envisioned a universe that is hospitable to human wonder and creativity, especially the creativity of dramatically new scientific discoveries. It would take many years of reading and rereading Lonergan's work for its wholeness to draw me in. But I was hooked.

My interest in science eventually led me to a doctoral dissertation and later several publications on the relationship between Albert Einstein's scientific work and his philosophical reflections on science. I was especially intrigued by Einstein's famous resistance to the statistical character of quantum mechanics. (In this regard he is often quoted as having said "God does not play dice!") I was surprised, therefore, to learn of his numerous significant contributions to statistical physics. My further studies of Lonergan's thought gave me a critical perspective on the paradox of this major scientist who was a master of statistical physics and yet rejected its implications.

My encounters with Lonergan's thinking about science also influenced my teaching in profound and rewarding ways. Under the auspices of a grant from the National Endowment for the Humanities, I worked with an interdisciplinary team of mathematicians, physicists, biologists, chemists, and philosophers in developing the mathematics-science curriculum of Boston College's well-regarded Perspectives in Western Culture program. This curriculum approaches undergraduate scientific education by emphasizing key moments of discovery in the history of Western science. Because of my studies of Lonergan's reflections on science, I was able to convince my colleagues of the importance of incorporating a unit on the rise of statistical methods in the natural sciences and the role of this development in transforming our vision of the universe. In addition to exposing students to the scientific discoveries of famous scientists, the program's pedagogy is also structured so as to guide students to become ever more refined in their observations of natural phenomena, and to awaken their wonder and inquiry about the new things that they come to notice. As a result, not only do our students learn about the discoveries of great scientists, but their learning is also cultivated in the spirit of careful scientific observation, inquiry, and insight. The very things that made science so exciting for me have now been explicitly incorporated into the scientific education of our students.

A Passion for Justice

Science was not my only passion. I was also passionate about justice and religion. Yet for many years the three passions ran along quite independent of one another. Although I was drawn to all three, I saw no way in which they had anything to do with one another. Still, I was also dimly aware that I wanted them to be connected. I desired some integration of these passions, without any reason to think that this was at all possible.

My passion for justice grew out of my father's example. His Irish heritage was most evident in his passion for telling and retelling stories. He would tell his three sons endless stories about growing up, school, church, his days in the marine corps, work, even his love for our mother. Among the many stories that affected me, one in particular stands out. I was very young when he first told us the story about an incident that occurred when he was stationed in California during World War II. He was walking along the sidewalk and noticed an African American couple—a navy ensign and his wife—standing outside a tavern and looking quite distressed. My father approached them and asked if there was a problem. The ensign told my father that the owner of the tavern had refused to serve them because they were black. My father's Irish temper flared at the indignity that another man like himself, prepared to sacrifice his life for his country, should be treated so unjustly. He went into the tavern and confronted the owner, who still refused to serve the couple. My father then ordered a round of drinks (and then a second) and went out on the sidewalk to socialize with the ensign and his wife.

In the grand order of things, this was a small incident, but it had a very powerful impact upon me. I strove to live up to my father's example. When I arrived at college I became involved in tutoring children who were consigned to inferior schools in a segregated urban school district. This initial involvement led to other activities, including civil rights and antiwar demonstrations. As with so many of my generation, a passion for justice and an optimism about changing the world gave way to frustration and impatience, and then to anger and rage. Aristotle says that anger is the emotion that feels injustice. I had that part down pretty well; I had become an angry young man.

But Aristotle also observes that "it is not easy to determine in what manner, with what person, on what occasion, and for how long a time one ought to be angry, and at what point right action ends and wrong action begins."[12] Anger at injustice needs to be tempered. It is only tempered when it is made part of a greater whole: "Justice is *complete* virtue."[13] Righteous indignation is indeed a virtue, but it is only one virtue. It needs to be integrated with other virtues: courage, gentleness, generosity, wittiness, and wisdom, both practical and theoretical. Authentic justice is a matter of wholeness.

This was a lesson I needed to learn. I did not realize for quite some time that my forceful passion for justice had gradually distorted me into an unjust person. I had become a person who was not capable of justice where I was most likely to achieve results. The area where I had the greatest likelihood of doing the work of justice was in my concrete effects upon the people I encountered from day to day. This was the work of justice and peace that my mother carried on in our family, in our community, and in our church. This was the work of justice in that small kindness that my father had performed, the one that had inspired me originally. This is the work that really does build up the wholeness that Martin Luther King Jr. called "the Beloved Community."[14] But my attention was turned elsewhere. This was a work of justice that utterly escaped my notice as an adolescent male. The big and difficult lesson that I needed to learn came when I received a deeply personal letter from my father, a letter that made me confront who I had become. For me this was the moment of what Lonergan calls "moral conversion."[15] That moment was a tentative new beginning; but how I should go about becoming more whole in virtue was very unclear. Although many people, including parents and teachers, would be instrumental in helping me along this path, Lonergan's contributions were also quite important.

Until the discovery of his early writings after his death, almost none of those who studied his published works realized that Lonergan too had shared a passion for justice.[16] In the light of these early writings, his social theory in *Insight* takes on a whole new meaning. His reflections on science and the evolution of natural environments (emergent probability) were brilliant in themselves, but they also set the stage for a theory of emergent justice. Not only in nature, but also in human affairs, genuine advance happens when new "schematic circles of events" emerge.[17] In the human realm, such schemes emerge because of intelligent responses to the conditions of the prior social environment. Human advance in justice is overwhelmingly a matter of developing patterns of cooperation and institutional schemes to meet genuine human needs—for food, water, shelter, health care, meaningful work, intimacy (sexual and otherwise), solace, education, acceptance, worship, and so on. This is the heart of Lonergan's social theory—that intelligent insights, critical reflection, and responsible choice and action are the origins of patterns of just social cooperation. Patterns that solve human problems emerge through insight and cooperation in one locale. They can be adopted and adapted by adding the further insights and free decisions appropriate to other places and times. This emergence of justice is a matter of raising "the relevant further questions: Can one's solution be generalized? Is it compatible with the social order that exists? Is it compatible with any social order that is approximately or even remotely possible?"[18] Lonergan taught me that an authentic concern for justice begins in small acts of being attentive to small things where one lives, and responding intelligently, reasonably, responsibly, and lovingly, as my mother and father had done so consistently. Authentic justice begins in attentiveness and creative intelligence and then pushes upward and outward. Authentic justice is an emerging justice.

It certainly took me by surprise to learn of such strong parallels between the way science works and the way authentic justice advances. Both are permeated by the same rhythms of attending to questions, invoking imagination, relentlessly pursuing insights that truly solve the problem at hand, and communicating the achievement to others. As with the wonder that motivates science, so also there are no limits to the desire for solutions that motivates the work of emerging justice.

A passion for justice often can contract, as it had in my case, into a narrow concern solely for the poor and the oppressed. Working for justice obviously includes care for the poor and the marginalized. Less obviously justice also includes care—a different kind of care—for the nonpoor. Working to make material prosperity a reality for all is not enough. Shockingly, material prosperity frequently produces people who are not at all whole persons complete in virtue. An authentic passion for justice desires a still greater social wholeness: a passion that acknowledges prosperity for all as an objective, but one that also realizes that prosperity itself sets forth conditions and problems calling for further insights and cooperative arrangements. No one is to be left behind in an authentically Beloved Community, neither the deprived nor the prosperous. An authentic concern for justice pushes ever upward and outward.

Lonergan helped me to realize that many different kinds of work are required to promote emerging justice. Practical works that meet human needs for sustenance, protection, healing, and worthwhile participation are needed, of course. Yet more than these practical works is needed for the wholeness of emerging justice. The work of theoretical science has made clear the shortsightedness of practicality and how it has jeopardized our natural ecosystems. Less obvious is the theoretical possibility that practicality has also compromised the human ecosystems of emerging justice. Lonergan makes a strong case that emerging justice requires also the works of theoretical minds in the human sciences, in philosophy, and in theology.[19] Increasingly, social policymakers rely upon experts from the human sciences to shape our patterns of cooperation. Human scientists in turn rely upon assumptions about what it means to be human. But because the human sciences merely take these assumptions for granted, their ideas about being human form very shaky foundations for genuine science or a trustworthy policy.

What it means to be human—the full meaning of the entire miserable and glorious record of human affairs—must itself be called into question, and that question must be approached methodically. The question of being human cannot be answered by a human science that takes the answer as its point of departure. Rather, it has to be answered by entering into the critical theoretical work of philosophy and theology.[20] This does not mean that only those with degrees in philosophy and theology have such answers, or that human scientists need to go to them, hat in hand, for "the truth" before they can start. It does mean, however, that there is need for real interdisciplinary work, where the provisional contributions of each approach are brought to the table to fertilize the emergence of ever better answers to the question of the wholeness of being human. Emerging justice requires the theoretical works of people who recognize the ultimate importance of this collaboration and who become "supremely practical by ignoring what is thought to be really practical."[21]

Lonergan enabled me to realize that there was a profound relationship between my passion for science and philosophy and my (transformed) passion for justice. These were not two passions but in fact one passion—a passion for a wholeness that is not yet. This wholeness emerges insofar as we learn to critically understand the passion that heads toward it and to cooperate with it. Although I continued my activism with more balanced practical involvements that addressed issues of justice, I gradually came to realize that I was called to contribute to emerging justice by making use of my abilities in the theoretical realm. I have attempted to do so in my teaching and writing and in my work to initiate programs at my university.

These lessons played a crucial role in the development of PULSE, our service learning program at Boston College. More than forty years ago I was involved in its founding and served as its first director. Now, more than four hundred PULSE students each year combine direct service in supervised human service agencies with academic reflection in courses in philosophy, theology, and other disciplines. At first the integration of traditional academic learning with the students' rich and often emotionally charged experiences from their service placements proved daunting. Gradually, however, we came to recognize that the students' personal encounters with the clients and staff of the human service agencies possessed the potential for conversion just as my father's letter had offered me. In moral conversion we are lifted out of our narrow, self-centered sense of what is right and wrong and are faced with the option of dedicating ourselves to bettering the larger world. But how best to respond to that option once opened becomes the major question for our students. They can come to see that being attentive to small things in their service work and responding intelligently to what they notice form major components of that response. Over the years we have also discovered rich resources in the philosophical and theological traditions that offer students insights that help them answer their questions for themselves. Among the most valuable insights for students are those regarding the wholeness of being human, what it means to be truly happy, and what the best ways to live might be.

Lonergan's conception of emerging justice has also had an impact upon the teaching in our service learning program. Typically, after a first semester of learning how to respond to individual clients at human service agencies, the enormity of their situations begins to sink into the consciousnesses of our students. They start to doubt that they are really accomplishing anything worthwhile, and eventually despair begins to set in. We have discovered that if we can teach our students to understand themselves as playing parts in institutions that can magnify their own contributions by integrating them with the contributions of others, then their naive enthusiasm can be transformed into more mature commitment and resolve to take on the task of emerging justice. We have drawn upon Lonergan's social theory to fashion exercises that enable students to analyze their institutions and the roles they play. These exercises have been effective in realizing these educational goals.

Because of these and other teaching experiences, I am currently at work on a book, *The Ethics of Discernment*, which I hope will pull together the sources of Lonergan's ethical thought into a unified philosophy of emerging goodness and justice.

Surrounded by Love

As with most human beings, my life has been constantly surrounded by love: the love of parents, grandparents, aunts and uncles, siblings, friends, teachers, and especially my wife and children. More subtly, more deeply, I have also been surrounded for my whole life by the love of God. Yet when I was young, I barely paid any attention to or appreciated the loves that engulfed me, whether human and divine. When love did become real for me, it did so, as is often the case, through my first real romance in adolescence. Being in love for the first time made love a powerful reality for me. It also enabled me to at least begin to notice the love that was all around me. I slowly noticed and even more slowly began to accept the love of my family, friends, and teachers.

As providence would have it, I went to Mass one Sunday when I was early in the throes of this adolescent romance, and I heard the reading from the first letter of John, 4:16: "God is Love; and whoever abides in love, abides in God, and God in them." There I was, abiding in love. No doubt I had heard this passage read in church many times before. But never before did I know the reality of love. The scripture reading allowed me to realize that I was in fact abiding in God. "God is love" was no longer just an abstract principle to me. It was a vivid experience: powerful, ecstatic, real.

From that point forward, my religion (and as I have come to think, all authentic religion) was about being cultivated in the arts of loving. I realize that this idea is not how most people regard religion, but it is what religion has meant for me from that day forward. Few people get beyond the idea of religion as being a matter of morality, and all too often a childish morality, one of rewards and punishments. My epiphany of love transformed all that for me. There is, of course, discipline in religions, but it is the discipline of learning to be genuinely, self-transcendingly loving. Even though I'd had many loving exemplars, both outside and inside explicitly religious contexts, I certainly needed (and continue to need) a great deal of cultivation (and discipline) in loving. At the heart of Christianity are the two great commandments that Jesus drew from the Hebrew scriptures: to love God with all one's heart, and to love one's neighbor as oneself. These two commandments (and the other more specific moral laws that they sum up) give direction to what it means to be loving. Living out such daunting commandments becomes possible only insofar as one already is in love—only if one abides in a love that embraces and values everything about everything and everyone. Nurturing that gift of love into active love requires examples and guidance of loving that knows no bounds. I began to find these first in religious writings and theological reflections centered on the example of Jesus the Christ, but also soon in writings about the great many other exemplars of unconditional loving, both Christian and non-Christian.

My first adolescent romance did not last, of course. It gave way to more mature love not only of God but also of my wife, children, and fellow human beings. More than anyone else, my wife has taught me by her example over and again what it means to be really loving, constantly saving me from my romanticized fantasies. The desire and ever renewed commitment to follow out this vocation to love has also played an important role in my commitment to justice—although it was originally a very limited notion of both love and justice. Lonergan's account of emergent justice would eventually help me to see that the two cannot be separated. In reality, institutions are, after all, those circles of social cooperation that people continuously adapt and originate. People exist and live and make their lives meaningful by their contributions and commitments to institutions, informal as well as formal. It is abstract and naive to believe that one can love a person but disdain the institutions that are part and parcel of that person's living.

I would, however, need still further guidance to help me understand that my call to be loving was also intimately related to my passion for science and philosophy. Lonergan eventually helped me to realize that love of God, love of neighbor, and love of the world of natural science are all caught up in one another: "Being in love with God, as experienced, is being in love in an unrestricted fashion. All love is self-surrender, but being in love with God is being in love without limits or qualifications or conditions or reservations. Just as unrestricted questioning is our capacity for self-transcendence, so being in love in an unrestricted fashion is the proper fulfillment of that capacity."[22]

Previously I had come to understand that authentic science and philosophy come out of our unrestricted questioning. Now Lonergan was asking, Where is this unrestricted questioning headed? The suggestion that our rational inquiry greets its *desideratum* in unconditional loving struck me as profoundly correct. I recognized a deep resonance between my experience of science and my experience of being surrounded by God's love.

We tend to believe that love and science are contradictory. We tend to believe that we cannot be objective about what we love. We tend to believe that love will interfere with our ability to be scientifically objective. After all, "love is blind," is it not? Although there is, of course, a grain of truth to this commonplace, I have come to regard it as fundamentally mistaken. Our scientific objectivity is compromised not when we love too much, but when we love too little. If we become obsessively attached to one of our ideas or theories or interpretations or worldviews, or to some object or person or race or nationality or gender, then we are not loving in an unconditional fashion. Bias against even further questions and considerations is protectiveness born of fear, not of love. Science is compromised not by unconditional love, but by ideology born of such fear. If we ignore or refuse to pursue further questions about something to which we are attached, we betray a fear that things will not work out all right. This is the dark heart of ideology, whether it cloaks itself in the mantle of religion or politics or ethics or science or philosophy or some "ism."

If God is the name for genuine unrestricted loving, then God loves everything about everything. God loves protons and galactic superclusters, earthquakes and hurricanes, viruses and mosquitoes, birds and deep-sea "monsters," and human beings even when they hurt and exploit and kill one another. God does not fear to understand anything precisely because God loves everything. A genuinely scientific, inquiring spirit is inspired by and yearns to comprehend what that divine, unrestrictedly loving being sees in all of the inhabitants of the universe.

Not only unrestricted scientific inquiry, but also finite scientific achievements—these are also intimations of the unrestricted passion that is God. Lonergan writes, "Our subject has been the act of insight or understanding, and God is the unrestricted act of understanding, the eternal rapture glimpsed in every Archimedean cry of 'Eureka!'"[23] That is, every scientific insight, and indeed every practical insight that contributes to emergent justice, is an opening into God's passionate love. I have come to realize that it was the natural world bathed in God's love, and the exhilarating glimpses into that rapture, that first attracted me to science.

The lack of objectivity, then, that is commonly attributed to the interference of love with objectivity comes not from too much love, but from too little. To paraphrase Saint Augustine, I would say that a guiding principle for a university career dedicated to wholeness is this: "First love God, and then research as you will."

My reflections on emerging catholicity are drawn from my own experiences and from the light cast upon those experiences by the work of Bernard Lonergan. These reflections have led me to the limited but assured knowledge that my emerging wholeness, such as it is, is caught up in the emerging wholeness of the whole universe and the whole human race. I do not know where all this is heading. But I do know that I am most at peace when I am confident that what I am doing is making a contribution to that unknown destiny.

Notes

1. Hans Reichenbach, *The Elements of Symbolic Logic* (New York: Macmillan, 1947), 2.

2. Ibid.

3. Bernard Lonergan, *Topics in Education*, ed. Frederick E. Crowe and Robert M. Doran, Collected Works of Bernard Lonergan 10 (Toronto: University of Toronto Press, 1993), 178; see also ibid., 146–53.

4. Bernard Lonergan, *Insight: A Study of Human Understanding*, ed. Frederick E. Crowe and Robert M. Doran, Collected Works of Bernard Lonergan 3 (Toronto: University of Toronto Press, 1992), 27.

5. Ibid., 28.

6. Ibid., 33.

7. Friedrich August Kekulé, quoted in "Benzene," Chemsoc Timeline, accessed April 14, 2011, www.rsc.org/chemsoc/timeline/pages/1864_benzene.html.

8. Lonergan, *Insight*, 156. Lonergan's technical term for an environment is "a conditioned series of schemes of recurrence." Ibid., 141ff.; see also 290.

9. Ibid., 477.

10. Ibid., 70.

11. Ibid., 497.

12. Aristotle, *Nicomachean Ethics*, trans. Martin Ostwald (Englewood Cliffs, NJ: Prentice Hall, 1962), IV.5.

13. Ibid., V.1.

14. See James H. Cone, *Martin and Malcolm and America: A Dream or a Nightmare?* (Maryknoll, NY: Orbis Books, 1991), 63–66, 297.

15. Bernard Lonergan, *Method in Theology* (New York: Herder and Herder, 1972), 240–42.

16. See for example Bernard Lonergan, "*Pantôn Anakephalaiôsis* (The Respiration of All Things)," *Method: Journal of Lonergan Studies* 9 (1991): 140–70.

17. Lonergan, *Insight*, 156.

18. Ibid., 245.

19. Ibid., 260–61, 423–24. See also Lonergan, *Method in Theology*, 248–49.

20. Lonergan, *Method in Theology*, 212.

21. Lonergan, *Insight*, 264.

22. Lonergan, *Method in Theology*, 105–6.

23. Lonergan, *Insight*, 706.

CHAPTER 2

From Discovery to Risk

Cynthia Crysdale

When I was an associate dean in the School of Theology and Religious Studies at The Catholic University of America, I regularly received calls from prospective students asking, "If I come to study at CUA, can I be assured that I will be getting the true teachings of the magisterium?" What always struck me about this question was the latent concern for certainty in faith, the assumption that theology is all about correct propositions. I was also struck by the canon within a canon—most of these students did not know the full body of magisterial teachings. I often replied that, indeed, our program adhered to magisterial teachings, which is why we expected them to take courses in religion and culture and to learn about world religions. The documents that promote the understanding of culture and dialogue with other religions clearly were not the ones these inquirers were referring to when they asked about magisterial teachings.

This concern for orthodoxy, the desire to have certainty in truth, reminds me of my own personal and intellectual struggles three decades ago. Coming from a Protestant tradition with an evangelical formation, I was determined to find educational programs that I could trust were safely grounded in biblical teaching. My peers at the time had very clear criteria for which professors, courses, and programs were theologically safe. I have come a long way from this concern for a clear litmus test for authentic theology. Rubbing shoulders with faithful inquirers in the Roman Catholic tradition, the ecumenical expansion of my world, has had a lot to do with the revision of my narrow worldview. In particular, the work of Bernard Lonergan contributed to a much more nuanced understanding of "true teachings"—one that has had a profound impact on my personal faith as well as my scholarly career. My objective in this chapter is to introduce a few key insights that Lonergan's work has offered me. I do this in the context of my own personal narrative. At the end I reflect on how these key concepts might influence an understanding of Catholic education on college campuses today.

How Do I Know Anything Is True?

I began my formal theological studies at the University of St. Michael's College, Toronto, in the mid-1970s. One of the core courses in the master's program was titled Foundations of Theology and, under the influence of Karl Rahner, was divided into sections on the "mediation of revelation"—via scripture, tradition, reason, and so on. Raised under the Calvinist influence of Presbyterianism, and affected in my college years by evangelical campus ministries, I was most distraught over the section on the mediation of revelation through scripture. How, I wondered, can anyone be assured that the Bible is truly the word of God? How could I know that what the Bible says is true? In an effort to make sure that what I was reading was correct, I had studied Koine Greek. But did that get me any closer to answering my skeptical friends, to reassuring me that the world of faith I had committed myself to was the real one? Increasingly disturbed by such questions as the semester unfolded, I finally visited my professor, Margaret O'Gara. When I concluded my barrage of angst-filled questions, she perceptively responded: "It sounds as if what you are really asking is 'How do I know *anything* is true?'"

Thus began my career in epistemology. I had no idea at the time that Dr. O'Gara's perceptive answer was the inroad to a host of complex further questions. I could not have even used the word "epistemology" at that point. I had never heard of Bernard Lonergan. But I was a precocious and bright student in my early twenties who would not settle for easy answers. I had spent the previous year at Wycliffe College because my evangelical Anglican friends had assured me this was a theologically safe place to study. I quickly discovered that "safe" meant that there were certain questions one did not ask and methods one did not use. Most notably, these methods included the higher criticism of scriptural texts that was taught at other schools in the Toronto School of Theology. The Introduction to the New Testament course at Emmanuel College was dubbed by my Wycliffe colleagues "Introduction to Heresy." The fact that my studies at Wycliffe coincided with the ordination of the first women priests in the Anglican Church of Canada did not help matters. Again, the interpretation of scripture was at issue. Reason and faith formed a dichotomy with no acceptable middle ground. Either one believed in the Word of God and was a Christian, or one used critical reason to analyze texts and started down the long road to heresy. Unhappy with such options, I jumped ship and crossed Queens Park to begin a master's program at the Institute of Christian Thought at St. Mike's.

Fifteen of us started the master's program that year. Seven were Protestants, ranging from Mennonite to Dutch Reformed to my own hybrid evangelicalism. Seven were Roman Catholic, including a middle-aged feminist and a young ex-Franciscan. One was a follower of Sun Myung Moon. My own discomfort with the questions generated by the mediation of revelation via scripture appeared quite odd to my Catholic colleagues. Then we got to the section in the course on the mediation of revelation via the magisterium. All hell broke loose in the Roman Catholic camp. "How can we trust what the magisterium tells us? How do we know that magisterial teaching is correct?" The perceptive question I had heard earlier came back to haunt me: How do we know that *anything* is true? At that point I knew nothing about the historical or theological differences between Catholics and Protestants. But the theological flashpoints of both traditions were graphically apparent. Underneath such graphic differences appeared to be a common question: How can I know that anything is true?

In spite of the clarity and the centrality of this basic philosophical question, I did not rush to embrace the task of answering it. I resisted anything that smacked of philosophy because I assumed it would be over my head, beyond my capabilities, something like undertaking quantum physics without a decent scientific background. One of my friends, Tatha Wiley, who had come to Toronto explicitly to study Lonergan, suggested that his philosophy might actually help me understand myself. Self-understanding and philosophy did not go together in my mind, but I nevertheless enrolled in a course called Conversion taught by Tad Dunne. Conversion was a category my evangelical brain could embrace, and indeed we were assigned many hours of writing reflection papers—again not my idea of philosophy. Before I knew it I was pondering not only "How can I know *anything*?" but "How can *I* know anything?"

Thus began my career, not only in epistemology but in self-appropriation. The remainder of the story unfolds as a story of my intellectual conversion. Those who are familiar with Lonergan's work will be familiar with both terms. For those not as familiar with Lonergan's work, there are two salient points here. The first is that knowing is not just a matter of looking—that what you see is not necessarily what you get. The process of determining that something as simple as "it's raining" is true is a matter not only of feeling wet blotches on one's skin or seeing dark droplets on the sidewalk. It involves engagement with a few other processes, what Lonergan calls operations. The experience of sense perception (or of memory, the data of consciousness) is only a first step—*experience*. We spontaneously try to make sense of this experience and consider a range of possibilities: a bird flying overhead making deposits on our heads, someone throwing liquid out of an upstairs window, a rainstorm. Such attempts to make sense of our experience are questions for *intelligibility*. But beyond such questions we go further, unsatisfied with the myriad of possible explanations. So we shift to questions for *judgment*: Which one of these possible explanations is correct? We determine this by considering our options in light of the evidence at hand—if the droplets are white and gooey, we conclude that we have been dumped on by a passing bird. If the droplets are clear and the sky is ominously black, we conclude it is raining.

So the first salient point is that knowing is not just looking: It involves a set of operations more complex than just sense perception, yet they are identifiable. The second salient point has to do with this identifiability. This is where self-appropriation comes in. Determining how I know something is true is a matter of catching myself in the act of determining something—noticing that I have just concluded that it is raining and then pondering what processes I used to come to that conclusion. What I continue to find compelling about Lonergan's critical realism is that it is grounded not in abstract and esoteric ideas but in concrete attentiveness to what I am doing as I do it. Indeed, undertaking this kind of philosophy was a matter of discovering something about myself. Discovering that I could and did make simple correct judgments such as "it is raining" led me to this simple but profound judgment: "I am a knower and can, not always but at least sometimes, make correct judgments." Such a simple but profound judgment gave me both a starting point for further questions and a bridge over the supposed chasm between mere fideism—something is true simply because you choose to believe it—and empiricism—only what we can perceive with our five senses is true, so any faith claims or propositions about intangibles such as God are ruled out a priori.

This intellectual conversion as I experienced it did not immediately solve my questions about the truth of the Bible or how one can interpret it in a valid way. There are a host of further and very complex questions under the guise of what we call hermeneutics—a German word for interpretation. Determining that it is raining is one thing. Giving an accurate interpretation of the meaning of a text, especially one from another historic or cultural era, is quite another. Whether and how such accurate interpretations are possible are a matter of debate, and such debates fill the tomes that populate library shelves. Then there are the theological questions concerning which texts are considered sacred, how these came to be so designated, and what impact such claims have on our daily lives today. None of these complex dilemmas were resolved by my conclusion thirty years ago that, indeed, I could and did regularly know things to be true. But my conclusion that this was possible, Lonergan's explication of the processes by which I do this, and my affirmation of the reasonability of his explanation granted a secure—and empirically verifiable—ground for both my life of faith and my academic pursuits.

This first autobiographical anecdote has introduced the basic *critical realism* of Lonergan's philosophy—a position that insists that we can and do know things in their realities, but that this process is complex and not merely a matter of *naive realism*, or just taking a look. As I was to discover, this was only a starting point.

The Knowledge Born of Belief

Having completed my master's degree in theology I decided, with some fear and trepidation, to go on to complete a PhD program, again at St. Michael's. I had discovered the delight of philosophy and theology as self-appropriation—personal reflection and serious analysis could go hand in hand. As I had resisted philosophical questions initially, so I resisted the challenge of doctoral study. A few Lonergan mentors, however, convinced me that learning was a matter not of filling in boxes but of asking questions—a quest, a journey, an exploration that amounted to an adventure rather than a burden.

I was soon to learn that discovery—asking and answering questions—never takes place in a vacuum. There is the matter of what sociologists call "social location." My social location in 1980 was that of a non-Roman Catholic woman undertaking theological studies at a Roman Catholic institution during my childbearing years. Born in the 1950s, living my formative years in the 1960s, and married in 1976, I was nevertheless subject to the gender expectations of a pre–women's liberation era. When the first women priests were ordained in the Anglican Church in Canada, I was the only woman in all my classes at Wycliffe College. One professor made a point of repeatedly mentioning something about "barefoot and pregnant in the kitchen" while pausing to stare in my direction. Although Lonergan's method promoted the asking of questions, asking questions was the one thing women were never to do—indeed, we have scriptural passages proving the point. I had decided not to pursue ordination, but undertaking doctoral studies in theology was no less a dangerous and controversial task. When I got pregnant in the middle of my doctoral work, I had a friend tell me that I would ruin my children if I did not give up my studies and stay at home. And when the handful of women in theological education in Toronto got together to explore our common concerns, my queries about academe and family life were met with stony silence—clearly childbearing was not a common concern among women in theology. When a British friend moved to Toronto to finish his doctoral work and joined my low Anglican evangelical church, he was immediately asked to deliver a series of sermons, tied to a set of Lenten Bible studies. Though I had been a member of the church and had been studying theology for more than eight years, I had never been asked to take a leadership role of any kind. Though not ordained, he clearly had the accent and the gender to qualify for lay ministry in the Anglican Church of Canada.

Thus began my career as a feminist. My mentors in this career had never heard of Bernard Lonergan, and my Lonergan mentors were all men, many of them Jesuits. Indeed, the critical analytical skills involved in understanding Lonergan's work, even the word "epistemology," seemed antithetical to the praxis-oriented anti-intellectualism of the newly emerging feminist theology. But although there were women in my Lonergan classes, none of them were mothers, and I am quite sure I was the first person ever to bring an infant and a breast pump to the Lonergan Workshop at Boston College.

The upshot of this personal journey was to add to my newly inspired enthusiasm for self-appropriation, the operations of knowing, and the sociology of knowledge. Academically this discovery of social location was fostered by working with Roger Hutchinson as a teaching assistant in social ethics and by taking courses with Gregory Baum. My Lonergan world expanded when I audited a full year of coursework with Robert Doran, as he refined Lonergan's notion of dialectic and developed his own dialectics of history.[1]

Lonergan enthusiasts often insist that the first element to be discovered about Lonergan's work—his critical realist position on the four levels of operations in knowing—is the sum and whole of his contribution.[2] If only everyone could see that we know things through the operations of experiencing, understanding, judging, and deciding, then everything else would be clear. Although this epistemological position is foundational, it does not tell the whole story of what we know. Michael Vertin, another mentor and the director of my dissertation, made the simple observation at one point that, in teaching, one must begin with the knowledge born of belief and then move on to introducing the self-appropriation of "immanently generated knowledge."[3]

Indeed, it turns out that we know most of what we know because someone else told us. Though I am in fact capable of determining that it is raining, most days I choose my clothes and weather apparel because of insights that a host of other experts—the local weather forecasters—have had long before I got out of bed. More important, what I know about auto mechanics or diabetes is not knowledge I have arrived at through experiencing, understanding, judging, or deciding. In these cases, my arrival at judgment is a judgment of value—determining the reliability of my sources and then trusting their judgments of fact to be accurate.

This other prong of knowing is an aspect of Lonergan's work that is often overlooked. Though my exploration of the knowledge born of belief, in Lonergan, did not resolve my feminist questions, it did provide a grounding for understanding the "different voice" of women—as highlighted by Carol Gilligan's psychological studies in the early 1980s.[4] The knowledge born of belief is not just a set of propositions, nor merely the acceptance of advice from an auto mechanic. It involves a whole set of intellectual assumptions, packaged in psychic garb, with emotional chemistry. And just as we can affirm the possibility of accurate knowing while admitting that mistakes are made, so we can affirm the validity of belief-knowledge while realizing that many aspects of our belief systems are distorted. And one of the most distorted set of beliefs that is often handed on is a set of beliefs about knowing itself. The gender implications are rampant—the history of (male) thought about women as being incapable of discovery, and the current sociological studies about women's ways of knowing, reveal a legacy in which women who claim any kind of epistemic autonomy put themselves in social jeopardy. No wonder studying theology as a woman in the 1980s felt liminal and dangerous.

So to my own discovery of discovery I added the dialectic between heritage and discovery.[5] We are born into a set of beliefs and, if we are lucky, gradually move toward the development of reason, such that we use the operations of knowing to discover things for ourselves. In the process we learn not only how to distinguish reality from fantasy but how to recognize bias and error. So we discover that some of what we believe is believed correctly, while other things we have taken for granted turn out to be the fruit of oversight, egoism, ignorance, and laziness, if not malice. We need to hone our skills not only of understanding and judgment of facts but of believing others. We need to learn how and when to believe whom for the right reasons. And we need to distance ourselves from the communities of distortion that lead us astray, while reforming communities of authenticity.

The Law of the Cross

By the time I had worked my way through these issues, along with the many questions about gender and knowing and about whether Lonergan's critical realism had any place in feminist theology, I was a tenured professor at The Catholic University of America in Washington, DC.[6] The naive optimism of thinking that Lonergan's epistemologically grounded method would clear up confusion in the theological world had given way to the recognition of the pervasive flight from understanding in all walks of life, and of the bias that clouds the understanding of women, men, feminists, and misogynists alike. In my personal life, encounters with those suffering from mental illness made the problem of evil and the need for grace and healing paramount. When given the opportunity to present the Glasmacher Lecture at Saint Paul University in Ottawa, Canada, in 1996, with a sabbatical on the horizon, I decided to plunge into the question of suffering and how it does or does not promote redemption.[7]

The more I researched both contemporary women's lives and the history of the Christian tradition, the more the distortion of a cult of suffering became apparent. The valorization of suffering, especially in women's lives, supposedly in imitation of the blessed sufferings of Jesus on the cross, is embedded sociologically and historically in twenty centuries of Christian teaching and practice. The imperialistic and triumphalist use of the cross as a symbol of tyranny, conquest, and hence oppression makes Christianity a system of abuse. The feminist critiques of the tradition, as found in such books as *Christianity, Patriarchy, and Abuse*, were telling.[8] No wonder women were leaving the Christian Church in droves or inventing earth-minded, women-centered alternative rituals and religions.

Nevertheless, the cross and Jesus's suffering and death are the centerpiece of the Christian gospel. Without them and the consequent claim that evil is eradicated by forgiveness rather than retribution, Christianity folds up completely. Once again I found myself caught between a rock and a hard place. My own experience of the dysfunction of forgiveness as enabling, and the psychological damage done by injunctions to surrender and submit to suffering in the name of redemption (my own or others), resonated with the scholarly feminist examinations of the Christian tradition's abusive side. Still, the gospel itself was what had held me to my vocation and what gave me hope in the face of dysfunction. I was not ready to jettison the gospel as nothing but patriarchal, misogynist, oppressive propaganda. How could suffering produce redemption? Was there a resurrection hope that was not a mere Pollyanna-like denial of oppression and pain?

In this case I came to struggle with what Lonergan talks about as the "law of the cross."[9] But my grasp of a new horizon in which I could accept this came from one of Lonergan's more mystical-minded followers: Sebastian Moore and his book *The Crucified Is No Stranger*.[10] Moore writes from a Jungian psychological perspective about how we perceive ourselves in the crucified Savior—in two ways. We discover ourselves as the ones responsible for his death—as sinners and betrayers. But we also discover ourselves with Jesus on the cross, as victims—of injustice, of misunderstanding, of violence. So I came to see that redemption has two sides—it is a matter of both forgiveness for sins (as the tradition has emphasized for years) *and* the healing of wounds. We are all both perpetrators who need forgiveness and wounded victims who need healing. As addiction recovery programs have long recognized, there is a cycle, in which victims become perpetrators in a distorted attempt to heal themselves and in the process create further victims, including themselves. This destructive cycle is the dilemma so well described by Saint Paul in the seventh chapter of his letter to the Romans: "For I do not do the good I want, but the evil I do not want is what I do" (Rom. 7:19, NRSV).

Aspiration and achievement fail us here—what is needed is the intervention of grace. Lonergan's work helps make concrete this advent of grace. He speaks of religious conversion as an "other-worldly falling in love"; and just as falling in love comes unexpectedly and shifts our horizons, so God's love, and our response, alters the cycles of betrayal and victimization.[11] It does so in two ways. First, new insights, born of transcendent love, convert our understanding to a new level, so that sins and wounds are seen in a larger perspective. This faith vision grants us a new horizon of wisdom to understand ourselves, our world, our relationships, our time-bound narratives, in a hope-filled light. Second, grace shifts our decision making. The otherworldly falling in love transforms our values concretely by shifting our desires. This is what the ancient fathers described as our appetites. As our desires change, so our habits—cycles of recurrent feelings and actions—are altered. Habits of love replace habits of bitterness and jealousy. The practice of allowing ourselves to be loved builds safe interior space for habits of healing.

A few key insights became clear to me. The resolution of evil is not about one person, perspective, social system, or political regime winning the day over the evil opposition. Such success inevitably succumbs to the tactics of coercion, hence, in one way or other, violating its enemies. The resolution of grace is of quite a different sort—it involves a transvaluing of values, a complete reversal, upheaval, conversion, such that the world and its issues are transformed into a faith-based, love-filled perspective. In sum, the solution to the problem of evil lies in love, not retribution. Although retribution and right relations—justice—may flow from redemptive love, or be its catalyst, the quest to fix evil most often only perpetuates it.

This does not mean that acquiescence or the acceptance of suffering is the route to redemption. Rather, having fallen in love, we abide in the divine life of love, such that our suffering is transformed from meaningless pain to a meaning-filled narrative. So far from a denial of suffering, this love-filled horizon transforms evil by negating its power. Resurrection is not a denial of death but the mockery of the powers that believe they can discern and control good and evil. Further, to live an integral life of transcendent love, whether nascent or mature, will be countercultural—sometimes to the point where others consider this integral living a source of evil itself, as was the case with Jesus and has been the case with countless martyrs through the ages. The point is that Jesus did not choose suffering as the means of grace. He chose love and accepted suffering. So we, too, as redemption unfolds in our lives, receive the gift of God's love and accept the realities that constitute the cross we inhabit. So far from a cult of suffering or the valorization of pain, this is a horizon of elevated understanding and transformed desire. It is a matter of surrender, for it leaves us dependent and out of control, but it is also a matter of empowerment—liberation as well as confession, healing as well as forgiveness.

One final element became clear to me at this point in my life and academic work. This is the importance of narrative and voice. Lonergan does not discuss these matters under this terminology, but he does explicate the role of meaning and the process of interpretation at length. The salient point for me, especially with regard to suffering, was the question of who gets to tell the story. Indeed, this has been an issue throughout Christian history—men have been the interpreters and storytellers, defining the meaning of women's lives for women. Women often have not been permitted to discern for themselves whether to surrender to difficult situations or resist them. Resistance to oppression, when defined as sinful disobedience, or at best benign ignorance, leaves women and minorities confused over their own intelligence and even sanity. It is a mark of oppressive regimes to define the underclass as less than human, incapable of discernment and judgment, thereby justifying injustice in their regard. In agreement with Lonergan's critical realism I believe that meaning is not entirely a matter of social construction—there are correct interpretations and incorrect ones. Nevertheless, in determining what constitutes valid meaning, the question of epistemic power—who gets to make this determination—must be asked. So far from a relativism that leaves everyone's perspective with equal validity, a critical hermeneutics combined with a suspicion of hegemony can allow hidden validity to emerge.

Emergent Probability and the Ethic of Risk

My book that addresses all these issues was published in 1999. By then I had been at The Catholic University of America for ten years. I had teenage children and a heartbreaking marriage. Struggles with manic depression had left my household with financial as well as emotional difficulties. The precariousness of daily life sent me contemplating the ethic of risk.

I had encountered Sharon Welch's book *A Feminist Ethic of Risk* when it was published in the late 1980s and had used it in my own work on retrieving the cross for today.[12] Welch develops a distinction between an ethic of risk and an ethic of control. She uses the nuclear arms race of the early 1980s as her case study and relies on literary works of African American women as her theological resource. An ethic of control assumes that moral action produces clear results. It leaves little room for ambiguity, using decisive action that renders one invulnerable to evil. One has a clear plan, a strategy, that will not only rid the world of the current problem but protect one from further threats. This model of moral action relies on "the equation of responsible action and control—the assumption that it is possible to guarantee the efficacy of one's actions."[13]

An ethic of risk, in contrast, is "responsible action within the limits of bounded power" and involves "persistent defiance and resistance in the face of repeated defeats."[14] This approach attends to that which may yield only partial results. The goal of moral action is not complete success but the creation of new conditions of possibility for the future. It accepts the long-term struggle involved in changing difficult situations. In such situations, an ethic of risk engages one in a community of risk takers, committed to the struggle over the long haul. It involves strategic risk taking in the face of overwhelming odds and recognizes the irreparable damage of structural evil. Although Welch's approach is quite different from my own or Lonergan's, statements such as the following struck me as worth exploring from a Lonerganian position: "Responsible action does not mean the certain achievement of desired ends but the creation of a matrix in which further actions are possible, the creation of the conditions of possibility for desired changes."[15] Specifically, though Welch was advocating an ethic of risk *prescriptively*, as an approach one ought to undertake, it seemed to me that Lonergan's analysis of moral deliberation gives a *descriptive* account of what we do in fact do when we make decisions, and that risk is inevitably involved.[16]

At the beginning of the chapter I explain Lonergan's delineation of how we know something to be true: "It is raining." It was this position of knowing facts that had grasped me in my initial intellectual conversion. But Lonergan also explicates a further level of knowing that has to do not with facts but with values—this is the level of deliberation and decision. In decision making—both the mundane and the monumental—one determines not what is the case but what might be the case. One weighs not the sufficiency of evidence to determine what is so but projected courses of action and their potential outcomes. As one considers these possible courses of action, one also considers the various values that will be created, or disvalues mitigated, by one's actions. This kind of consideration—though it does come to an end once we make a value judgment and act on it—nevertheless always involves an element of provisionality, since we are dealing with an incompletely known future.

Let me expand on this a bit further. Questions for deliberation—What ought I to do in this situation?—do not come out of a vacuum but arise in conjunction with concrete discoveries of fact. My car won't start in the morning—what I ought to do depends on the reasons why it isn't working. A bit more seriously, I visit my mother and find her not breathing on the floor of her apartment. My course of action must begin with at least a rudimentary determination of what has happened to her.

So "what am I to do?" (value judgments/decisions) and "what is the case?" (judgments of fact) are questions that often emerge simultaneously. And the validity of my actions does rely on my accurate grasp of the facts of the situation. Still, judgments of value and decisions go beyond a mere determination of the current facts to a determination of the probable outcomes of various courses of action. This latter determination involves calculating probabilities, and such probabilities, by their very nature, involve risk.[17]

Thus, for example, once I get my mother to a hospital I seek expert advice about her condition. A resuscitation process has started her breathing again, but it is unlikely that she will make it through the night without an artificial respirator. Intravenous medication may help her breathing but brings other side effects. No treatment at all, other than bed rest and vigilance from nursing staff, is also a possibility, but repeated resuscitation, if thought necessary, would further damage her fragile heart.

The point is to show that the choices involved here all include a consideration of probabilities. The more accurate the predictions are, the more informed our choices will be. But no matter how accurate certain predictions are, it is the nature of probability to involve uncertainty and therefore risk.

This account of decision making fits in with Lonergan's analysis of development as a matter of emergent probability. The world, including the world of human living, is dependent on the regularities of schemes of recurrence. Whether we are talking about the hydrological cycle by which water evaporates, accumulates, and then precipitates, or about the monthly deposit of my paycheck into my bank account, certain phenomena depend on schemes of recurrence that occur on a regular basis as parts of larger schemes. There are recurring cycles of schemes of recurrence, and in all cases the underlying routines are the basis for the continuation of more sophisticated schemes. If my blood sugar stops metabolizing properly, or my hormonal production becomes unbalanced, my thinking won't be very clear.

Emergence is a matter of novelty in these sets of schemes—at times made possible because of an imbalance or malfunction of what should be regular routines. One can purposefully alter routines or establish new habits in an effort to allow novelty to emerge. But in all cases, when something new does emerge, it is dependent on underlying elements and reintegrates them into a higher configuration of regularities. Further, the emergence of novelty and its survival are a matter not of direct causality but of probabilities.

While classical science studies the regularities of schemes of recurrence, statistical science studies the likelihood of emergence. One can take the number of home runs hit by a baseball star throughout his career and determine the likelihood of his hitting another home run during the World Series championship. One can take a survey of people who have used a certain drug to help them with heart problems, determine how many have had which side effects under which conditions, and then predict the likelihood of a new patient having the same side effects. But in all these cases, the actual instances revolve nonsystematically around an average; and the average, however accurately calculated, will not determine which actual instances will occur in the future. Knowing that the chance of rolling a six is one in six does not tell you whether *this* throw of the die will yield a six or not.

The significant point that I came to realize out of all this was that my own model of moral action was incorrect. I had been taught to think of moral deliberation and choice as a matter of choosing to do A and having B result. I was thinking in terms of direct causality: A causes B. If B did not occur—if I could not fix a disturbing situation—it was because I had not performed A correctly. Indeed, I now realized, I had been latently assuming an ethic of control, as if I could take decisive action with a guaranteed result. In fact, such a model of moral action is not only ethically inadvisable but performatively impossible. Whatever I choose, the actions that I take set up a matrix of possibilities out of which something new—what I am hoping to accomplish—may or may not emerge. I can try to affect the likelihood of its emergence—through chemotherapy, psychotherapy, fertilizer, irrigation— but whether the intended end comes about is not in my direct control. The key phrase here is "conditions of possibility." Lonergan's phenomenology empirically grounds the profound point Welch makes about the ethic of risk: "Responsible action does not mean the certain achievement of desired ends but the creation of a matrix in which further actions are possible, the creation of the conditions of possibility for desired change."[18]

Implications for Catholic Higher Education Today

In light of my journey, let me draw out what I see to be the implications of my insights, generated by Lonergan's work, for teaching and learning in the context of Catholic education. The first piece, critical realism grounded in empirical self-appropriation, defines a starting point for Catholic higher education. The pedagogical point is that one must incorporate some kind of self-reflective self-appropriation in the teaching-learning process in order for education to be adequately grounded. To think of Catholic education merely as a catechesis of basic Catholic teachings in which one inculcates and advocates certain doctrines will produce ineffective results at best. The philosophical point, which is controversial, is that epistemology comes before metaphysics. This is controversial because many see epistemology—questions about the nature of knowing—to have been the great erroneous turn of the Enlightenment. It was this tangent, many claim, that led us into the bind of relativism. To start with the human agent and how he or she knows leads to a morass in which nothing is certain and the truths of Catholic faith are peripheral if not altogether lost.

Some students as well as teachers on Catholic college campuses today believe in the need to retrieve certainty in truth. Philosophically the trend is to start with metaphysics—the nature of reality—in order to avoid the relativism that supposedly comes with the introduction of epistemology. Theologically, the approach is to begin with dogma, the explicitly proclaimed teachings of the magisterium. Just as I sought certainty in biblical truth in a world of pluralistic meanings, so some students and teachers today want assurance of objective propositional truth.

The problem with this approach, as I see it, is that it overlooks the prior question: Where did these truths come from? Indeed, the doctrines we currently hold in the Christian tradition, and the dogmas officially proclaimed throughout history, were at one time answers to very concrete questions. These questions were asked by active Christians trying to live faithful lives in previous eras. The just war tradition is the fruit of the concrete struggle of newly converted Christians in late antiquity who were trying to decide if serving in the Roman army was compatible with their newfound faith. Indeed, even the central tenets of Christology came from a variety of believers trying their best to explain to their pagan neighbors how Jesus could be both human and divine.

The point is that doctrines are answers to questions; and the best way to understand the doctrines is, therefore, to understand the questions that they originally answered.[19] This necessarily engages one in living history, not just the history of ideas. It also, however, raises the question of questioning itself. How does religious conviction become religious teaching? What is the process by which practicing faith turns to systematic questions that need resolution? To understand this process one is best served by understanding both one's own religious experience and one's own processes of questioning. One engages necessarily in theological method and hence in self-appropriation. To merely promote the answers to questions—the doctrines—without simultaneously promoting self-appropriation—how anyone comes to valid answers to the questions—is to build on shifting rather than secure ground.

This relates to my second insight—the role of belief in knowledge. Indeed, earlier generations came to conclusions about what their religious experience meant, the truths that needed to be proclaimed, and the best way to systematically understand these propositions. Cumulatively these have become the deposit of faith that we hand on to succeeding generations. Both the deposit of faith and the process of coming to faith need to be examined in Catholic higher education. Both heritage and discovery are matters for examination in promoting Catholic identity.

Note, however, a few things about this relationship. First, the knowledge born of belief comes to us through individual acts of trust in the people handing on that knowledge. Hence, to find a trustworthy mechanic, a reliable doctor, or a discreet and wise confessor is valuable beyond measure. Likewise, the credibility of the content of what we teach is determined by the credibility of ourselves as teachers. No curriculum, no set of textbooks, no fancy audiovisuals or web-based learning can alter the basic fact that students accept and trust what is given to them by acceptable and trustworthy agents. For good or for ill, this fact requires that the foundation of good Catholic higher education is the intellectual, moral, and religious conversions of those who teach and administer. It also means that one of the skills we need to teach is critical credulity. Not everything that passes for "Catholic" comes from a reputable source—especially in a cyber-driven world. We need to teach students not only a historically and theologically grounded tradition but also ways to make critical judgments about whom to believe.

Second, we must distinguish the complementary dialectic between heritage and discovery from the contradictory dialectic between authenticity and inauthenticity.[20] The deposit of faith and its rediscovery by each succeeding generation constitute a creative tension that is not to be disparaged. Often, the discussion of Catholic identity on college campuses breaks down into a polarity between the traditionalists and the progressives. However, it is not the case that the way of heritage is the enemy, such that we need to recreate the wheel over and over again. Nor is it the case that innovations are always distortions, such that we need to return to truths as expressed in previous eras. In other words, authenticity, or orthodoxy, is the domain of neither the traditionalists nor the innovators. Rather, both the tradition as received and our processes of discovery suffer from oversights, mistakes, blind spots, bias. Both the knowledge born of belief and the operations we use in discovery need to be constantly and consistently purged of individual, group, and general bias.

My third nexus of insights had to do with grace, redemption, and the law of the cross. This is the most difficult insight to apply to Catholic higher education, since the gospel itself is inherently paradoxical. Rosemary Haughton, in *The Transformation of Man*, discusses this paradox as the relation between formation and transformation.[21] As a church and as educators we are in the business of formation. Our liturgical life, our family lives, our educational institutions mold the intellects, imaginations, relationships, and affects of the upcoming generation. Nevertheless, the gospel message is that no amount of achievement will on its own eradicate the consequences of evil. Indeed, the good news is the law of the cross—that human effort in the end will come to naught, that our formation will be upended in transformation. So we are in the odd position of trying to establish educational institutions that are meant to lead to failure—that is, that are meant to be undone by a transformative experience whereby students see the ultimate futility of their professional, educational, and even spiritual goals.

In fact, of course, we are not in the business of promoting failure in the name of transformation. At the same time, suffering and experiences of crucifixion abound—many of our students are too well aware of the brokenness of human relations and the futility of human effort in trying to fix the world's ills. The question becomes how to incorporate this suffering and the need for grace and healing into our pedagogy, into our bureaucracies. This takes some creative imagination; but it seems to me that when we consider the values base of Catholic higher education, we need to think not only of the virtues we want to propound but also of the healing and forgiveness that are available through God's grace. "Catholic values" are not just a matter of religiously correct positions on sexual and social issues. They are also a matter of recognizing and embracing our own sins and wounds, the ways in which we have hurt and been hurt. Though a college or university is not a church and should not try to be one, nevertheless it can exhibit a pastoral pedagogy that promotes the downward mobility of servant leadership rather than merely advocating the upward mobility of professional and financial success.

This, then, leads to my final set of insights about an ethic of risk that sets conditions of possibility. The pastoral pedagogy mentioned above comes necessarily with a humility about what we intend and how we accomplish what we desire. An ethic of control would presume that we can come up with a formula that guarantees the efficacy of our actions. Catholic identity would be a matter of having the right policies and procedures, enforcing Catholic values on a college campus. In fact, though learning can take place through coercion and control, insights are novelties that emerge not by direct causality but by emergent probability. As teachers we try to affect the probabilities that desired insights will occur. Indeed, this is the heart of all pedagogy. But the best we can do is to set up the conditions of possibility for the requisite insights and conversions to take place. In the end we are not in control of what learning and growth does or does not happen. To the degree that we believe that our goal is not only the upward mobility of education but the transformation of gospel love, we will set up conditions of possibility not only for learning but for an otherworldly falling in love.

Catholic higher education is about setting up the conditions of possibility for transformation—intellectual, moral, and religious. Catholic identity is not a matter of labels, demarcations, categories, or doctrinal proclamations. Though Catholic education deals with the content of the tradition, it must also attend to the learner and promote his or her cognitive, moral, and religious self-appropriation. Learning how one asks and answers questions will ground the truths that are taught as enduring doctrines. And perhaps the best way to promote such learning is to have an authentic learning community. The Catholic heritage will be accepted to the degree that there are appealing and credible persons teaching it. These teachers will be credibly believed if they themselves are asking critical questions in a spirit of humility. An ethic of risk combined with faith in a God who is not too small, and who is certainly not under our control, will create a matrix of action in which new and wonderful transformations can emerge.

Notes

1. See Robert M. Doran, *Theology and the Dialectics of History* (Toronto: University of Toronto Press, 1990).

2. So far in this chapter I have discussed only the first three operations of consciousness, as explicated by Bernard Lonergan. These have to do with the determination of facts. Lonergan also outlines the operations involved in a fourth level—those operations involved in deliberation and decision making. For a fuller explication of these, see Bernard Lonergan, *Method in Theology* (New York: Seabury Press, 1979), chap. 1.

3. For a discussion of belief in relation to immanently generated knowledge, see ibid., 41–47.

4. See Carol Gilligan, *In a Different Voice: Psychological Theory and Women's Development* (Cambridge, MA: Harvard University Press, 1982). See also Cynthia S. W. Crysdale, "Gilligan and the Ethics of Care: An Update," *Religious Studies Review* 20 (1994): 21–28; Crysdale, "Gilligan's Epistemological Challenge: Implications for Method in Ethics," *The Irish Theological Quarterly* 56 (1990): 31–48.

5. See Cynthia S. W. Crysdale, "Heritage and Discovery: A Framework for Moral Theology," *Theological Studies* 63 (2002): 559–78. See also Frederick E. Crowe, *Old Things and New: A Strategy for Education* (Atlanta: Scholars Press, 1985).

6. See Cynthia S. W. Crysdale, "Lonergan and Feminism," *Theological Studies* 53 (1992): 234–56. See also Crysdale, "Women and the Social Construction of Self-Appropriation," in *Lonergan and Feminism*, ed. Crysdale (Toronto: University of Toronto Press, 1994), 88–113.

7. This lecture was published as "Feminist Theology: Ideology, Authenticity, and the Cross," *Église et Théologie* 28 (1997): 245–63.

8. Joanne C. Brown and Carole R. Bohn, eds., *Christianity, Patriarchy, and Abuse: A Feminist Critique* (Cleveland: Pilgrim Press, 1989).

9. Bernard Lonergan, *De Verbo Incarnato* (Rome: Gregorian University Press, 1964).

10. Sebastian Moore, *The Crucified Is No Stranger* (London: Darton, Longman, and Todd, 1977).

11. Lonergan, *Method in Theology*, 240.

12. Sharon Welch, *A Feminist Ethic of Risk* (Minneapolis: Fortress Press, 1990); Cynthia S. W. Crysdale, *Embracing Travail: Retrieving the Cross Today* (New York: Continuum, 1999), especially chap. 3.

13. Welch, *Feminist Ethic of Risk*, 23.

14. Ibid., 19.

15. Ibid., 20. Although I use Welch's work to facilitate my own understanding of the redemption, in the end my theology of God is quite different from hers. See Crysdale, *Embracing Travail*, 170n51.

16. For those familiar with Lonergan's distinction between "description" and "explanation," this is not what I am referring to. Rather, I am just making the simple comparison between prescriptive and descriptive claims. Welch is prescriptively advocating an ethic of risk, whereas my point is that the ethic of risk is in fact what we do in any case.

17. Note that Michael Vertin has pointed out, based on Frederick E. Crowe's work on Aquinas, that there are judgments of value that do not look toward change but recognize and accept value as it already exists. Thus, Vertin makes the distinction between complacency and concern. Most notably, he contends that to interpret Lonergan's analysis of moral deliberation as having only to do with predicting and planning future change is a misinterpretation. See Vertin, "Judgments of Value, for the Later Lonergan," *Method: Journal of Lonergan Studies* 13 (1995): 221–48. See also Crowe, "Complacency and Concern in the Thought of St. Thomas," *Theological Studies* 20 (1959): 1–39, 198–230, 343–59. Crowe's articles have been edited by Vertin and published in book form: Crowe, *Three Thomist Studies*, ed. Vertin (Chestnut Hill, MA: Lonergan Institute of Boston College, 2000).

18. Welch, *Feminist Ethic of Risk*, 20.

19. See Charles C. Hefling, *Why Doctrines?* (Boston: Cowley Publications, 1984).

20. Robert Doran has nuanced Lonergan's discussion of dialectic by distinguishing between two forms of dialectics, those that are complementary and those that involve radical disagreement—what Doran calls contradictory differences. See Doran, *Theology and the Dialectics of History*, 10.

21. Rosemary Haughton, *The Transformation of Man* (Springfield, IL: Templegate Press, 1967; repr., 1980).

CHAPTER 3

Professional Education as Transformation

Robert J. Deahl

I have been for the last thirteen years the dean of the College of Professional Studies at Marquette University in Milwaukee, Wisconsin. The college is one of eleven colleges and schools at Marquette and is committed to educating working professionals—adult, nontraditional students—throughout southeastern Wisconsin.

While writing this chapter, I have been working with my staff, faculty, and advisors in completing a strategic plan for the college as we prepare to celebrate the fifteenth anniversary in 2011. This plan is part of a university-wide effort designed to meet one of the critical needs that we face in Catholic higher education in the years ahead, namely, the need to achieve a wholeness and a unity that are easily overlooked despite our best efforts to work in concert with one another across disciplines, among diverse faculty, and throughout the university.

One of the cornerstones of our planning is to create, fund, implement, and launch a Center for Community Transformation. This center will be at the heart of the college's undergraduate, master's, and community learning programs and will provide a central, unifying place to bring together diverse individuals and groups to help restore and heal the problems we face throughout our local and regional communities.

As I think about these plans and the work that I have been involved in as dean, it strikes me that the nearly lifelong influence of Bernard Lonergan has played a pivotal role in how I approach my personal and professional life and work both within and outside the academy. This chapter explains how Lonergan has helped me with my own vision and commitment to bring a better sense of wholeness and unity to my college, to the university, and to the Milwaukee community. This book has used the term "catholicity," a notion that John Haughey embraced and elucidated in *Where Is Knowing Going? The Horizons of the Knowing Subject* to capture this sense of wholeness. Haughey notes,

> We are all hopers about any number of things. There is the ever present need and hope to keep moving from obscurity to clarity or to see the fuller picture, or to answer elusive questions. By getting past our ever importuning immediacies, we should be able to appreciate the fact that we are scripted to pursue some kind of *pleroma*: a completion, a fullness, just as surely as we are scripted to know what is so and what is good. The notion of catholicity keeps

beckoning us on to a more, to something yawning out before us, leading us on, that is in the genre of is and is good, but also of a more that is not more of the same.[1]

Striving toward Wholeness: Catholicity in Personal Reflection and Shared Conversations

I had the joy and honor of meeting and speaking with Bernard Lonergan at the Lonergan Workshop held at Boston College in 1981. I was in the middle of writing my dissertation, *Doing Ethics in the Third Stage of Meaning: Retrieving Ethics through the Generalized Empirical Method of Bernard J. F. Lonergan as a Disclosive and Transformative Function of Interiority*, under the direction of mentor and friend Josef Fuchs, and was home for the summer between my fifth and sixth year of studies in Rome. The dissertation focused on adapting the early work of Robert Doran to Lonergan's method and applying both to the field of ethics. Lonergan's positive comments about the focus of my work provided a great source of encouragement and support.[2]

As I think about my personal life journey and the professional work that I have been involved in as a faculty member and dean, it becomes clear that Lonergan has influenced me in two primary ways. First, his focus on intentionality analysis by way of integrating the discipline of the transcendental precepts has convinced me of the need for the personal practice of self-appropriation. This is not a one-time event but a regular, sustained reflective practice in which I consciously and intentionally take stock of what I am doing and why I am doing it.

In this regard I resonate strongly with David Orr's notion of slow knowledge as he explains it in *The Nature of Design: Ecology, Culture and Human Invention*. Orr argues for the need to engage in slow, reflective knowledge: "Because new knowledge often requires rearranging worldviews and paradigms which we can only do slowly. Instead of increasing the speed of our chatter, we need to learn to listen more attentively. Instead of increasing the volume of our communications, we ought to improve its content. Instead of communicating more extensively, we should converse more intensively with our neighbors."[3] Taking this time is, I believe, the key to unlocking Lonergan's method of accessing self-appropriation. Many years ago, even before leaving to study and live in Italy, I began the practice of taking a retreat at least once a year to actively seek out the space and time for quiet reflection, reading, and writing. In fact, the one constant in my life's journey is the regular practice of retreating into interiority and remapping my conscious intentionality that keeps me in the present in a way that allows the future to emerge in fresh and new ways.

I see this reflection as absolutely necessary in my role as dean. Many decisions that affect many peoples' lives are made in the boardrooms or the offices of corporate and academic leaders who may have no sense of self-appropriation and no regular practice of reflection. Such leaders make decisions and actions pell-mell in the rush of doing too much with insufficient information or context and therefore operate more in the world of a conceptualized, unappropriated immediacy and less out of a reasonable, responsible context of fully human knowing.

Second, Lonergan's focus on intellectual conversion that draws a sharp distinction between the world of immediacy and the world mediated by meaning and motivated by value has influenced my attempts to make judgments and decisions and to act in ways that are consciously aligned with what is real, here and now, and what is of and for the good. This kind of process, this kind of praxis, represents—for me, in my experience—the kind of alignment that Lonergan calls for when he points to the nexus of genuine objectivity and authentic subjectivity. Lonergan's attention to the subject made it more likely that objectivity could be attained. Haughey points out, "Rather than despairing about whether or not we'll ever understand one another because of the increasingly differentiated universes of discourse developing in the world, he became convinced that objectivity can be achieved and dialogue can become fruitful where authentic personal and collective subjectivity is operating in a more explicit manner."[4]

Personal reflections and shared conversations are the tools we have available as we strive toward self-appropriation and a collective achievement of the real and the good in our midst. These are also at the heart of the Western, Catholic theological tradition of *actio* and *contemplatio*, of action and contemplation, of action grounded in the discernment of reflection. And this is where I experience this dynamic pull of catholicity.

This notion of catholicity, a heuristic that pushes for a further whole, its dynamic always moving us toward an entirety, is what informs and motivates and energizes my own work as dean of our college. I envision a future of Catholic higher education as developing a praxis catholicity more than a doctrinal catholicity: a catholicity that has transformative power that resides in and emerges from our interiority rather than from a static set of assumptions about the true and the good.

Embracing Catholicity through the College of Professional Studies

I have had the privilege of being involved in a number of highly productive and challenging conversations over the past thirteen years in my roles as dean, chief administrator, and faculty member at Marquette University. Working with students, faculty, alumni, leaders in the community, and people from a wide variety of industries and disciplines, we have created an environment that invites adult students to embark on a journey of self-identification and self-appropriation. The liberal arts courses that are at the core of our curriculum provide the context in which students can explore who they are in relation to their world.

Many of our adult students initially balk at the notion of having to take theology and philosophy courses, and they ask us how this or that course could possibly be helpful or relevant to their job or profession. As the dean I am often asked to write a letter to a student's employer to explain how a theology or philosophy course will benefit the employee's personal life and professional career, and how the company can justify providing employee reimbursement for taking such a course. I welcome these requests and have tried to carefully articulate the value—and even the return on investment—that our liberal arts courses, such as theology and philosophy, offer the employer and their student.

Our staff and faculty hear time and again how these courses that our students once viewed as unnecessary or irrelevant have become the most important courses that they have taken and, in many cases, have changed lives in ways that have truly been transformative and liberating. My colleagues and I have seen scores of our adult students move from a more hardened, biased, literal, fundamentalist way of thinking, judging, and acting to a much more complex, nuanced, considered approach to the world around them. We see our students moving toward higher—indeed, wider—viewpoints: a largeness and largesse of understanding. This change becomes apparent in how they begin to speak differently about their lives, in the complex questions that they pose, and in the way that they express their hopes and aspirations.

This overall, potentially transformative, educational experience in our college has been the "symbolic operator," to use Lonergan's term, the trigger that activates the transcendental precepts that Lonergan speaks of—be attentive, be intelligent, be reasonable, be responsible—and makes them alive and engaged in our students' lives.[5] This is an educational experience that focuses on the student's capacity for self-transcendence: morally, intellectually, and religiously inviting, prompting, and challenging our students to embrace the world in a more holistic, attentive, intelligent, reasonable, responsible, and inclusive way. In very real ways students begin to undergo an intellectual conversion in Lonergan's sense and begin to see their own self-appropriation as an essential part of their lifelong learning.

I'd like to share four examples in which my own appropriation of Lonergan's insight and method and the challenge of his transcendental precepts have affected how I approach the work of our College of Professional Studies at Marquette University. It is in these examples that this notion of catholicity keeps beckoning my colleagues and me on to something more, something more whole within the university, within the community, within the curriculum, and within our faculty working across various disciplines.

Catholicity and the University

Fifteen years ago Marquette University launched its first degree program designed specifically for adult students and working professionals. Since then the College of Professional Studies has been developing and implementing an expanding repertoire of undergraduate and graduate degree programs, noncredit and certificate continuing education programs, and a workforce learning program that customizes training and education programs for corporations and other organizations throughout the community. The college utilizes a variety of nontraditional models and frameworks to manage and deliver its student services, online and classroom student instruction, and faculty development.

Many faculty and administrators along the way have been reluctant to embrace new ways of delivering our courses to these nontraditional adult students. Over the past decade the staff and faculty of the college have had to advocate for and defend these models and promote a broadened understanding of how teaching and learning can take place in new and different ways within the confines of a very traditional university framework. I have tried to make sure that we have implemented these changes in a very intentional way—one as intelligent, reasonable, and responsible as possible—through our advocacy on committees, the representation of our students and programs to other offices on campus, and our efforts to inform as many of our colleagues as possible about the meaning and value inherent in our mission of educating adult students.

Although there remains a great deal of work to be done to help full-time traditional faculty and administrators appreciate and embrace both our nontraditional adult student population and the different ways in which we engage student learning, I believe that the College of Professional Studies, by following Lonergan's transcendental precepts in the work we have done, can continue to help create better conditions throughout the university community for the possibility of a more "catholic" appropriation of alternative models for teaching and learning. Other colleges within Marquette have now adopted our delivery models and frameworks, and several have enlisted our assistance to design and implement faculty development programs based on our college's model.

Catholicity and the Community

Thirteen years ago the college forged a strategic partnership with Harley-Davidson Motor Company, whose global corporate headquarters is located in close proximity to the Marquette University campus in the heart of Milwaukee. For the past thirteen years the college has delivered its bachelor's degree in organization and leadership to the employees of Harley-Davidson on-site at the plant. In developing this unique educational partnership between an urban Jesuit Catholic university and a world-renowned American motorcycle company, we quickly discovered a rich synergy between the organizational values of the company and the mission of the university and of the college. We both find common ground in our commitment to develop a values-based learning organization dedicated to the personal and professional growth of our employees and students.

Under the inspirational leadership of former chief executive officer and chairman Richard Teerlink, Harley-Davidson was one of the first participants in the work being done in the early 1990s at the Massachusetts Institute of Technology with Peter Senge and Daniel Kim in applying systems thinking to the development of learning organizations. Harley-Davidson committed itself to creating effective organizational conditions for the emerging possibilities of dynamic and sustained economic growth by empowering its employees to participate fully in the recreation of the company. Teerlink's conviction that "people are our most important sustainable advantage" came alive through the company's engagement of employees in learning circles and regular cycles of intellectual development.[6] Harley-Davidson empowers its employees by engaging as many employees as possible in conversations about how to make the company better. The company does this as long as it takes and until they get it right. This is very much like Lonergan's notion of the "self-correcting process of learning"—asking the questions until we get it right.[7]

Our Harley-Davidson–Marquette partnership is a model that we have since duplicated with a growing number of companies throughout southeastern Wisconsin. Through the sustained development of these corporate relationships and our attentiveness and responsiveness to their needs, we contribute to a growing awareness of how companies make a difference in people's lives by how they support and interact with their employees, their customers, and their stakeholders. These relationships are helping our community develop a capacity for an appropriation of the kind of meaning and value that empowers people to live and act in responsible ways.

Catholicity and the Curriculum

Since the inception of Marquette's College of Professional Studies, its primary focus has been leadership education for adult working professionals. Recently, the college faculty designed a new professional master's degree in leadership studies. We intentionally designed the core courses for this master's degree based on Lonergan's transcendental precepts: Be attentive, be intelligent, be reasonable, be responsible, be loving.

The new master's program presents the student with a conscious focus on leadership and ethics from the inside out, beginning with the self and moving through an ever-widening scope of leadership and interrelationships, leadership and society, leadership and the world. We have designed specific outcomes suited to each of the courses, and student assessment is based on an ever-deepening appropriation of leadership and ethics on both a personal and a professional level. In every course the students are challenged to understand their own experiences as leaders and to explore and affirm their own roles as leaders within the different contexts of their lives.

Lonergan's method and his map of intentionality in this master's program, though not always immediately transparent, provide the operating principles for how students will progress through this degree program, culminating in a praxis-based learning experience that integrates reflection and application of what has been learned and appropriated throughout the degree and how this learning is applied in their personal and professional lives. Students are challenged at every turn to consciously examine their assumptions and their judgments, and they are asked to constantly stretch beyond and sometimes break out of their past learning patterns to reach toward a more complex, intelligent, reasonable, responsible way of constructing their world mediated by meaning and motivated by values.

This is a learning journey that embraces complexity and ambiguity and works actively to create the conditions for the possibility of moving out of a literalist, dualist, and fundamentalist approach that displaces authority onto something or someone other than oneself. Students begin to understand their unique roles and contributions as leaders and learn that authentic leadership comes from within their own understanding of their places in the world. This is a learning journey that directly challenges students to become the authors of their own lives in every sense of that word.

Catholicity and the Faculty across Disciplines

The college has implemented a program for faculty development. Three times a year, the faculty of the college gathers over a meal and spends either part of a day or an evening engaged in focused discussion on some aspect of student learning and classroom teaching.

Faculty from all disciplines in the college come together to share best teaching practices, discuss student assessment, explore new models and methods of pedagogy, or simply share stories about the successes, challenges, and lessons learned from their own practice. We have held these sessions on a regular basis for the past eleven years and have gradually created a community of shared learning and collegial support in which faculty feel safe, respected, supported, and challenged in their reflections and practice.

This program has had an impact on the life and growth of the college and contributes to the broadening and deepening of individual faculty members' understanding and appreciation of one another's disciplines. In this sense the college has created the conditions for real interdisciplinary conversation and collaboration.

One of the activities that we experience together in these faculty development sessions is the sharing of an "intellectual hero." Individual faculty tell about a mentor, author, or teacher whose craft and insights and impact have made a profound difference in the life of that faculty member. We have heard stories of parents, painters, philosophers, poets, scientists. The sharing of the intellectual hero has been the occasion for faculty from diverse disciplines to consciously articulate just how their thinking, their teaching, and their practice have been formed and shaped and how they have personally and professionally appropriated those influences in their lives.

Many of us in the program have been challenged to reflect upon our own discipline and our own thinking and practice because of these presentations. And if there is one clear place where I can palpably point to a feeling of catholicity, a sense of the wholeness of what we do, however different and diverse we are across disciplines, this is the place. This program can surely be a model for other faculty conversations that reach across disciplinary lines and reach toward a unity that we seem so seldom to experience in the siloized tendencies that run so rampant through university life. Indeed, how do we create—and sustain—this kind of culture of intellectual conversion among our students and our faculty, throughout our community, and build across our divisions toward the wholeness that we desire?

On the heath Lear asks Gloucester, "How do you see the world?" And Gloucester, who is blind, answers, "I see it feelingly." Our Catholic liberal arts tradition helps us see the future feelingly and can fire and inspire our moral imagination in ways that lead us out of the confines of a world too narrow, too immediate, too literal, too restricted, and into something more.

It is a tradition that stands on the depth of history and embraces a breadth of meaning and value in a way that at once honors pluralism and difference while calling forth our human capacity for wholeness. I believe it is a tradition that can reach across boundaries and, while committed to the education of the whole person, can bring together the multiplicity of disciplines in ways that allow us to see that we are more authentic when we are together than when we are fragmented and apart. It is a tradition that embraces this notion of catholicity, pushing us further and striving toward wholeness.

The Liberal Arts and Professional Education

The ancient Chinese word *hua*, which means "change through teaching," captures the essence of liberal arts education. *Hua* consists of two characters: on the left, the character for human being; on the right, a character depicting an inverted human being. Education turns us and our world upside down. As

Meg Wheatley states in *Leadership: The New Science*, "Knowledge is disruptive."[8] As its name suggests, the goal of liberal education is to free us from prejudices, misconceptions, biases, and assumptions about the world around and within us.

Therein lies the difference between liberal arts and vocational education. Vocational instruction assumes that students already know what they want. It takes the student's goal, such as becoming a computer technician or an electrician, as a given and then teaches the student how to perform tasks associated with that goal. Vocational education is often termed "training"—we train by performing one task repeatedly until we have mastered it. In this respect vocational training is primarily instrumental. And unlike liberal arts education, it affirms the learner's view of himself or herself and his or her place within the immediate world.

I believe liberal arts education goes beyond the instrumental training and seeks formally to create the conditions by which the learner is challenged to (re)consider his or her place in a world mediated by meaning and motivated by value. William Sullivan's recent call for renewing professional education in *Work and Integrity: The Crisis and Promise of Professionalism in America* echoes this sentiment and emphasizes the need for a new model of education that concerns itself with shaping the consciousness and character of our students.[9] Rather than merely providing an educational environment that consists of an unreflective immersion in one's occupation and culture, Sullivan calls for a recovery of what he calls the "formative dimension" of education. Lonergan's invitation to intellectual conversion and self-appropriation is very much in alignment with Sullivan's work.

This formative education is above all a kind of shaping of the person, providing an educational environment that is not just informative but potentially transformative. An appreciation of this dynamic, heuristic notion of catholicity could help us see more clearly this point of institutionalized learning. As Haughey notes in *Where Is Knowing Going?*, "What is missing in educational theory is this notion of catholicity, a heuristic that pushes for a further whole, a connectedness between partial knowns known as partial."[10] My life experience tells me this is so.

Past to Present: An Emergent Catholicity

Indeed, when I look back on my own educational experiences, I see the profound impact that the Catholic liberal arts tradition, the work of Lonergan, and the influences of other cultures and religions have had on my life. I see a whole more than I see divisions; I see a breadth of viewpoints and perspectives more than I see the constraints of a single point of view. It is from the richness of these experiences that I turned my own focus and energies toward a life in professional education and my work as dean of our College of Professional Studies. Lonergan mapped a cartography of subjectivity, his insight and method providing illumination for the journey.

I grew up in a quintessential, traditional Catholic home in the Midwest attending Catholic grade school, part of all that was Catholic culture and piety in the late 1950s and early 1960s. Praying in Latin at mass as an altar boy, participating in May Day processions to honor Mary, and participating in weekly rosaries and the seasonal rituals of Advent and Lent shaped and formed my young view of the world in the safety and sacredness of American Roman Catholicism.

It was during my years at Saint Francis de Sales Seminary High School in Milwaukee that I began to get a peek at a different way of understanding my Catholic religious roots. Though we all drank deeply from the rich wells of a classical education, our teachers—young Catholic priests who themselves were beginning to change how they understood their own roles and identities within a new people of God that was just emerging at that pivotal moment of Vatican II—began to expose us to a different, less literal way of understanding the faith and culture that so deeply surrounded us.

I remember listening to the musical *Jesus Christ Superstar* in religion class and accessing the symbols and metaphors of the life of Jesus and the Christ of the early Church in ways that sounded and felt quite different from the pious Jesus depicted and recounted through the Holy Name Society and the Serra Club. As the Church and the seminary began to shed many of their devotional accoutrements, and as the liturgy became more accessible, demystified, and less unknown, my own sense of self and authority began to quietly shift from an immediacy of "out there" to a more mediated "in here" that was prompted, encouraged, and cajoled with great care by my seminary spiritual directors.

But it was surely during my college years at Saint Francis Seminary College that I moved from what Lonergan calls the realm of common sense to the realm of theory, and out toward that great space of liberation and freedom that he calls the realm of interiority. My college seminary, in those days of the late 1960s and early 1970s, is still looked upon by many of us who lived and studied there as a golden age in the life of the local church. Not only did I continue my studies in Latin and Greek and feast on the full menu of theology courses—from biblical to historical, from systematic to moral to sacramental—I also immersed myself in philosophy, literature, sociology, and psychology, all of which opened up a whole new set of perspectives on the world around and within me. But it was through my studies in theology in particular that my life began to change.

When one of the priests, Tom Suriano, introduced me to Rudolph Bultman, and Richard Sklba, today a bishop, opened up a whole new way of understanding the Hebrew scriptures, I was jerked out of the perfunctory way of reading and interpreting texts that I was used to and was thrust into a whole new world of myth and metaphor and hermeneutics. Horizons and viewpoints shifted in radical ways.

It was in my third year of college that another priest, John Yockey, introduced me to Lonergan's *Insight* and began to speak about his books *The Subject* and *Method in Theology*.[11] Yockey talked about cognitional theory in a way that began to sketch out the broad lines of how I would begin to reconstruct my way of thinking about the world around me—a world that became less immediate, less literal, and more complicated, more dense, more mediated by new meanings and values. He did all of this in a course titled the Theology of Nonviolence, in which I also read Gandhi, Thomas Merton, and Martin Luther King Jr. and examined the just war theory that was being tossed about as Vietnam wound down and the Cold War cranked up.

In retrospect it seems quite fitting that Lonergan first appeared on my horizon in a course on nonviolence. During the last two years of my college seminary days, I began attending the noon Mass in the Joan of Arc Chapel on the Marquette University campus and listened to scores of sermons by Sebastian Moore. In my senior year I took an independent study course at Marquette with Matt Lamb titled Political Theology, and I worked with Lamb, Jim Groppi, and others to prevent the deportation of Michael Cullen. Cullen was the charismatic leader of the Milwaukee Fourteen who, along with Jim Forrest and a dozen others, burned draft cards in protest against the war in Vietnam in 1968. Cullen was in touch with Daniel and Philip Berrigan, brothers who had taken similar actions, and a strong and growing group of Catholic leaders in Milwaukee became quite involved with the civil rights movement, the women's movement, and the antiwar protests that were spreading across the country.

As I look back on this heady time, I can see how my growing understanding of self-appropriation, as Lonergan outlined this, provided a framework for me to stretch beyond the previously set and entrenched boundaries of a more static self-understanding of faith and church and world. Lonergan's invitation to negotiate the realm of interiority pulled me into a new world, a new way of connecting myself to the world around me. Seeds were planted that would eventually break new ground and stir new growth. Like a living heuristic, I found something new here, something yet unknown but known enough to pursue and explore, something pushing for a further whole.

In 1976 I was sent to Rome, Italy, to continue my studies at the Pontifical Gregorian University. I never expected to spend six years of my life living and studying in Rome and traveling, studying, and working around the world. Many of my contemporaries at the time assumed that since I was studying at the Gregorian University in Rome, I would be immersed in a world of conservative, doctrinaire theology. Nothing could be further from the truth. Professors from Latin America, India, Eastern Europe, Africa, and Asia brought new and emerging perspectives on a staggering array of topics. My Jesuit mentor, who became a dear friend, Josef Fuchs, directed my dissertation and worked with me for four years as I applied Lonergan's work in the field of moral theology.

Fuchs, sometimes known as the Silver Fox to his peers in Rome for his clever and yet reasoned ways of remapping the traditional models of moral theology, had known Lonergan when both taught at the Gregorian University and understood his approach to cognitional theory and intentionality analysis. My weekly conversations with this great scholar remain one of the highlights of my life, and I will forever remember him with affection and appreciation for his commitment to excellence in his scholarship. I was one of the last Americans he directed before he fell into ill health. His depth of scholarship and breadth of application of his discipline remain a powerful intellectual complement to my work with Lonergan. Fuchs's challenge to become and remain an authentic person will forever resound in me alongside Lonergan's call to self-appropriation.

During my years in Rome I had the good fortune to live and study in Paris, Jerusalem, Calcutta, and Cape Town and Durban in South Africa. These travels exposed me to cultures and religious traditions far afield from the Western, Judeo-Christian world in which I had grown up. I experienced once again a shift from a more literal, dichotomized way of seeing the world to one that began to recognize and appreciate a more holistic, interconnected world, one in which peoples and cultures share a common bond—a bond that Lonergan would locate in interiority.

It was during my studies in Israel and my travels through the Middle East that I found the growing cultures of fundamentalism—be it Islamic, Jewish, or Christian—to be in such sharp contrast to the liberating effects of Lonergan's method for self-appropriation. Something felt wrong; something did not ring true. The metaphors and symbols of those traditions that were supposed to be resilient and malleable, rich in tradition and shot through with an energy toward transcendence, seemed hardened, truncated, and manipulated by the controlling dynamics of a fundamentalist viewpoint of the world, of God. This seemed in such contrast to the more expansive, heuristically charged notion of catholicity that was clearly informing my own educational experience.

Upon completion of my dissertation, return to the United States, and priestly ordination in Milwaukee on August 8, 1980, and after four years in the priesthood, my embrace of Lonergan's path to self-appropriation once again changed how I understood the world and my place in it. After a long retreat at the Camaldolese Monastery in the mountains above Big Sur, CA—a place I have returned to many times since then—I made the difficult decision to leave active ministry. Rembert Weakland, whom I had come to know from the day he was named the archbishop of Milwaukee in 1977 while he lived in Rome as the abbot primate of the Benedictine order, received my news with sadness but encouraged me to stay close to the world of Catholic higher education that had so deeply shaped me from my years in the seminary to my studies in Rome. It was not the life and work of ministry in the Catholic Church that led me to leave but rather the mandate of a life of celibacy, a charism that is to be cherished—and one that perhaps should be freely chosen.

All along on this journey from my college years throughout the six years of study at the Gregorian University and on to travel, work, and study around the globe, the self-appropriating methodology of Lonergan provided a liberating framework for growth and understanding, for judging, discerning, learning, and reconstructing the world I live in, mediated by rich new meanings and motivated by the tug and pull of new insights and values.

It has been Lonergan's map of our conscious intentionality that helps lead me out of the biased cul-de-sacs of unappropriated assumptions and absolutes about how the world is supposed to be according to some "already out there, now real." This map pushes me to recognize a much more organic, (w)holistic way toward meaning and truth and value.

Moreover, it has been my life experience both as a student and as an educator that the liberal arts tradition indeed can create the conditions for the possibility of personal liberation and transformation. It is largely because of Lonergan's lifelong influence on how I understand myself and the world around me that I see my role, my vocation, as dean as one of creating those conditions for personal liberation and transformation for our students.

Striving toward Wholeness

This chapter has been a brief personal account of the process of my own intellectual conversion. I have explained how my particular self-appropriation of Lonergan's method and the zeitgeist of his transcendental precepts—be attentive, be intelligent, be reasonable, be responsible—continue to liberate me from the constraints of a prevailing culture of what I would call intellectual fundamentalism that seems to prevent individuals and communities from reaching a richer sense of self and of life. Rather, I hope to embrace this notion of catholicity that pushes us toward a completion, a fullness—indeed, toward God.

Master Nan Huai Chin, who is regarded by many in China as the most important living *chan* (Zen) Buddhist master and who is also a Taoist master and an eminent Confucian scholar, has stated, "What has been lacking in the twentieth century is some *central cultural thought* that would attempt to unify all these things: economy, technology, ecology, society, matter, mind and spirituality" (emphasis added). Nan states that this "central integrating thought" will emerge from building three integrated capacities: "A new capacity for *observing* that no longer fragments the observer from what's observed; a new capacity for *stillness* that no longer fragments who we really are from what's emerging; and a new capacity for *creating alternative realities* that no longer fragment the wisdom of the head, heart and hand" (emphasis added).[12]

My experience is that Lonergan provides a method—a way—to reach toward that central integrating thought that Master Nan speaks of and shows us a way toward a newfound wholeness. In Lonergan's words: "Thoroughly understand what it is to understand, and not only will you understand the broad lines of all there is to be understood, but you will possess a fixed base, an invariant pattern, opening upon all further developments of understanding."[13]

Notes

1. John C. Haughey, *Where Is Knowing Going? The Horizons of the Knowing Subject* (Washington, DC: Georgetown University Press, 2009), 95.

2. I have likewise deeply appreciated other Lonergan influences along the way: Sebastian Moore and Matt Lamb at Marquette University; Jerzy Szaszkiewicz and Giovanni Sala at the Gregorian University; Joe Komonchak and David Tracy, who were scholars in residence in Rome; Dick Liddy at the North American College; Archbishop Dennis Hurley of Durban, South Africa; Gabriel (Gabey) Ehman, a priest in Edmonton, Canada; Michael O'Callaghan, Terry Tekippe, Phil McShane, Fred Lawrence, Shawn Copeland, Fred Crowe, and other friends at the Lonergan Workshops at Boston College that I attended during and after my Rome years; and John Haughey and my colleagues who have been collaborating on this book for three years.

3. David Orr, *The Nature of Design: Ecology, Culture and Human Intention* (New York: Oxford University Press, 2002), 42.

4. Haughey, *Where Is Knowing Going?*, 92.

5. Bernard Lonergan, *Philosophical and Theological Papers 1965–1980*, ed. Frederick E. Crowe and Robert M. Doran, Collected Works of Bernard Lonergan 17 (Toronto: University of Toronto Press, 2004), 400.

6. Richard Teerlink, *More Than a Motorcycle: The Leadership Journey at Harley-Davidson* (Boston: Harvard Business School Press, 2000), 33.

7. Bernard Lonergan, *Insight: A Study of Human Understanding* (New York: Philosophical Library, 1958), 174.

8. Margaret Wheatley, *Leadership and the New Science: Discovering Order in a Chaotic World* (San Francisco: Barrett-Koehler Publishers, Inc. 1999), 32.

9. William M. Sullivan, *Work and Integrity: The Crisis and Promise of Professionalism in America* (San Francisco: Jossey-Bass, 2005).

10. Haughey, *Where Is Knowing Going?*, 120.

11. Bernard Lonergan, *The Subject* (Milwaukee, WI: Marquette University Press, 1968); and Lonergan, *Method in Theology* (London: Darton, Longman & Todd, 1974).

12. Nan Huai Chin, quoted in C. Otto Scharmer et al., "Science Performed with the Mind of Wisdom," chap. 14 in *Presence: An Exploration of Profound Change in People, Organizations and Society* (New York: Random House, 2005), 211.

13. Lonergan, *Insight*, xxvii.

CHAPTER 4

Learning to Love the Law of the Sea

William P. George

For many if not most doctoral students, the choice of a dissertation topic is a matter not only of importance but, until the choice becomes clear, also of obscurity. At least it was for me. Late in my first year of doctoral studies in the mid-1980s, I had yet to settle on a general topic that would shape my remaining coursework and outside research. Having spent four years in Zambia, and with a background in philosophy and theology primarily in the Catholic tradition, I entered the University of Chicago Divinity School's program in ethics and society with vague ideas about exploring natural law, property rights, or especially some aspect of international economic justice—perhaps the ethics of international debt. But nothing seemed quite right.

Then one evening as I was thumbing through political science indexes in search of material for a paper on military intervention on humanitarian grounds, I chanced upon entries on a very different topic: the 1982 Convention on the Law of the Sea (hereafter "Law of the Sea"). This was a topic about which I knew next to nothing at the time. Yet almost out of the blue it suddenly, silently dawned on me that this would be—not could be, but would be—the topic of my dissertation. Not everything was clear. There was of course much to learn and much to do. But I had found my general topic, I was sure.

In the months that followed, I began to see striking continuities and discontinuities between this experience and what had gone before. Despite my lack of knowledge about the Law of the Sea, the topic did not emerge from nowhere. Rather it embraced, in one way or another, the very subject matter (natural law, property rights, international economic justice, and more) that I had been mulling over for some time.[1] But there was at least this point of discontinuity: Before I entered the Regenstein Library that evening I did not have a dissertation topic, and when I left I did.

This single, simple experience pointed me in new directions, leading to intellectual landscapes (or seascapes) and personal relationships I could not have anticipated even days or weeks before. Among my many memories of that period, two pertain especially to the aim of this chapter and the broader theme of emergent catholicity. One was the attempt at what Mark Morelli calls "horizontal diplomacy"—the movement back and forth between significantly different horizons.[2] Within a few months of the library epiphany, I found myself immersed in things international—law, relations, economics—through courses, readings, and discussion groups. A political scientist (later one of my dissertation readers) with an interest in international cooperation introduced me to game theory and to the then burgeoning work on international regimes.[3] Twice a week for one term I trudged across the Midway— a tract of land that separates the law school from the divinity school and the main campus of the University of Chicago—to attend a class in international law. Later I frequently made the same trip to settle on the sixth floor of D'Angelo Law Library, where texts and journals in international law are shelved.

Especially at first, it was like moving into an uncharted world. In fact, it was while reading a text on international regimes that first I came across the inscription found on the margins of ancient maps: "*Cave! Hic dragones*" (Beware! Here be dragons). Crossing over from theology, where I felt at home, to international law, where I did not, was a little like reaching the edge of my intellectual map. Yet deeper down it seemed not so totally different—for was this not, I asked myself, still ethics (my field of study) writ large? And might there not be something theological in it after all?

A second memory relevant to this chapter was the reaction of one person somewhat removed from academic life when I told him, in response to his query, that I was writing a dissertation on the Law of the Sea. "You mean the Holy See?" he asked. For in his mind, what else could a divinity school dissertation be about? In misunderstandings there are meanings to be found. And so this misunderstanding of a single word is worth keeping in mind, for it gets to the heart of this chapter as a contribution to this volume. That is, I do wish to say something about catholicity—including that found or desired in Catholic universities. And I even want to say something about the divine. It's just that the entry point and avenue are international law and not the Vatican.

Although my library experience might be interpreted and accounted for in more ways than one, Bernard Lonergan's description of "insight" is surely apt. Insight, Lonergan says, "(1) comes as a release to the tension of inquiry, (2) comes suddenly and unexpectedly, (3) is a function not of outer circumstances but inner conditions, (4) pivots between the concrete and the abstract, and (5) passes into the habitual texture of one's mind."[4] The pages that follow in this chapter could undertake a careful analysis of the particular insight I reached in the library that night and the manner in which that experience matches each component of Lonergan's description. Autobiographically that would be appropriate, since Lonergan's "understanding of understanding" has influenced me greatly. But my intent in this chapter is not simply autobiographical. Or to be more precise, if it is autobiographical, it falls along the lines of another element of Lonergan's thought that has shaped my understanding not only of the Law of the Sea but also of other matters of fundamental (one might say, with qualification, "metaphysical") importance.[5] I refer to isomorphism, or the dynamic correlation that exists between cognitive operations of the knowing subject, on the one side, and the object of his or her search, on the other.[6] So in the present instance one may posit a correlation between the operations of the knower—and, I would add, the decider—and that which is to be known or engaged in concrete ways, namely, the Law of the Sea.[7]

My focus then is isomorphism or correlation. But to sharpen the focus I need to add to the above description of insight another element discussed by Lonergan—the notion of emergence. "Add" is surely not the right word, for as Lonergan explains, insight is the "prototype of emergence."[8] The matter of settling on a dissertation topic was a matter of emergence. I did not have a topic, and then I had one—at least in inchoate form. The topic was not known to me, and then it was: It emerged. But emergence pertains to the topic of my dissertation in another crucial sense. As an enormously complex carrier of meaning and value, the Law of the Sea, along with international law in its other aspects, is itself characterized by the fact and dynamics of emergence. More specifically, in a manner explained more fully below, the existence and development of the Law of the Sea—as well as its breakdowns—may be understood within the framework of what Lonergan calls "emergent probability."[9]

Emergence, then, is the controlling or heuristic theme for what follows in this chapter. But to this I must yet again add—or simply emphasize, for it is not foreign to the notion of emergence—another element, that of fragility. I suppose the word "contingency" would serve as well. What I am emphasizing is the absence of a guarantee in international law—as in any number of other spheres of life, including academia—that emergence will occur or that the new reality that emerges will endure. There is no guarantee that children will really learn, that families will thrive, that businesses or nations or universities will prosper. For emergence is a matter of conditions, and these may or may not be met. So in the library incident described above, if certain "inner conditions" had been absent, the event—the insight—could not have occurred. Furthermore, a single insight will not do. Not only are insights a dime a dozen, subject to verification in acts of judgment, but insights along with judgments and decisions also accumulate.[10] There is a huge difference between a bright idea for a dissertation and a completed work. At this point I simply wish to comment that international law is subject to myriad conditions and a dialectics of emergence that may render it fragile.[11]

In what follows I first discuss the notion of emergence in relation to international law generally and then turn to the Law of the Sea for a more extensive and illustrative example. If I do not present here a complete or even adequate account of international law, this is due not only to the still-emerging character of my own grasp of this vast field of meaning and value, but also to the still-emerging character of international law itself. In the final section I return to personal narrative and draw some connections between my engagement of international law and my experience in Catholic higher education, where catholicity, too, displays a fragile, emergent character.

International Law and the Dialectics of Emergence

Since it happens that the work of Bernard Lonergan and international law share a common, if only partial, mooring in the thought of Thomas Aquinas, it may be appropriate to begin a discussion of the dialectics of emergence with a statement much like one might find in *Summa Theologica*: "It would seem that international law is of little substance."[12] This complaint against or dismissal of international law takes various forms. Some have proposed, for instance, that international law is simply what the present sole superpower, the United States, says it is; that no one obeys international law; that it is all theory and no practice; that international law is not real law; and that international lawyers are not real lawyers.[13]

Though these and similar criticisms of international law may cause problems for the apologist, they are not insuperable. If one considers the recognized sources of international law, namely, treaties, custom, and general principles accepted by the world's major legal systems, it is easy to show that the body of international law is considerable and growing.[14] As a system of norms and as an operating system, international law daily and usually silently governs, among other things, international travel, trade relations, space exploration, disaster relief, the conduct of war and preparation for it (including the development of weapons of mass destruction), care for the environment, and a wide range of human rights.[15]

Surely one must concede to its deniers that international law is far from perfect and that compliance is often a problem, but to dwell only on its imperfections is to overlook the remarkable fact of its achievement. This achievement could be spelled out at length, but perhaps a succinct, oft-quoted statement from a leading international lawyer can suffice: "It is probably the case," says Louis Henkin, "that *almost all nations observe almost all principles of international law and almost all of their obligations almost all of the time*" (his emphasis).[16] In short, the criticisms of international law are often overstated. International law is very real, and in multiple forms it has emerged.[17]

Still, there is no denying the fragility inherent in the dynamics of the emergence and sustenance of international law. For instance, Geoffrey Best concludes from his study of war and law since 1945 that the international legal record, though in some respects remarkable, has been anything but stellar at least in terms of compliance.[18] And for many, the recent practices of the United States, a supposedly strong supporter of international law, seem to show that the cynicism of international law's deniers is not totally ungrounded.[19] I will introduce some examples of how fragile the emergence of international law can be; but first it is helpful to say a bit more about emergence in general, and emergent probability in particular.

A key to emergence is the notion of conditionality: If certain conditions are met, then something (perhaps an insight) may occur. But that something may be not a single event but rather an entire scheme of recurrence. As Lonergan puts it, "if A occurs, then B, and if B then C, and if C then D, and if D then A again."[20] This A to D to A chain is made simple for the sake of explanation only; the limited number of terms should not obscure the enormous complexity of the many schemes in which human beings actually participate—both in the natural world (such as biological evolution, or the nitrogen or hydrological cycle) and in human history.

Think, for example, of all the conditions that must be met to ensure the more or less smooth, safe, and recurrent flow of traffic in and out of O'Hare International Airport. Consider what is required to get the planes fueled and up and running, to see that the ticketing goes off without a hitch, to make sure the luggage gets loaded in a timely fashion and gets off at the right place. And it would be a mistake to think of these things solely in terms of impersonal operations. "Operations" is a good word, but only if it includes, for instance, countless cognitive acts of attention to and proper interpretation of norms and protocols, along with the range of acts of intelligence (questioning, insights, judgments, decisions) that gave rise to those norms and protocols in the first place. And though my intent at this point is not to discuss international law, but rather to introduce the notion of emergent probability, it is worth noting that some of the conditions that must be met include the observance of international law—for example, norms regarding airspace and overflight.[21] Consider the number of ways in which this set of recurrent schemes may be interrupted: a thunderstorm in Chicago or snowstorm in Denver, a labor strike, a mechanical failure, the sudden dissolution of the airline due to financial failure, a terrorist attack that grounds all commercial flights for several days, a devastating hurricane that hits coastal states. Dwelling on such interruptions or stoppages will by no means produce an exhaustive list of conditions necessary to actualize air travel, but it may bring home the critical—in some instances life-and-death—importance of meeting any one, or any one set, of such conditions.

For Lonergan emergent probability is the worldview wherein higher schemes of recurrence are understood to emerge, according to schedules of probability, from lower schemes. A historical study of O'Hare International or United Airlines will not overlook the lower schemes of recurrence in engineering; research and design; manufacturing; financing; labor relations; negotiations with local, state, and federal government; legal compliance; and so on that condition the emergence of an airport or a major airline.[22] Nor are these lower schemes always relegated to the past. Current labor relations within a company, for instance, may be invisible to travelers. But they are no less important for being unseen, and if they severely sour then sooner or later the average passenger may learn the hard way of their importance when a slowdown or strike occurs.

The emergence of higher schemes from lower schemes is a matter of probability. The probability jumps when the conditions for the emergence of the higher scheme are met, and it jumps again when the higher scheme actually emerges.[23] Major airports are very difficult to get up and running, but once the obstacles have been cleared the odds for emergence are greatly increased.[24] And it is easier to maintain an airport than it is to build one. But increased probability is not inevitability. The initial emergence is not guaranteed, and neither is the sustenance of the schemes that do emerge. In the extreme, airports may be put out of commission by a hurricane or during war, and at times United Airlines, for example, has appeared on the verge of going out of business if persistent internal wrangling and extreme financial difficulties could not be resolved.[25]

At least four more critical aspects of emergent probability need to be noted, if not fully explicated, before returning to international law. The first is that of defensive circles. Lonergan explains that, in almost paradoxical fashion, recurrent schemes that could condition real progress "bind within their routines the material for the possibility of later schemes and thus block the way to full development."[26] In other words, the very thing that gives schemes their stability may also impede the emergence of new schemes. Now in some instances defensive circles may be highly desirable. For example, a working immune system can stave off the emergence of disease. But the defensive circles may also be undesirable: for instance, when loyalty to one's fellow police officers, so necessary in the field, becomes a "blue wall of silence" that thwarts the emergence of a more honest and humane police force.[27]

And this draws attention to the second point: Schemes of recurrence contribute to, and in certain respects constitute, the good of order—not just food for a day, but the developed means of growing, harvesting, processing, and delivering the food. But the good of order is not the good in its entirety.[28] There is also the question of the values (or disvalues) served by the schemes.[29] So a fleet of airplanes might be up and running, and the planes may leave and return only to take off again, day after day—but their ongoing mission may be to destroy entire population centers.[30]

Third, a notion of the good that transcends the good of order calls attention to something else—the idea that emergence and emergent probability in human affairs are conditioned in part by conversion (intellectual, moral, religious) or its absence. This huge topic cannot be dealt with sufficiently here, but it may at least be said that various kinds of bias—dramatic, individual, group, and the general bias of common sense—will impede or skew the emergence of new schemes that actualize the common good.[31] To give an example that brings us back to international law, one may consider the manner in which racism, a deeply embedded and pernicious form of group bias, could support the defensive circles that sought to defeat the emergence of nascent human rights laws proscribing the slave trade with its particular cooperative schemes, or good of order. More generally, if the human subjects engaged in schemes of recurrence at various levels lack conversion, or if that conversion is only partial, then this will shift the probabilities of emergence or, if emergence does occur, will shift the likelihood that the schemes to be sustained are truly humane.

I have stressed the manner in which lower schemes condition development through the probable emergence of higher schemes. The fourth and final point is that the emergence that takes place recalls that which occurs in cognitional processes when, successively, a novel experience gives rise to questioning (What is it?); insights into that experience beg for criticism and judgment (Is it really so?); and settled matters of fact urge sound decisions about the good to be pursued (What should we do?). But it should also be stressed that such development is also promoted from above, for instance in the form of an affectively moving visionary agenda, inherited values, or especially the experience of falling in love that radically shifts one's horizons.[32] For present purposes, development from above is especially important to keep in mind for at least two reasons. On the one hand, we should not underestimate the manner in which international law, with its long and in some respects venerable tradition, develops from top down, as well as from bottom up. On the other, religion can play, and has played, a crucial role in providing the visions, the values, and even—or especially—the unrestricted love that can aid in that development from above.[33]

A Return to International Law

My point is not simply to discuss the workings of airports or airlines, but rather to say enough about emergent probability to provide a basis for seeing how international law fits within this framework and at the same time is marked by fragility. Consider then a few examples. The first is the League of Nations as an operating system for international law. As is regularly pointed out, the catalyst for the growth of international law is often the horror of war.[34] So in briefest terms, the disaster of World War I gave rise to the emergence of the League, which was to advance international law with, for instance, a judicial arm (the Permanent Court of International Justice). It was also to be a security regime established to protect its weakest members. With a strong push from Woodrow Wilson, the League was established—it did emerge. But it could not be sustained. And one of the reasons that might be suggested is that defensive circles operative within the US Senate blocked support for this later, higher regime grounded largely in Wilson's vision.

A second example regards the League's successor, the United Nations—an institution again integral to international law as both an operating system and a generator of new norms. From a certain point of view—namely, an egalitarian one—the United Nations is hardly a perfect institution. And this imperfection has partly to do with the original design of the organization, especially with the veto power of the "big five" in the Security Council. Indeed, in its early years, the one time the United Nations actually functioned as the security regime it was intended to be—in the UN action in Korea—it was able to do so only because the Soviet Union was at the time boycotting the Security Council (a short-lived experiment on their part).

Now at the inception of the United Nations, such an imperfect arrangement was hardly satisfactory to certain "idealists." But it might be argued that the conditions for an alternative were simply not in place. Those who envisioned a new world order without any inequality, without any necessary balance of power, were in Reinhold Niebuhr's view "naive children of light" who did not understand that a new initiative of this magnitude could not be produced by fiat—for example, through drawing up a "constitution for the world."[35] In terms of emergent probability, it might be suggested that Niebuhr understood that the schemes of recurrence (related to what he called "social tissue") were not sufficiently developed to give rise to an institution and a global good of order that would fully satisfy the idealists. The emergent institution could not run ahead of the lower schemes that made its emergence probable or indeed possible. Or to put it in Lonergan's rather than Niebuhr's terms, it might be suggested that the truly worthy ideal is not something unattainable but rather is "the next stage in the development of the concrete"—for the good is always concrete.[36]

A third example regards the emergence of international human rights law. This area of law has seen almost spectacular development since the 1948 arrival on the international scene of the Universal Declaration of Human Rights. This document has pretty much attained the status of customary international law and has conditioned or inspired the emergence not only of the two great human rights covenants but also of a raft of declarations, conventions, tribunals (such as for the former Yugoslavia and Rwanda), nongovernmental organizations (NGOs), institutes, academic courses, books and scholarly journals, and websites.[37] The importance of these developments—this complex of emergences—should not be underestimated. Yet neither should the fragility of the existing human rights regime be denied. As Mary Ann Glendon has shown, the emergence of the Universal Declaration was in part a matter of taking advantage of a small window of opportunity—a set of conditions—that might have been missed.[38] The groundbreaking declaration was therefore no sure thing. Neither has the success of subsequent human rights efforts been assured. East-West ideological splits required that the Universal Declaration be advanced through two separate covenants (or treaties), and these have yet to gain full endorsement. Just as importantly, issues of compliance and enforcement on a day-to-day basis continue to hinder real advancement in the area of human rights. And of course the philosophical grounding for universal human rights remains a question for many.[39]

Though these examples could be further developed, they may be sufficient to intimate the heuristic potential of emergence and emergent probability for understanding the dynamics of international law, a potential that must be qualified as fragile. This intimation may be advanced by a closer examination of the Law of the Sea.

Emergence and the Law of the Sea

I began this chapter with a personal instance of insight-as-emergence and then introduced the notion of an isomorphism or correlation between the emergence that occurs on the side of the knower and the reality to be explored and possibly known. In this case the reality to be understood is the Law of the Sea. My dissertation did not employ directly either Lonerganian terms or the notion of emergence.[40] Rather, the focus in that work was the theological character of a key and bitterly contested principle in the 1982 Convention on the Law of the Sea: the "common heritage of mankind."[41] The study involved three Christian thinkers—Reinhold Niebuhr, Jacques Maritain, and Gustavo Gutiérrez—in a sort of thought experiment, asking what each might make of a principle and set of issues none had ever dealt with in any explicit way. I concluded that each would likely have construed the common heritage principle as a tensive concept pivoting between an eschatologically anticipated world, on the one hand, and the world as it is, finite and flawed, on the other.[42] It turns out, however, that the tensive and heuristic character of this concept fits well the notion of emergence, and here I briefly expand on the manner in which emergence and emergent probability offer a way to understand what was and is at stake in the Law of the Sea.

The history of sea law is long and complex.[43] But for present purposes it may be simplified by saying that for several hundred years the oceans, which constitute about 70 percent of the Earth's surface, were governed by two principles of customary international law. The first was that coastal states would have jurisdiction over a narrow strip of adjacent waters, usually set at three miles according to the "cannon shot" rule.[44] The second principle, espoused most famously by Hugh Grotius, was that of freedom of the high seas, which allowed for use (trade, travel, fishing, and so on) of the open seas by all so long as, in the fashion of John Locke, one left "enough and as good for others."[45]

By the end of World War II and then increasingly into the 1960s, this earlier paradigm of sea law was no longer deemed satisfactory, for a variety of reasons. For one thing, with decolonization numerous new states had emerged—states not always happy to abide by international rules not of their own making. For another, the assumption that the oceans were a virtually inexhaustible storehouse of living resources was factually challenged. New fishing technology (sonar and refrigeration) encouraged the fleets of one nation to raid the traditional fishing grounds of others, sometimes far away, thereby giving rise to bitter disputes, which were sometimes brought before the International Court of Justice. A third reason for dissatisfaction with existing sea law arose in 1945 with the issuance of the Truman Proclamation, a claim of US jurisdiction over its continental shelf for the purposes of hydrocarbon and mineral exploitation, with a view toward US postwar energy independence. This action spurred similar unilateral declarations of coastal jurisdiction by other countries, especially by some Latin American states. Among other things, these claims called into question the free passage of navies, especially through straits—a question that got the attention especially of the United States and the Soviet Union. A fourth concern about existing sea law involved growing threats to ocean ecology due to dumping of biological and other wastes—including nuclear material. Nuclear material also gave rise to a fifth concern: The ocean bed stood as a potential site for the placement of nuclear weapons, to go along with the nuclear weaponry already coursing beneath the ocean surface aboard nuclear-powered submarines. And finally, estimates in the late 1960s that deposits of polymetallic nodules on the ocean floor were both massive and, with developing technology, actually recoverable raised pressing questions of who should have claims on the deep seabed and its resources.[46]

To explain it in language made famous by Thomas Kuhn, these "anomalies," which the existing paradigm of ocean law and management could not handle, made pressing the need for a new ocean regime.[47] To put it in Lonergan's language, there was a need at this point in history for a "creative" response to a changed situation.[48] The probabilities that a new regime would actually emerge were greatly increased in November 1967 when Arvid Pardo, representative to the United Nations from the tiny state of Malta, galvanized the UN General Assembly with a lengthy speech that not only laid out in great detail the facts of the present situation, but also insisted with high rhetoric that humanity was at a turning point. "The dark oceans," Pardo said, "were the womb of life": "from the protecting oceans, life emerged. We still bear in our bodies—in our blood, in the salty bitterness of our tears—the marks of this remote past. Retracing the earth, man is now returning to the ocean depths. His penetration of the deep could mark the beginning of the end of man, and indeed for life as we know it on this earth: it could also be a unique opportunity to lay solid foundations for a peaceful and increasingly prosperous future for all nations."[49]

Key to Pardo's vision of a new ocean regime was his urging that ocean space beyond existing national jurisdictions be declared the "common heritage of mankind."[50] This novel concept became part of the accepted set of negotiating principles that informed the most extensive and complex negotiating process in history, a process that concluded in December 1982, when the completed treaty was opened for signing by individual states. Though the common heritage concept was accepted as a heuristic principle, with its precise content to be worked out through negotiation, it did have certain initial agreed-upon meanings: that the area so designated could not be appropriated by any state; that its resources were to be rationally managed; that the area was to be used for peaceful purposes only; and very significantly, that it was to benefit "mankind as a whole," with special regard for less developed nations.[51]

To retell the history of this process of negotiation in the terms I have been employing would be to examine in great detail the various conditions from which the treaty eventually emerged.[52] Obviously, that exceeds the scope of this chapter. But it is possible to highlight certain aspects of the process and its product that reveal both the emergent character of international law and its fragility. First, although it is generally acknowledged that Pardo's UN speech was crucial as a catalyst for the emergence of the new law, significantly, the eventual treaty fell quite short of his original vision in which all of ocean space would be beyond national jurisdiction (and not just the deep seabed).[53] Second, the emergence of the common heritage of mankind as a fully accepted legal concept was not a sure thing. Its early status as a legal term was vague, and attempts to invest it with more meaning than it could sustain became apparent.[54] In the midst of the negotiations, the United States attempted to pass unilateral mining legislation that ran counter to at least some internationalist and socialist interpretations of the common heritage principle popular among the less developed nations. When leaders of these nations protested the US action on the grounds that the common heritage principle was now an established part of international law, having attained the status of *jus cogens* (peremptory law), the United States simply denied the claim: "Common heritage of mankind" was at best a heuristic principle to guide the negotiations; legally, it would mean what it meant when the negotiations were complete.[55]

In fact, the negotiations did not come to a satisfactory end, at least in the minds of many. The United States' early involvement in the negotiations, which included having a sympathetic attitude to the notion of common heritage and the international sharing it promised, was absolutely crucial to the success of the negotiations. But in a manner suggestive of Lonergan's analysis, this high-level support morphed into a defensive circle with the arrival of the first administration of Ronald Reagan. Concerns about threats to laissez-faire international economic relations and the prospect of losing national sovereignty to a centralized international authority to govern mining operations (the Seabed Authority) led to a decision not to sign the convention. So as far as the common heritage concept is concerned, at least in its more egalitarian or socialist-leaning interpretations, the outcome of the negotiations was disappointing. The very concept suggestive of a common humanity became the flashpoint for global fissure. In fact, the most divisive aspect of the convention, Article XI, which dealt with deep seabed mining and which was inspired by the common heritage concept, was soon opened for renegotiation in the hopes that dissenting nations, and the United States in particular, could be coaxed back on board.[56]

From a Lonerganian perspective, this turn of events is surely open to a more nuanced interpretation in terms of the dialectics of progress and decline. For instance, even prior to the Reagan administration, the tide was turning toward freer trade and more open markets—the kind of economic view skeptical of the heavily centrist and bureaucratic weight the common heritage concept acquired in the process of the negotiations.[57] One might even suggest that the history of the Law of the Sea negotiations was signaling an emergence away from the nation-state and toward a new kind of state— the market-state.[58] My only point is that the emergence of a new ocean regime to match Pardo's vision would have required that certain conditions were fulfilled. They were not.

A final point about emergence and the Law of the Sea needs to be emphasized. When the topic is international law, it is easy to get the impression that emergence is a matter simply of big, powerful nations exerting their individual or collective wills. And I do not underestimate the importance of this view. As just explained, the election of Ronald Reagan and the subsequent shift in US policy with regard to the emerging convention are of undeniable importance. But if the so-called Reagan Revolution had an effect on the Law of the Sea, it is important to recall that this revolution itself emerged on a number of different levels—with lower schemes conditioning higher schemes, even as the lower schemes may have been inspired by a vision, however packaged for mass consumption, that it was "morning in America again."[59] And if the Reagan Revolution served as a defensive circle inhibiting the emergence of a new ocean regime grounded in the common heritage philosophy, it should not be overlooked that the positive thrust toward a new law was also conditioned by lower schemes inspired by a vision of a new world of international economic justice that differed considerably from that of the Reagan administration.

Exemplary here is the activity of the Neptune Group, a small citizens organization that was visionary—indeed, some members were religiously inspired—but not so blinded by vision that it overlooked the pragmatics of successful negotiations. Put in terms of emergent probability, this group was keenly attuned to the manner in which higher schemes are conditioned by the lower schemes at which they so adeptly worked. As a result, this faith-inspired but diplomacy-savvy and informed group was remarkably successful in pressing its agenda to a successful conclusion, however limited by coun-teractive defensive circles that conclusion turned out to be.[60] Nor should we forget that perhaps the most important mover and shaker when it comes to the Law of the Sea, Arvid Pardo, represented one of the world's smallest na-tions, Malta.

International Law and Emergent Catholicity

Whether "isomorphism" between knower and known, between the one who engages and that which is engaged, is the best terminological bridge from the autobiographical to the topical and back again to myself, I cannot say for sure. But I can attest to an enlargement of self that accrues from for-getting oneself and turning to broader topics such as the high seas, and to deeper matters such as the ocean depths. In these closing pages I reflect upon that gain in view of my present circumstances as an educator in a Catho-lic university. Along with teaching courses in theology and occasionally in international law, I have for several years served as director of the core cur-riculum in a small but vibrant and growing Catholic institution, Dominican University. Thus I have been called to reflect a little more deeply upon the core, the very heart, of education in such an institution. My own reflections on the core of Catholic higher education do not stray too far from some of the issues—emergence, horizonal diplomacy, the possibilities and pitfalls of global community—that I have been discussing here.

What I may in fact offer is a twist on an old theme. About seventy years ago, it was debated whether international law originated with Grotius or, as John Brown Scott (himself a Protestant) argued, whether it in fact had Catholic origins, namely, in the Salamanca school of Francisco de Vitoria, Francisco Suárez, and others.[61] Here I am asking a similar question, but I am less interested in origins than in the direction we are headed. I am suggesting that, whatever its origins, an engagement of international law may lead—it has led me, at least—to a relatively nuanced and dynamic understanding of catholicity, a sense of the whole, that may be illuminating as we seek to make sense of Catholic higher education.

So what have I learned from delving into international law and the Law of the Sea? And what has that to do not only with curricular matters but with something deeper, the very core of Catholic higher education? First, of course, is the matter of both emergence and fragility, both on the side of the individual subject, namely myself, and on the side of world processes. My attempts to understand the international legal battles, especially over the ocean floor, have helped to illumine the conflicts—the clashing of loves, in

Augustine's terms, or the alluring flight from understanding and insight, as Lonergan might put it—in the depths of my own soul. Conversely, awareness of my own interior struggles, my own fragility, has left me more understanding of the difficulties of resolving conflicts besetting whole peoples and nation-states.

It need not be this way. One could, I suppose, attend to the world of laws and clashing armies and be oblivious to one's interior life. Conversely, one could get caught up in endless spirals of self-absorption and pay little attention to world events. My own attempts to steer between the Scylla of self-absorption and the Charybdis of escape into various intellectual corners of the world out there leads to at least two conclusions. First, education requires a balance of self-awareness and engagement of an ever-expanding world. To put it in Lonergan's terms, self-appropriation cannot bypass engagement with that which transcends the self.[62] Second, for teacher as for student, negotiating the straits of education is not easy. There is no guarantee that one will emerge a balanced and integral human being, just as there is no guarantee, for instance, that the goods of the earth will in theory or in practice be regarded as humanity's common heritage. But things may be done to shift the probabilities in the right direction.

Next, my attempts to understand the dynamics and the fragility of emergence in the world of international relations and law have both informed and tempered my personal involvement in Catholic higher education. Although I still tend to think in terms of ideals, I find myself becoming more sensitive to the manner in which change occurs. This includes thinking in terms of shifting probabilities, rather than guarantees or inevitabilities, and thus nurturing the lower schemes of recurrence. For example, the semester before I was to assume the position of core curriculum director, I was given a course release to prepare for this transition. I used much of that time meeting one-on-one with the eighty or so faculty teaching in the core. In addition to being some of the best and most enjoyable experiences I have had in higher education, these conversations alerted me to what was going on at lower (that is, personal or departmental) levels, to the possibilities for the emergence of a stronger core, and to possible defensive circles hindering change.

Similar observations might be made of my involvement in conversations and efforts over the years regarding strategic planning at Dominican, an institution that seeks to maintain its Catholic identity in the midst of growth and a commitment to diversity. The worldview of emergent probability and all that it entails has helped me to name, at least for myself (and sometimes within myself), the biases that seem to cripple authentic institutional development. All the biases discussed by Lonergan are no doubt present, as are moments of grace and signs of the biases' reversal. But I would highlight as a particular problem the general bias of common sense. For it appears that this bias, and the closely allied problem of conceptualism as a substitute for true understanding, can run deep even in institutions supposedly devoted to the life of the mind. It is not unusual for universities rightly to address in conferences and workshops such crucial matters as racism or sexism, but similar efforts to eradicate anti-intellectualism appear to be less common.

Although emergent probability has turned my attention to the lower schemes of recurrence within the university, it has also made me more attuned to development from above. I have, for instance, tried to emphasize repeatedly that *Caritas Veritas*, Dominican University's motto, must be understood theologically, as the school's founders surely understood it, lest everything we are about be reduced to human effort and initiative. So also I detect the need to nurture and authentically to transmit the heritage of the school even as it enters a new age. Forgetting the past may not be on Lonergan's list of biases, but it certainly can have deleterious effects. This is as true in Catholic higher education as it is in international law.[63] At the very end of *Insight*, Lonergan writes of the importance and the difficulty of learning what the *vetera*—the ancient things— really were so that they might be augmented and perfected by means of the *nova*.[64] This is a huge challenge to Catholic institutions, and a challenge not always met.

My engagement with the Law of the Sea also suggests that life—including the intellectual, moral, and religious life of Catholic colleges and universities—is a matter of order and possibly harmony (law), on the one side, and uncontrollable power and murky depths (the sea), on the other. *Logos* and *mythos* seem to be joined in the subject I chose to explore in my dissertation, and I see no reason why they may not be joined in higher education as well. I realize that *logos* may be understood in such a way that feeling and wonder are not destroyed, and *mythos* need not mean the denial of reason. Still, I've found it is good to keep in mind *mythos*, in the sense of the primordial and unfathomable (suggested by Pardo's UN speech), lest we neglect narrative and feeling or too quickly think we understand. The sea and the rest of creation demand our respect before they invite our efforts to control—as an unpredicted tsunami or even a well-predicted hurricane can remind us all too well. As one who is now charged with thinking about the very heart of undergraduate education in a Catholic university, I try to keep the balance of *logos* and *mythos* in mind. This sense of balance is regularly found, I think, in excellent programs in the liberal arts, where not only science and philosophy and critical thinking but also art and literature and a symbolically rich religion and theology all find their place.[65]

The issue of control and its limits suggests another connection between international law and an emergent catholicity in Catholic schools. It may be suggested that those who cannot conceptually or practically distinguish law from command, with coercion to back that command, will likely be disappointed by international law. But international law as it actually exists—in all its messiness—appears to outstrip such narrow definitions. So too command

and coercion, the preferred modus operandi of some when it comes to the Catholic character of colleges and universities, represent too narrow an approach. An emergent catholicity appropriate for Catholic universities is arguably more akin to the fragile dynamics of international law, with its fits and starts and growing ends, than it is to a seemingly airtight institution that stakes its identity on authority structures backed by heavy-handed sanctions.

This need to appreciate multiple disciplines, along with the need to sort through the pluralism of multiple perspectives, has been driven home not only by Lonergan but also, in rather different ways, by one of my mentors at the University of Chicago, the eminent theological ethicist James M. Gustafson. In his teaching and writing Gustafson seemed to have two worries—that theological claims would not be taken seriously, and that theologians would isolate themselves from those in other fields, especially the natural sciences.[66] Indeed, inspired in part by Gustafson's example, one of my scholarly aims has been to encourage religiously and theologically minded people to take international law more seriously and on its own terms.[67] So too in Catholic institutions theologians need to attend to ways in which not only other disciplines but also those not sharing the Catholic faith contribute to the Catholic character of the institution.

Having said that, I cannot end without some reflections on the other side—not the failure of theologians, including myself, to see beyond theology or to regard everything only in theological terms, but rather the possible exclusion of theology from both international law and the university. For just as some might claim, as pundits sometimes do, that "Catholic university" is an oxymoron, assuming that a dogmatic and authoritarian theology will preclude the free exchange of ideas, so most international lawyers would likely agree with the late sixteenth- and early-seventeenth-century international lawyer Alberico Gentili, who warned theologians not to encroach upon their domain ("*Silente, theologi, in munere alieno*").[68] Though it may be true that both the university and modern international law had their origins in a Catholic world that presumed faith in God, such origins are not immediately visible today. Thus, just as the great Protestant theologian H. Richard Niebuhr could ask, in a famous article, "Is God in the War?," I have often asked myself, Is God in international law?[69] And I have just as frequently asked, Is God in the university?

This sort of question was at the fore in my dissertation as I inquired about the theological character of the common heritage of mankind, that pivotal principle in a monumental treaty. And I do not want that radical question to be dropped when the topic is Catholic higher education, lest obscurantism rule the day. In the Catholic university, I believe, the question of God needs to be pressed. Otherwise, as John Henry Newman warned, the vacuum left by theology's silence will soon be filled by some other mode of discourse and inquiry all too eager to overstep its bounds.[70] Or to use Lonergan's terminology, the danger is that the transcendent realm of meaning will be eclipsed.[71] This would be to forget that the question of God is the "question that questions all our questioning," whether that questioning occurs within the walls of the Catholic university or beyond.[72]

Here I do not hope to press, much less answer sufficiently, questions regarding God's presence in the university or in international law. An answer cannot be a simple return to the medieval university that synthesized faith and reason, or to the theologically comfortable international law of Vitoria, Suárez, or even Grotius (whom many too quickly credit with severing international law from theology).[73] For one thing, international law must now reckon with its future in a multicultural world, and Catholic universities cannot sidestep their own issues of diversity, whether religious or otherwise.[74] To address these issues, other insights from Lonergan barely mentioned here—regarding pluralism, for example, or the move from classicism to historical mindedness—may be of great help. And whatever the future holds for international law or Catholic higher education, the dynamics of emergence, progress, decline, and redemption are bound to be operative, whether we attend to them as we should or not.

Such lines of inquiry must be left aside for now. The point I wish to close with is a simple one. In thinking about Catholic higher education, I have been helped not simply by having a great thinker as a guide but also by turning my attention to a topic that transcends the university and its sometimes constricted concerns. In my case, the realm of meaning and value that has allowed me to enter more deeply into the reality of the Catholic university has been the dynamic world of international law. Its complexity is worthy of respect, and its fragility is worthy of care. It deserves to be taken on its own terms, however much those terms may be related to disciplines closer to home. That is why here I give it so much space. It is my hope that others will find an entry point at least as rich for considering questions of an emergent catholicity in Catholic higher education today and in the years ahead.

Notes

1. It even turned out that, unbeknownst to me while I was there, Zambia had been taking a vital interest in negotiations over the Law of the Sea. Because the country is a landlocked "less developed nation" (the term employed by the Convention) dependent on the export of copper for over 90 percent of its foreign exchange earnings, the prospect of deep seabed mining disrupting its own already tenuous share in the global metals market was of no small economic concern.

2. Mark Morelli, "Horizonal Diplomacy," in *Creativity and Method: Essays in Honor of Bernard Lonergan*, ed. Matthew L. Lamb (Milwaukee, WI: Marquette University Press, 1981), 459–74.

3. Duncan Snidal was at the time the chair of the Committee on International Relations in the Political Science Department. He suggested I attend weekly meetings of the Program on International Politics, Economics, and Security (PIPES), a funded discussion group with guest presenters from around the country.

4. Bernard Lonergan, *Insight: A Study in Human Understanding*, 5th ed., ed. Frederick E. Crowe and Robert M. Doran, Collected Works of Bernard Lonergan 3 (Toronto: University of Toronto Press, 1992), 28.

5. That is, the metaphysics to which I refer takes into full account the "turn to the subject." See Bernard Lonergan, "Metaphysics as Horizon," in Lonergan, *Collection*, ed. Frederick E. Crowe and Robert M. Doran, Collected Works of Bernard Lonergan 4 (Toronto: University of Toronto Press, 1998), 188–204.

6. For a discussion of this isomorphism, see Lonergan, *Insight*, 470–71, 473–74. I might add that in the background of my thinking here is also Saint Augustine. I have been deeply impressed by the fact that one and the same person could write both the *Confessions*, so deeply personal and psychological in character, and *City of God*, with its global reach.

7. For some further comments on isomorphism between the act of deciding and the good to be achieved, see William P. George, "Anticipating Posterity: A Lonerganian Approach to Contingent Future Persons," in *Contingent Future Persons: Philosophical and Theological Challenges*, ed. Jan C. Heller and Nick Fotion, Theology and Medicine Series (Dordrecht, Netherlands: Kluwer Academic Publishers, 1997), 191–208.

8. Lonergan, *Insight*, 506.

9. On emergent probability, see Lonergan, *Insight*, 146–51; and Kenneth Melchin, *History, Ethics, and Emergent Probability: Ethics, Society and History in the Thought of Bernard Lonergan* (Lanham, MD: University Press of America, 1986).

10. Bernard Lonergan, *Method in Theology* (New York: Herder and Herder, 1972), 13; Lonergan, "Healing and Creating in History," in *A Third Collection: Papers by Bernard J. F. Lonergan, S.J.*, ed. Frederick E. Crowe (Mahwah, NJ: Paulist Press, 1985), 103.

11. The notion of fragility used here recalls the ancient Greeks' appreciation for tragedy and contingency in their accounts of the moral life. See Martha C. Nussbaum, *The Fragility of Virtue* (New York: Cambridge University Press, 1986). Fragility is also a word that lends itself to theological reflections on the human condition.

12. Every one of the individual articles in the *Summa* begins the same way: "It would seem. . . ." See Thomas Aquinas, *Summa Theologica*, trans. Fathers of the English Dominican Province, 5 vols. (Westminster, MD: Christian Classics, 1948). The Thomist roots of Lonergan's works are fully evident and documented. When it comes to international law, I have in mind Aquinas's influence especially on early shapers of international law, such as Francisco de Vitoria, Francisco Suárez, and Hugo Grotius. See also E. B. F. Midgley, *The Natural Law Tradition and the Theory of International Relations* (New York: Harper and Row, 1975).

13. For an articulation of these "myths" and their rebuttal, see David J. Bederman, *International Law Frameworks* (New York: Foundation Press, 2001), 6–11; and John H. E. Fried, "International Law—Neither Orphan nor Harlot, Neither Jailer nor Never-Never Land," in *International Law: Classic and Contemporary Readings*, ed. Charlotte Ku and Paul F. Diehl (Boulder, CO: Lynn Riener Publishers, 1998), 26–27.

14. The authoritative listing of these sources is Article 38 of the Statute of the International Court of Justice. "Judicial decisions and the teachings of the most highly qualified publicists of the various nations" are listed there as "subsidiary" sources: art. 38(1)(d).

15. For this distinction between a system of norms and an operating system, see Charlotte Ku and Paul F. Diehl, "International Law as Operating and Normative Systems: An Overview," in Ku and Diehl, *International Law*, 3–16. In the immediate aftermath of the 2005 tsunami disaster, one could find on the home page of the American International Law Society's website links for international law pertaining to disaster relief.

16. Louis Henkin, *How Nations Behave: Law and Foreign Policy*, 2nd ed. (New York: Columbia University Press, 1979), 47.

17. The fact of various forms of emergent international law over the course of history is emphasized by, among others, Philip Bobbitt in his remarkable and provocative work *The Shield of Achilles: War, Peace, and the Course of History* (New York: Random House, 2002).

18. Geoffrey Best, *War and Law since 1945* (Oxford: Oxford University Press, 1994).

19. Such a record includes the length of time it took for the United States to ratify the genocide treaty (nearly forty years); its refusal to accept the jurisdiction of the International Court of Justice in the Nicaragua case and, more recently, in death penalty cases involving questions of diplomatic relations; the "unsigning" of the Rome Treaty to establish the International Criminal Court; the fact that the United States is virtually the only nonparty to the Convention on the Rights of the Child; apparent attempts to give the Geneva Conventions very wide interpretation when it comes to detaining and interrogating prisoners of war; and the strong objection by Justice Antonin Scalia and others that US court decisions on the execution of minors might be influenced by international standards. It should be stressed, however, that some of these actions can be read quite differently—for instance, that the United States takes international law very seriously and thus is slow to bind itself.

20. Lonergan, *Insight*, 143.

21. See, e.g., the 1944 Chicago Convention on International Civil Air Travel and subsequent conventions, some dealing with terrorism.

22. I choose these examples because of my close proximity to one of the world's busiest airports and because Chicago-based United Airlines, the world's second-largest air carrier, has in the past averted labor strikes that, had they occurred, would arguably have spelled the doom of this huge corporation. And when an outdated (2002) story about United Airlines' imminent bankruptcy made it onto Internet trading screens on September 8, 2008, the company's stock fell drastically in one hour (from $12 to $3), ending the day with an 11.2 percent loss—fragility on display. See Michelle Maynard, "United Airlines Shares Fall on False Report of Bankruptcy," *International Herald Tribune*, September 9, 2008, www.iht.com/articles/2008/09/09/business/AIR.php.

23. Lonergan, *Insight*, 144–45.

24. Over several years there were repeated attempts to build a third Chicago-area airport in south suburban Peotone, but these were largely blocked by political forces that instead have sought the expansion of O'Hare International—expansion that in turn has been resisted by the defensive circles of neighboring municipalities wary, in part, of more noise and declining real estate prices.

25. As an example of the extreme effect of war on air travel, I was in Zambia in 1979 during the waning days of the war in Rhodesia (now Zimbabwe) when Ian Smith's regime conducted an air strike against Zimbabwean freedom fighter camps across the Zambian border. The story goes that the Rhodesian air force radioed the airport in Lusaka to say that they would be conducting their "business" for about thirty minutes, during which time if any planes took off the airport would be leveled. No planes took off.

26. Lonergan, *Insight*, 141.

27. Jerome H. Skolnick, "Code Blue," *The American Prospect*, November 2, 2002, http://prospect.org/cs/articles?article=code_blue.

28. On the good of order and its broader context, the human good, see Lonergan, *Method in Theology*, 27–56.

29. For a discussion of values, see ibid., especially chap. 2, "The Human Good."

30. I give this example because it is one of the few definitive moral condemnations by the Second Vatican Council. See also John C. Ford's classic article "The Morality of Obliteration Bombing," *Theological Studies* 5 (1944): 261–309.

31. On the various conversions, see Lonergan, *Method in Theology*. See also Lonergan, *Insight*, 232–69.

32. On development from below and above, see Lonergan, "Healing and Creating." Note that this bottom-up and top-down imagery—already limited—should not be construed as the equivalent of "grassroots" and "halls of power." People working at the grassroots may be informed by a love that reorients all, by inherited values, and by visions of an alternative world, just as people at the highest level may be working from the bottom up, seeking to chart truly new territory, step by step, one insight or solid judgment or sound decision at a time.

33. The overly functionalist view of religion notwithstanding, this point is made at some length by James A. R. Nafziger, "The Functions of Religion in the International Legal System," in *Religion and International Law*, ed. Mark L. Janis and Carolyn Evans (The Hague: Martinus Nijhoff Publishers, 1999), 155–76.

34. Thus the UN Charter begins: "We the peoples of the United Nations determined to save succeeding generations from the scourge of war, which twice in our lifetime has brought untold sorrow to mankind."

35. See Reinhold Niebuhr, "The Myth of World Government," *The Nation*, October 21, 1944: 313; and Niebuhr, "The Illusion of World Government," *Foreign Affairs* 27 (April 1949): 379–88.

36. Bernard Lonergan, *Topics in Education*, ed. Frederick E. Crowe and Robert M. Doran, Collected Works of Bernard Lonergan 10 (Toronto: University of Toronto Press, 1993), 29.

37. See the two great human rights covenants: Covenant on Political and Civil Rights, www2.ohchr.org/english/law/ccpr.htm; and Covenant on Social, Economic, and Cultural Rights, www2.ohchr.org/english/law/cescr.htm.

38. Mary Ann Glendon, *A World Made New: Eleanor Roosevelt and the Universal Declaration of Human Rights* (New York: Random House, 2001).

39. John Haughey discusses this problem and draws upon Lonergan to address it. See John C. Haughey, "Responsibility for Human Rights: Contributions from Bernard Lonergan," *Theological Studies* 63, no. 4 (December 2002): 764–85.

40. The fact that the dissertation was not explicitly Lonerganian was itself, in part, a function of unmet conditions. None of the directors or readers available to me was conversant in Lonergan's thought, whereas individually or collectively these same scholars had a superb understanding of the figures on which I chose to focus.

41. William P. George, "Envisioning Global Community: The Theological Character of the Common Heritage Concept in the Law of the Sea," PhD diss., University of Chicago, 1990.

42. In my dissertation, "Envisioning Global Community," I argued that Niebuhr would regard the common heritage notion as an "impossible possibility" (chap. 4); Jacques Maritain would view it as a "concrete historical ideal" (chap. 5); and Gustavo

Gutiérrez would view it in terms of a "utopia" that pivots between faith and concrete social programs (chap. 6).

43. See D. P. O'Donnell, *The International Law of the Sea*, 2 vols., ed. I. A. Shearer (Oxford: Oxford University Press, 1981, 1984); and Lawrence Juda, *International Law and Ocean Use Management: The Evolution of Ocean Governance*, Ocean Management Policy Series (London: Routledge, 1996).

44. H. S. K. Kent, "The Historical Origins of the Three-Mile Limit," *The American Journal of International Law*, 48, no. 4 (October 1954): 537–53.

45. On the connection between Grotius's freedom of the seas doctrine and John Locke's view of property and government, see Alexandra Merle Post, *Deepsea Mining and the Law of the Sea* (The Hague: Martinus Nijhoff Press, 1983), 93. Traditional sea law included, of course, principles besides these two. Some, such as proscriptions of piracy, remain crucial today.

46. These potato-sized polymetallic nodules were found to contain cobalt, zinc, copper, and other metals. They were first discovered about one hundred years previously by the explorer ship *Challenger*, but the extent of the deposits was unknown at that time.

47. The 1958 and 1960 conventions left unresolved especially the crucial question of the width of the territorial sea.

48. Lonergan, "Healing and Creating," 103.

49. UN GAOR 1st Comm., 22d sess., 1515th mtg. at 2 par. 7, UN Doc. A/C.1/ PV.1515 (November 1, 1967).

50. UN GAOR 1st Comm., 1516th mtg. at 2 par. 13, UN Doc. A/C.1/PV.1516 (November 1, 1967).

51. *Declaration of Principles Governing the Seabed and the Ocean Floor*, GA Res. 2749, at 24–25, UN GAOR, 25th Sess., 1933d plen. mtg., UN Doc. A/RES/25/2749 (December 17, 1970).

52. See O'Donnell, *International Law of the Sea*, and Juda, *Ocean Use Management*.

53. See Arvid Pardo, "An Opportunity Lost," in *Law of the Sea: U.S. Policy Dilemma*, ed. H. Oxam, David D. Caron, and Charles L. Buderi (San Francisco: ICS Press, 1983); and Aaron Danzig, "A Funny Thing Happened to the Common Heritage on the Way to the Law of the Sea," *San Diego Law Review* 12 (1975): 655–64.

54. Steven Gorove, "The Concept of 'Common Heritage of Mankind': A Political, Moral, or Legal Concept?" *San Diego Law Review* 9 (1972): 390–403.

55. H. Roberto Herrera Caceres, "La sauvegarde du patrimoine commun de l'humanité," in *La gestion des ressources pour l'humanité: le droit de la mer* [The Management of Humanity's Resources: The Law of the Sea], Workshop, The Hague, October 29–31, 1981, ed. René-Jean Dupuy (The Hague: Martinus Nijhoff Publishers, 1982), 125–34.

56. The Law of the Sea took full legal effect in 1994. The United States has since signed the treaty but has yet to ratify it. It does, however, recognize the vast majority of the treaty's provisions as codification of binding customary law.

57. Christopher C. Joyner and Elizabeth A. Martell, "Looking Back to See Ahead: UNCLOS III and Lessons for Global Common Law," in Ku and Diehl, *International Law*, 245–72.

58. On the emergence of the market-state, see Bobbitt, *Shield of Achilles*.

59. "It's morning in America again" was the message of a popular Ronald Reagan television ad. See "Ronald Reagan TV Ad: 'It's Morning in America Again,'" accessed April 9, 2011, www.youtube.com/watch?v=EU-IBF8nwSY.

60. Ralph B. Levering and Miriam L. Levering, *Citizen Action for Global Change: The Neptune Group and the Law of the Sea* (Syracuse, NY: Syracuse University Press, 1999).

61. See Christopher R. Rossi, *Broken Chain of Being: John Brown Scott and the Origins of Modern International Law* (Boston: Kluwer Law International, 1998).

62. For a discussion of self-appropriation and warnings about the difficulty of achieving it, see Lonergan, *Method in Theology*, chap. 1, "Method."

63. For some caustic remarks on an international legal profession negligent toward history, see David Kennedy, "Image of Religion in International Legal Theory," in Janis and Evans, *Religion and International Law*, 121–22.

64. Lonergan, *Insight*, 769.

65. Speaking autobiographically, this concern for balance between rigorous analysis and the riches of narrative reflects a long-term concern to relate the intellectual and the affective, including a master's thesis on the theme of conversion in the works of Saint Ignatius of Loyola, Bernard Lonergan, and C. G. Jung. William P. George, "Imagination and Conversion," MA thesis in philosophy, Gonzaga University, 1978.

66. See James M. Gustafson, *An Examined Faith: The Grace of Self-Doubt* (Minneapolis, MN: Fortress, 2004).

67. See William P. George, "Looking for a Global Ethic? Try International Law," in Janis and Evans, *Religion and International Law*, 483–504.

68. Alberico Gentili, *De jure belli ac pacis* (1588).

69. Virgil Aldrich and H. Richard Niebuhr, "Is God in the War?," *The Christian Century*, August 5, 1942.

70. John Henry Newman, *The Idea of a University*, discourses 1–3. This is available in several editions.

71. See Lonergan, *Method in Theology*, 83–85.

72. Ibid., 103.

73. See William P. George, "Grotius, Theology, and International Law: Overcoming Textbook Bias," *The Journal of Law and Religion* 14, no. 2 (1999–2000): 605–31.

74. René-Jean Dupuy, ed., *The Future of International Law in a Multicultural World*, Hague Academy of International Law Workshop, November 17–19, 1983 (The Hague: Martinus Nijhoff, 1984). For a more theoretical argument, see Surya Prakash Sinha, *Legal Polycentricity and International Law* (Durham, SC: Carolina Academic Press, 1996).

CHAPTER 5

Catholicity and Faculty Seminars

Richard M. Liddy

When I was a young student in the 1950s I came across a book titled *The Wisdom of Catholicism*.[1] I liked it very much and bought a copy as a present for my parents. It was edited by Anton Pegis of the Medieval Institute in Toronto and contained selections from the Catholic classics: Augustine's *Confessions* and *City of God*, Thomas Aquinas's *Summae*, Dante's *Divine Comedy*, the *Imitation of Christ*, Teresa of Avila's *Interior Castle*, John of the Cross's *Ascent of Mount Carmel*, Blaise Pascal's *Pensées*, and John Henry Newman's *Apologia pro vita sua*. There were also more recent selections: papal encyclicals on Christian philosophy and on the reconstruction of the social order, as well as literary pieces, such as Charles Péguy's *Vision of Prayer*, Paul Claudel's *The Satin Slipper*, and selections from Helaire Belloc, G. K. Chesterton, Christopher Dawson, Sigrid Undset, Etienne Gilson, and Jacques Maritain. At the time it provided evidence for me of the superior wisdom of Catholicism. It was a wisdom achieved in the past, and our job was basically one of appropriating it and passing it on.

In recent years there has again been much talk about the Catholic intellectual tradition—often in relation to Catholic studies programs—and I ask myself what difference there is between "the wisdom of Catholicism" as I conceived it in the 1950s and this wisdom as I look on it today.[2] In this chapter I first focus on the problem of an inadequate, often classicist, conception of the Catholic intellectual tradition and contrast it with a more dynamic, historically conscious understanding. Second, I link the Catholic intellectual tradition to the person of Christ, the "incarnate carrier of meaning."[3] Then I trace the trajectory of the carriers of the meaning of Christ through three stages: from the symbolic or commonsense understandings expressed in scripture and the ordinary life of Christians, to the doctrines and theologies that have tended to use theoretical language, and finally to modes of expression rooted in an understanding of human interiority. These are stages in the Catholic intellectual tradition, and the transition from common sense and theory to interiority captures the cultural change that I have experienced in my own lifetime. In the final section I call attention to the pastoral orientation of the Second Vatican Council and to the present orientation of the Catholic intellectual tradition toward pastoral communication and the healing of all areas of human culture. I use an example of this process from my own experience at Seton Hall University.

Historical Consciousness

The historian Eric Voegelin wrote of "the hardening of the symbols," that is, the cultural process whereby an authentic tradition becomes disconnected from its roots in authentic living.[4] Bernard Lonergan has referred to one version of this as classicism, that is, an ahistorical mode of thinking in which "all the answers are in the book," meaning somewhere in Aquinas or the Code of Canon Law or books and manuals that summarize all of the above. Somewhere one can find all the answers, a well-defined block of knowledge.[5]

On the other hand, a more contemporary view of the Catholic intellectual tradition sees it not merely as an achievement completed in the past, but rather as a living tradition affecting diverse cultures and challenging persons to do in our day what that tradition at its best accomplished in cultures gone by. For the Catholic intellectual tradition is not a pile of books or writings "out there"—it is not some "thing." It is rather a living meaning, very alive to some, less alive, perhaps even dead, to others.

In his *Essay on the Development of Christian Doctrine*, John Henry Newman wrote that the authenticity of a tradition—he called it "a living idea"—bore fruit in its "power of assimilation": that is, its power to enter into various cultures and to assimilate the best elements of those cultures into its own self-expression.[6] Such inculturation is the ability of Christianity to be truly and authentically itself while being at the same time truly and authentically Japanese, African, American, and so on. The Catholic intellectual tradition is not a closed canon of Western works only. For many, Shusaku Endo's *The Silence* has become a classic of the Catholic intellectual tradition arising from Japanese Catholicism.[7] And Vincent Donovan's *Christianity Rediscovered* appeals because of its respect for the native patterns of east African cultural life—in terms of which alone the gospel message can there be proclaimed.[8]

Consequently, if the Christian message is to be communicated to all nations, preachers and teachers need to enlarge their horizons to include an accurate understanding of the culture and language of the people they address, as Lonergan says: "They must grasp the resources of that culture and that language, and they must use those resources creatively so that the Christian message becomes, not disruptive of the culture, not an alien patch superimposed upon it, but a line of development within the culture."[9]

Incarnate Meaning

Cardinal André Vingt-Trois, the archbishop of Paris, remarked to a journalist: "Just because Christianity is two thousand doesn't mean it's old." Then he added: "Becoming Christian means adhering to Someone who is not a cultural object. Christ has certainly been carried by the culture called Christian, but it's not about that, it's about the person of Jesus."[10]

Does this mean that the person of Jesus is the meaning of the Christian tradition? One way to think about the question is to reflect on the way a tradition is carried—from one person to another, from one generation to another. Lonergan in his *Method in Theology* writes of various "carriers of meaning": intersubjectivity, art, symbols, language, and finally "incarnate meaning."[11] For meaning passes from one person to another through our very intersubjectivity, our very presence to each other. We communicate with one another by every gesture, frown, facial movement, smile. Certainly Christ communicated through his very presence. There was something about him; he spoke with authority. By his very presence he evoked attachment and generated resistance.

Art is another very concrete carrier of meaning. The patterns in musical sounds communicate deep feelings; so also do the forms and colors of a painting. Christ encouraged people to pay attention to their experience: "Look at the birds of the air and the lilies of the fields!" One's aesthetic sense can spot a seed fallen on the side of the road or a bit of sawdust caught in another's eye.

So also do symbols communicate meaning. They are images that concretely evoke feelings or are evoked by feelings. A young man sends a keepsake to his beloved. Jesus took bread and broke it and gave it to his disciples to eat. He physically touched those who were ill. The symbols he left speak.

But by far the most obvious carrier of meaning is language. These seemingly inconsequential sounds or marks have meaning. They have the meanings constituted by the understanding, judgments, and decisions of people in concrete situations.[12] So Jesus told stories and parables; he said, "Do this in memory of me." Though rooted in the here and now, words can also transcend the moment and strain toward a more universal perspective, a distant past and a future beyond us. Jesus's words broke open the limits of ordinary speech to open people to deeper meaning.

But besides intersubjectivity, art, symbol, and language, Lonergan names one further carrier of meaning, and that is incarnate meaning. Quoting Newman's motto, *cor ad cor loquitur*—heart speaks to heart—Lonergan lays out the meaning of incarnate meaning: "Incarnate meaning combines all or at least many of the other carriers of meaning. It can be at once inter-subjective, artistic, symbolic, linguistic. It is the meaning of a person, of his way of life, of his words, or of his deeds. It may be his meaning for just one other person, or for a small group, or for a whole national, or social, or cultural, or religious tradition."[13]

The incarnate meaning of Jesus is central to Christianity: the meaning of his life, the meaning of his person. The meaning of the person of Christ was central to his first followers and to the early Christian community. That meaning found particular expression in the Eucharist, where scripture was read and reflected on, songs were sung, the bread was broken and cup passed—and all expressed the incarnate meaning of Jesus of Nazareth. At this breaking of the bread there were songs and acclamations acknowledging Jesus as Lord, confessions that God had raised him from the dead, as well as gradually developing and expanding formulas of belief. It was to provide a context for such acclamations, confessions, and formulas, to clarify their meaning and preclude misinterpretation, that memories of Jesus's earthly ministry were recalled and the classics that we call the gospels were written.[14]

Symbolic Consciousness

A curious aspect about the phrase "Catholic intellectual tradition" is the word "intellectual." Does that constrict this tradition? If we agree with Aquinas that the human person is especially the human spirit or the human mind— "*homo maxime est mens hominis*" (the human person is especially the human mind)—then any genuinely human tradition is an intellectual tradition.[15] Of course a tradition may fade, become watered-down and lifeless; but it will only revive to the extent that people begin again to use their heads. Such intellectual activity is not limited to theorizing—to theology and philosophy— it can also find expression in art and music, symbol and dance, architecture and poetry, myth and ritual. Fyodor Dostoyevsky caught this ground-level intellectual activity in the songs of the Russian peasants, because even during persecution they kept alive the image of Christ: "The people acquired their knowledge in churches where, for centuries, they have been listening to prayers and hymns which are better than sermons. They have been repeating and singing these prayers in forests, fleeing from their enemies, as far back as the time of Batzi's invasion; they have been singing: *Almighty Lord, be with us!* It may have been then that they memorized this hymn, because at that time nothing but Christ was left to them; yet in this hymn alone is Christ's whole truth."[16]

The Catholic intellectual tradition finds expression, then, not just in philosophical and theological works but also in poetry (the *Divine Comedy*, the poems of Gerard Manley Hopkins) and art (frescoes, mosaics, icons; medieval, Renaissance, and Baroque painting); in architecture (Romanesque, Gothic, Baroque, modern) and music (Gregorian chant and polyphony); as well as in medieval mystery plays and the fables of J. R. R. Tolkien.[17]

In addition the Catholic intellectual tradition has found literary expression in works of practical spirituality that at least for some communities within the Church have attained the status of classics: the *Rule of Saint Benedict*, the *Imitation of Christ*, the *Cloud of Unknowing*, the *Spiritual Exercises of Saint Ignatius*, Teresa of Avila's *Interior Castle*, John of the Cross's *Ascent of Mount Carmel*, Francis de Sales's *Introduction to the Devout Life*, and so on. These works, for certain communities within the Church, have attained the status of classics, in that they have become the focal point for the concrete living of people. Thus, David DeLaura writes about Newman's *Apologia pro vita sua*:

The special distinction of the *Apologia* is that it does make its way, as any prophetic book must in the modern world, on its own and literarily; it creates its own authority and authenticity; while it constitutes our whole experience for a time, its inherent thrust is to transform us in some more permanent way. In this sense, the book's literary power, as the subtle revelation of the religious progress of a highly gifted human being, makes the *Apologia*, as it touches the deepest springs of the religious impulse in man, an ever renewable force in the contemporary world, in ways in which most of even the highest of modern art does not.[18]

Now what all the "Catholic classics" have in common is that they invite one to change. They operate as mediators of conversion. Christ changed people; he brought them to a deeper spot. Through his word of forgiveness he brought them out of the darkness within themselves and enabled them to envision a new reality, a new world, the kingdom coming. In such a world people are graced to be and to do what previously they were not at all interested in being or doing. Through the gift of the Holy Spirit the Catholic intellectual tradition, even in its symbolic expressions, has aimed to do the same thing.

All such expressions of the Catholic intellectual tradition are expressions of what Lonergan calls "symbolic consciousness":

> The universal style is symbolic. Its language is instinct with feeling. At its liveliest it is poetry. At its profoundest it is rhetoric. It lacks neither attention to detail nor keen insight nor balanced judgment nor responsible decision. But it has all these, not stripped of feeling, but permeated with feeling. The calm, the detachment, the clarity, the coherence, the rigor of the logician, the mathematician, the scientist—these are just beyond its horizon. Such by and large is the language of the New Testament. . . . Such also in the main was the language of the Church Fathers, and down the ages it has remained the straightforward simple language of mainstream Christianity.[19]

Theoretical Consciousness

> In a developed culture, religion has to be pluralistic; it needs some measure of symbolization for all; it needs only a limited measure for the few that get beyond symbolic thinking; and it needs a bounteous dose for the many that do not.
>
> —Lonergan, "Sacralization and Secularization"

Though massively prevalent, the symbolic style of consciousness is not the only one in the Catholic tradition. History also reveals a move to another type of consciousness, that is, theoretical consciousness. As is evident even in the pages of the New Testament, as the word of God began to be preached throughout the Mediterranean world, those who preached it faced new situations and new questions. Disputes arose: What is the exact meaning of the word of God? What are its implications in this situation—in Antioch? in Corinth? in Rome? Early Jewish-Christians wanted to hold Gentile converts to the whole Jewish law. Those influenced by gnosticism wanted to reduce the Gospel to an esoteric sect. Innovators formed schools that splintered off in various directions and by their very separation and diversity emphasized a main, unchanging tradition.[20]

That main tradition itself encountered ever deeper issues, including the question raised by Arius: In what sense can it be said that Jesus is the Son of God? Is this just a metaphor in the sense that all humans are children of God? Or as Saint Athanasius held, is Jesus truly the Son of God, in the sense that what is said of him is also said of the Father, except that he is the Son and not the Father? To express this truth Athanasius and those gathered at the Council of Nicea in 325 adopted the nonscriptural, quasi-technical term *homoousios*—"consubstantial"—to express and protect what they considered to be scriptural truth.[21]

For just as "the Law" in the Hebrew scriptures implicitly contains the idea that the Law is to be obeyed, so "the Word" in the New Testament is something to be spoken, believed, and acted upon; and from that idea quite practical consequences follow. One was the care of the bishops, leading up to the early Councils, for the integrity of the meaning of the Gospel.[22] Such concern for the truth of Christianity arose out of the Church's life and preaching in ever new situations. Eventually this concern also found expression in a specifically theoretical way, preeminently in the great *summae* of Aquinas, the *Summa contra gentiles* and the *Summa theologica*. This theoretical expression was a natural consequence of the movement of the Christian religion into the highly sophisticated culture of the medieval university. Here was a world of careful distinctions, of the natural order and the supernatural order, of the autonomy of the natural order and the use of the most sophisticated philosophy of the time—that of Aristotle, mediated by the Arabian philosophers—to provide a conceptual and theoretical framework for understanding all these distinctions and levels of being. It was that scholastic philosophy that provided the background for preaching the Catholic faith up to our own time.[23] It was that background that I was schooled in and that I brought to my own encounters with modern philosophies. But a new stage of meaning has arisen in modern times, one concerned with rooting both symbolic and theoretical consciousness in the interior world of the person.

Interiority

Modern philosophy, modern psychology, and modern concerns with the interior life of the person have all reflected the trend to identify and appropriate the interior foundations whence flow both common sense and scientific-theoretical consciousness. Lonergan thematized this trend toward interiority in his philosophical writings, but perhaps it can best be described by the analogy with the experiential education proposed by the psychologist Abraham Maslow. Maslow emphasizes the fact that at their best, human persons actualize themselves through peak experiences: that is, through experiences of goodness, of love, of beauty, of clear communication, and so forth. The trouble, Maslow contends, is that most people are unaware that these peak experiences go on within them. Many are even unaware of their innate capacity for such experiences. As a result, he suggests, very few people are self-actualizing, that is, responding to their own most creative capacities. What is needed, then, is an education in which people are encouraged to become aware of their own capacities for self-actualization. Such education involves people personally. At its best education does not just point to other people's experience and understanding; it points to one's own. Maslow formulates this experiential education in the following way:

All this implies another kind of education, that is, an experiential education. . . . It also implies another kind of communication. . . . What we are implying is that in the kind of experiential teaching which is being discussed here, what is necessary to do first is to change the person and to change his awareness of himself. That is, we must make him aware of the fact that peak-experiences go on inside himself. Until he has become aware of such experience and has this experience as the basis for a comparison, he is a non-peaker; and it is useless to try to communicate to him the feel and the nature of peak-experience. But if we can change him, in the sense of making him aware of what is going on inside himself, then he becomes a different kind of communicatee. He now knows what you are talking about when you speak of peak-experiences; and it is possible to teach him by reference to his own weak peak-experiences how to improve them, how to enrich them, how to enlarge them, and also how to draw the proper conclusions from them.[24]

But what has this to do with the Catholic intellectual tradition in our time? Well, in an analogous way the Catholic intellectual tradition in our time is marked by this concern to relate the Gospel of Christ to human interiority. From Newman's concern with identifying how we make judgments and the role of conscience in decision making, to Edith Stein's concern with linking accounts of human consciousness with the Gospel, to Lonergan's concern with tracking the levels of human consciousness—modern Catholic writers have constantly been working to link the Gospel with interiority.[25]

Such a concern with interiority is not just a concern for inner individuality. For the patterns of human consciousness find expression in the human worlds we create together, in the civilizations and cultures that express our communal self-transcendence as well as in the stagnation and sinful social structures that reveal our need for healing. Let me conclude with a practical example of communicating the dynamism of the Catholic intellectual tradition today.

Communicating the Tradition

If one wanted a short mantra or formula expressing moments in the Catholic intellectual tradition—peaks along the way—then one could point to scripture, Augustine, Aquinas, Newman, and Lonergan. The whole is a movement from symbolic to theoretical to interiorly differentiated consciousness. But the whole flow, the whole progression, is that the word of God be communicated in the present and to the future; and in that whole process, conversation is key. After Jesus opened up the meaning of scripture to the disciples on the road to Emmaus, they said to each other, "Were not our hearts burning within us as he explained the Scriptures to us on the road?" (Luke 24:32, NAB).[26] He set their hearts on fire to bring that meaning—the meaning of his life, death, and resurrection—to others.

In an article titled "Pope John's Intention" about the convening of the Second Vatican Council, Lonergan emphasizes the council's pastoral nature, its concern to speak to all cultures in ways distinct from more formal or theoretical previous modes of discourse: "The inspiration he [Pope John XXIII] had had in calling the council was hope for a widespread and more fervent renewal in the life of the church. It was for a new and more vigorous spread of the gospel in the whole world. He wanted our contemporaries to be made aware of the church's striving for the spiritual and, no less, for the material betterment of the whole of mankind."[27]

The Catholic intellectual tradition is not static but dynamic; it heads toward the future. Its fundamental concern is to proclaim the love and support of the Good Shepherd for all peoples as together we build our world. Such a proclamation is ecumenical and interreligious. It involves caring for people of all cultures and all religions, and even persons of no religion. It involves a special concern for the poor. That is why Bernard Lonergan spent many of his last days studying and writing on economics.

In order to communicate the Catholic intellectual tradition to all cultures, my own university—Seton Hall University—has for a number of years been engaged in interfaith and ecumenical conversations among faculty from all the disciplines and professions in the university. I have asked questions along two lines to animate these faculty dialogues:

1. How is it that you personally came to teach your particular discipline, your particular profession? What is your story? What deep drives have brought you to this point?

2. Where is your particular discipline or your particular profession going? What is your profession or discipline contributing to the human family, the common good, the building of a better future?

All such questions relate to communicating the Catholic intellectual tradition in our day: the good news as catholic, that is, as penetrating every area of culture. For every area of human culture has its blind spots, and such blind spots can most effectively be healed in and through community discernment. The Seton Hall seminars aim to facilitate faculty conversations on broad humanistic themes. The topics during the past twelve years have been as follows:

1998:   Knowledge and Wisdom
1999:   Divine Madness
2000:   Spirituality and the Academic Vocation
2001:   Reflections on the Core Curriculum
2002:   Religious Horizons and the Vocation of the University
2003:   Faith at Work
2004:   The Call of Poetry
2005:   Augustine and Culture
2006:   The Call of Two Cities: Citizenship and Christian Identity
2007:   Postmodernism and Religion
2008:   Kierkegaard and Catholicism
2009:   Strategies and Themes of Luke

These seminars have taken place for three or four days every May. More than 150 faculty members have participated in these seminars, which have allowed faculty to gather, to get to know one another, and to wrestle together about the meaning of being human in the light of the Catholic intellectual tradition. All the seminars have been guided by an outside facilitator, persons with their own expertise; and all kinds of faculty have responded: Catholics and Protestants, Jews and Muslims, Hindus and those professing no faith. Community has been built, deep issues vented, and good will generated. People have often asked me about the secret to the seminars, and my flippant answer has been, "It's not rocket science. Just get people into the same room, have a good facilitator and ask good questions." It's as simple as Jesus asking questions of the disciples on the road to Emmaus. Let me present just one evaluative comment from Susan Leshnoff, a professor of art. She had this to say about her experience:

Regarding the Catholic seminars, I attended "Divine Madness" with Jerry Miller in 1999, and please know that to this day, that week remains the most intellectually stimulating week I've had with colleagues to date. We faculty in attendance came from diverse backgrounds, and the discussion crossed religious boundaries, yet helped us all see that within the Catholic philosophy discussed was core content that not only applied to all of our lives but enriched our perceptions of Catholic thought. The faculty bonding during that week even 6 years later is still alive among so many of us.

There is a theological dimension to these conversations. The Hebrew word for church is *Qahal*, meaning the assembly called forth. Previously those journeying in the desert were a motley crew, and then they were called forth, gathered together, inspired by a common word, called to be in touch with the word of God within them—in Augustine's terms, "the teacher within"—so that they could become a people.[28] I am convinced that this process takes place very simply by calling people together and sharing with them an interesting, inspiring, open, and up-building word. High points for myself have involved hearing a fellow faculty member tell his or her personal story; a professor from the art department describe how certain art works can express depths of feeling; a person from the communications department describe the difficulties of balancing family life with academics; or an accountant describe a humanistic vision of accounting. A high point for me is just sitting at lunch with participating faculty and saying to myself, "I am glad I'm here— this is what it's all about."

It is in service to such encounters that the Catholic intellectual tradition points. It appeals to personal depths and concrete practical involvements. If its roots are in the past, still it points to a dynamic future. In this it coheres with a historically conscious worldview. I like the way Lonergan says this:

> Modern culture is the culture that knows about other cultures. It is aware that they are man-made. It is aware that the cultural may sustain or destroy or refashion the social. So it is that the modern person not only individually is responsible for the life he leads but also collectively is responsible for the world in which he leads it. So modern culture is culture on the move. It is not dedicated to perpetuating the wisdom of ancestors, to handing on the traditions it has inherited. The past is just the springboard to the future. . . . The future will belong to those who think about it, who grasp real possibilities, who project a coherent sequence of cumulative realizations, who speak to the human longing for achievement.[29]

I found a lot of the "wisdom of Catholicism" in the books I read as a young man. What the intervening years have taught me is that that wisdom not only existed in the past but penetrates the present and the future as it encounters in new ways all kinds of people from all kinds of communities. The Catholic intellectual tradition has a practical and future-directed orientation. The Letter to the Hebrews puts it succinctly: "The word of God is living and effective, sharper than any two-edged sword, penetrating even between soul and spirit, joints and marrow, and able to discern reflections and thoughts of the heart" (Heb. 4:12).[30]

Notes

1. Anton Pegis, ed., *The Wisdom of Catholicism* (New York: Modern Library, 1955).

2. See Richard M. Liddy, "Catholic Studies and the Mission of the University," in *Here Comes Everybody: Catholic Studies in American Higher Education*, ed. William C. Graham (Lanham, MD: University Press of America, 2008), 40–47. An earlier version of this chapter can be found in Richard M. Liddy, "The Catholic Intellectual Tradition: Achievement and Challenge," in *As Leaven in the World: Catholic Perspectives on Faith, Vocation, and the Intellectual Life*, ed. Thomas Landy (Franklin, WI: Sheed and Ward, 2001), 3–16.

3. Bernard Lonergan, *Method in Theology* (New York, 1974), 73.

4. See John Ranieri, *Eric Voegelin and the Good Society* (Columbia, MO: University of Missouri Press, 1995), 110–11; and Glenn Hughes and Fred Lawrence, "The Challenge of Eric Voegelin," www.mmisi.org/pr/24_01/hl.pdf.

5. Bernard Lonergan, "Belief: Today's Issue," in *A Second Collection* (Philadelphia: Westminster Press, 1974), 92.

6. John Henry Newman, *An Essay on the Development of Christian Doctrine*, www.newmanreader.org/works/development/index.html. See chap. 1, "The Development of Ideas," and chap. 8, "Assimilative Power."

7. Shusako Endo, *The Silence* (Marlboro, NJ: Taplinger Publishing Co., 1980).

8. Vincent Donovan, *Christianity Rediscovered* (Maryknoll, NY: Orbis Books, 1982).

9. Bernard Lonergan, *Method in Theology* (Toronto: University of Toronto Press, 1996), 362–63.

10. Steven Englund, "The French Connection," *Commonweal*, November 7, 2008, 14.

11. See Lonergan, *Method in Theology*, 57–73.

12. On the emergence of language, see ibid., 86–90.

13. Ibid., 73.

14. Bernard Lonergan, "Christology Today," in *A Third Collection* (Mahwah, NJ: Paulist Press, 1985), 84. There Lonergan refers to the works of Heinrich Schlier and Franz Mussner.

15. Thomas Aquinas, *Summa theologiae*, 1–2, q. 29, a. 4 c.

16. Fyodor Dostoyevsky, quoted in Denis Dirschel, *Dostoyevsky and the Catholic Church* (Chicago: Loyola University Press, 1986), 63.

17. To use a modern example, the paintings and prints of Georges Rouault articulate a truly catholic vision of Christ's presence in the poor and the suffering.

18. David DeLaura, "Newman's *Apologia* as Prophecy," in John Henry Newman, *Apologia pro vita sua*, ed. David J. Laura (New York: Norton, 1968), 496.

19. Bernard Lonergan, "Questionnaire in Philosophy," in *Philosophical and Theological Papers 1965–1980*, ed. Robert Doran and Robert Croken, Collected Works of Bernard Lonergan 17 (Toronto: University of Toronto Press, 2004), 363.

20. Lonergan, *Method in Theology*, 138. Helping to clarifying within ourselves these distinctions between the symbolic and the theoretical was the aim of much of Lonergan's work, beginning with his magisterial *Insight: An Essay on Human Understanding*, ed. Frederick E. Crowe and Robert M. Doran, Collected Works of Bernard Lonergan 3 (Toronto: University of Toronto Press, 1992).

21. See Bernard Lonergan, "The Origins of Christian Realism," in *A Second Collection*, 239–61.

22. See Bernard Lonergan, *Early Works on Theological Method I*, ed. Robert Doran and Robert Croken, Collected Works of Bernard Lonergan 22 (Toronto: University of Toronto Press, 2010).

23. See Lonergan, *Early Works*, passim, for what Lonergan called the developing "dogmatic-theological context." It is what has been built up in the Church, is taken for granted by Catholics, and is handed on and communicated in seminaries, theological schools, and theological writings.

24. Abraham Maslow, *Religions, Values, and Peak Experiences* (New York: Viking Press, 1970), 89–90.

25. See Alisdair MacIntyre, *Edith Stein: A Philosophical Prologue 1913–1922* (Lanham, MD: Rowman and Littlefield, 2007).

26. *New American Bible*, www.usccb.org/nab/bible/luke/luke24.htm.

27. Lonergan, "Pope John's Intention," in *Third Collection*, 225.

28. For Augustine on "the teacher within," see "On the Teacher," Augnet, accessed May 14, 2011, www.augnet.org/default.asp?ipageid=279.

29. Lonergan, "The Absence of God in Modern Culture," in *Second Collection*, 115. See also "Theology and Man's Future," in *Second Collection*, 135, on the emerging role of the university: "The correlation between the accelerating explosion of knowledge and socio-cultural change confronts the contemporary university with a grave problem. For the university has ceased to be a storehouse whence traditional wisdom and knowledge are dispensed. It is a center in which ever-increasing knowledge is disseminated to bring about ever-increasing social and cultural change."

30. *New American Bible*, www.usccb.org/nab/bible/hebrews/hebrews4.htm.

CHAPTER 6

The "Real World" of Business

J. Michael Stebbins

When I completed my doctorate in systematic theology at Boston College in 1991, I fully intended to spend the next few decades of my life teaching courses in that field in a university setting. As it turned out, the years I spent in graduate school prepared me for a somewhat different future.

At its root systematic theology is the effort to produce a fully integrated Christian worldview. It is carried out from the perspective of faith (in Anselm of Canterbury's famous twelfth-century formulation theology is found *fides quaerens intellectum,* "faith seeking understanding"). Systematic theology takes as given the truth of the content of Christian faith and proceeds to ask, What is the meaning of what we believe? Beyond explaining how Christian doctrines are consistent with one another, its further goal is to integrate what Christians affirm through faith with whatever truth has been discovered in every field of human knowledge: history, literature, the arts, philosophy, the natural sciences, the social sciences, communications, and the innumerable varieties of common sense generated by people living and working in different times, places, and cultures. At its best, systematic theology attempts to embrace the world in its totality. It does so not by claiming detailed expertise about every aspect of every part of the universe—an obvious impossibility—but rather by finding intelligible connections between what is affirmed by faith and what is affirmed by reason, and by showing that, far from contradicting the truths of faith, anything known via science or any other kind of legitimate human knowing is compatible with, and indeed can be meaningfully related to, Christian doctrine. More than any other field of learning, systematic theology is concerned with the whole—everything that exists, Creator and creation, the ultimate whole of which all other wholes are only a part.

University positions in systematic theology were not plentiful in the early 1990s. My first job after leaving Boston College was a two-year contract at Gonzaga University teaching Christian ethics, which had been my minor area of specialization in graduate school. During that time I was asked by Jim Connor to come periodically to the Woodstock Theological Center in Washington, DC, to discuss ways in which Bernard Lonergan's theological method might serve as an interdisciplinary resource for the center's programs, which dealt with a variety of social, political, economic, and ecclesiastical issues. Before long I was asked to join the Woodstock staff as a senior fellow and director of a newly launched program in business ethics. Its intended audience was not university students but rather business people in the context of their everyday work lives. The program was supposed to use some of Lonergan's insights in order to pursue a twofold goal: enhancing the ability of managers and executives to assess and guide the ethical performance of their organizations, and providing a framework that would allow managers and executives to explore the relationship between their faith and their work.

In 2000, after six years at Woodstock, I returned to Spokane, Washington, to assume the directorship of the new Gonzaga Ethics Institute, a position I held until the end of 2008. In that role I often taught one to two courses per semester (both graduate and undergraduate) and pursued a variety of ethics projects and programs for both on- and off-campus audiences.

So despite the fact that I earned my PhD in the field of systematic theology, the jobs I was hired for after graduate school had to do with ethics instead. Moreover, during that period the vast majority of participants in the various off-campus workshops, classes, seminars, and retreats I presented were people of a decidedly practical bent: managers and executives in business, the nonprofit sector, and government; members of the engineering and legal professions; leaders at the parish or diocesan levels of the Catholic Church (priests, deacons, religious women, lay people, and even a few bishops); alumni of Jesuit high schools and universities; and ordinary Catholic parishioners. By and large these people participated voluntarily in the programs I offered, and they came because they wanted concrete guidance for the everyday choices they faced. They had little interest in the kinds of theoretical issues that tend to occupy academic ethicists and theologians.

When I first began working in the area of business ethics, I had to enlarge my horizon. I knew something about ethics, but I knew only a little about business, the economy, and organizational life. There was a lot to learn. It wasn't just a matter of learning from textbooks, although I did a fair amount of that; and it wasn't just a matter of reading journals in the areas of business and management, although I did and continue to do quite a bit of that as well. More than anything else it was a matter of talking with business people, with executives and managers and employees: getting to know them, getting a feel for their interests and concerns, for the way they think and speak, for the way they understand themselves and their work. I quickly discovered that my habitual academic style of teaching was not very effective with this group. I wanted to speak in generalities; they wanted very specific examples. I wanted to give them a solid, coherent theory; they wanted to know precisely how that theory would affect their practice. I wanted to present them with pages of carefully wrought, polysyllabic, footnoted prose; they wanted a one-page summary with bullets. They wanted to know what the payoff was—not in a cynical way, but because they were willing to invest time and energy in learning from me only if what I offered could be applied in a significant way to their lives, to their organizations, to their ways of doing business. So I had to adjust my thinking, language, and style accordingly. I had to reduce the amount of content that I presented, because I was usually dealing with severe time constraints and with people who were not used to extended presentations on deep topics. I had to adjust my starting point, and I had to speak much more concretely than I had been accustomed to. And I had to do all of this without losing the substance of what I was trying to communicate.

Perhaps most fundamentally, I had to grow in my understanding of what ethics and systematic theology are all about. Having to respond regularly to people who wanted to learn not just ideas, but ideas that helped explain the meanings and values at stake in their lives, forced me to recognize more clearly than I ever had before that ethics is an eminently practical field of investigation. Ethical theories, no matter how elegant or rhetorically appealing, are useful only to the extent that they can help actual human beings grapple effectively with who they are and with the decisions they have to make. The same kind of practical orientation also holds for systematic theology. It is not a prop for wishful thinking or pietistic idealism; its function is to present a robust, dynamic framework for making sense of the world as a whole, in all its natural and supernatural reality. It has to help people work out the meaning of their faith in the world as Christians believe it actually is—a world in which human beings are called to friendship with God but in which sin and human frailty also exercise their deforming effects.

I found the task of meeting this challenge occasionally daunting, but more often freeing and exhilarating. I found that I could not adopt anyone else's approach wholesale. No one had yet produced a full-blown theory based on Lonergan's powerful but incomplete set of insights about ethics, much less worked out in detail how those insights could be applied specifically to economics and business ethics or to issues of faith and work.[1] I had to explore new territory, picking up clues where I could, having whatever insights I could muster on my own or learn from others, trying things out, and proceeding by trial and error.[2] Eventually I came up with an approach that the various groups I have worked with seem to find valuable. In the following pages I present some of the basic elements of that still developing approach.

Although I do not usually state it in these terms, my primary aims are to give people a framework that helps them better understand themselves and the world, and to heighten their sense of responsibility for doing their part to bring good into the world. I invite people to try out this framework in order to see whether it helps them make sense of things. Frequently I find that I'm not changing people's minds so much as helping them achieve greater clarity about what they already think and feel and value. Below I discuss the key elements of the framework.

The Distinction between "My World" and "The World"

At the outset I try to get people thinking about the fact that the way in which each of us makes sense of the world is never completely accurate. First, we don't know everything about the actual world, because it is obviously too extensive and deep and complex for us to grasp fully. We cannot even understand everything that there is to be understood about ourselves, our family members and friends, or the events going on around us. Second, our way of making sense of the world is always partly mistaken. Some of what we think to be true is actually false, and vice versa; and at the level of feeling, the tumult of our desires sometimes leads us to pursue lesser goods, or objects that are actually harmful, instead of the goods that would actually lead to greater happiness for ourselves and others. The hope is that as the years pass, our understanding of the world broadens and becomes increasingly accurate, and our feelings gradually align themselves with an authentic scale of values. The point of introducing this topic is not to promote scorched-earth skepticism or relativism, but rather to underscore the difficulty involved in correctly making sense of the world, and to alert people to the need to take responsibility for the way in which we carry out that lifelong task.

Our Participation in Patterns of Cooperation

I have found it helpful to get people thinking about the extent to which human living is a cooperative enterprise. In the developed society in which we live, there is practically no want or need that we meet entirely on our own. The life we construct for ourselves always builds on the achievements of others who have preceded us in time, and it always involves our participation with others in ongoing patterns of cooperation—that is, recurrent, flexible systems or routines that meet wants and needs of various kinds on an ongoing basis.[3] Such patterns may be formal or informal, adverted to or unnoticed, large-scale or small-scale. As new needs, wants, or opportunities arise, old patterns may undergo adjustment or fall into disuse, and new patterns may arise. Although it is undoubtedly true that each of us is an individual human being, a person with our own identity and unique history, still our living is a communal project. Without patterns of cooperation, human living as we know it would be impossible.

Patterns of cooperation do not function automatically. The people in them have to play specific roles, acquire the knowledge and skills needed for those roles, develop relationships, maintain and develop routines and institutions, and so forth. And this means that every pattern of cooperation— a friendship, a family, a school, a nonprofit organization, a business firm, a government agency, an economy, a nation—contains, so to speak, its own ethical requirements. People have to function intelligently and responsibly within the pattern in order for the pattern as a whole to function effectively. If too many people lack the needed skills, fail to play their various roles, or operate in ways that disrupt relationships and undermine trust, the pattern of cooperation grows increasingly dysfunctional. It becomes less capable of meeting the legitimate human wants and needs that are its raison d'être. In some cases the pattern may become so distorted that its net effect is to hinder or destroy the greater good, even though no one intends that result.

One of the primary themes of Catholic social teaching is the need to promote solidarity, which Pope John Paul II defined as "not a feeling of vague compassion or shallow distress at the misfortunes of so many people, both near and far," but rather "a firm and persevering determination to commit oneself to the common good."[4] I would argue that being seriously committed to the common good means taking patterns of cooperation seriously. It is not enough to bewail the great economic, political, social, and cultural issues of our times and then assume that one's duty to the common good has been fulfilled by stating that one is on the side of the angels. Nor is it enough to be satisfied with actions that achieve some good on a small scale or in the short term, or that serve mainly to produce in oneself a glow of self-satisfied contentment. The spirit of solidarity includes, as an essential element, the recognition that particular wants and needs are met by patterns of cooperation, so it always prompts the question, How can this want or need be met in a way that works for everyone—that is, in a way that enhances, or at least doesn't significantly damage, our ability to live together? Given the complexity of the various patterns of cooperation in which we are involved, answering this question typically requires the input of many people, a relentless effort to get to the bottom of things, a refusal to accept one-size-fits-all solutions, and a willingness to experiment, to admit mistakes, and to keep trying to do the next intelligent and reasonable thing.

I am not advocating central planning. I am not envisioning a utopia. Rather, I am calling for the kind of thinking and deciding and concern for the whole that ought to characterize the citizens of a democracy. Solidarity, properly understood, is a democratic virtue.

Rethinking the Purpose of Business

One commonly hears that the purpose of business is to maximize profit, to maximize shareholder value, to maximize return on investment, or, more crudely, simply to make as much money as possible. Despite the fact that this notion has come under attack in recent years, in my experience it is still held by the majority of business people and tends to be the fallback position even of business people whose actual performance seems to belie it.[5] But once they have spent some time becoming familiar with the idea of patterns of cooperation, I have found that business people—even corporate managers and executives—often begin to realize some of the shortcomings of the standard account of the purpose of business. Any business, including a sole proprietorship, is a node in a set of intersecting patterns of cooperation (and in almost all cases can itself be thought of as such a pattern). To fully understand the functioning of a particular business requires investigating all the patterns of cooperation in which it participates (that is, how it is linked concretely to customers, employees, suppliers, lenders, government entities, communities affected by its operations, current networks and modes of communication, and so on); the various wants and needs that its operations help meet both directly and indirectly; and its dependence on other players to meet its own wants and needs.

Helping people view business in this way requires the use of concrete examples. Let me briefly describe one that I used with an undergraduate business ethics class in the fall semester of 2001. Earlier that year the town of Chewelah, Washington, located about fifty miles north of Spokane, had been stunned by the announcement that a nearby aluminum smelter that had been a major employer in the area would soon be permanently shut down. I had my students visit the smelter and the town, where they interviewed plant managers, current and former employees and vendors, local government officials, school teachers and principals, business people, leaders of charitable organizations, and church pastors. Often the dimensions of a pattern of cooperation become most apparent when the pattern breaks down. In this case my students quickly began noticing all the ways in which the community was experiencing pain as a result of the plant's closure. Each instance of pain—the lost jobs, the foreclosures and declining real estate values, the drop in school enrollments, the shuttered small businesses, the decrease in financial contributions to local charities, and perhaps most poignantly the personal relationships disrupted by all these changes—represented the many wants and needs whose satisfaction had depended, in one way or another, on the operations of the smelter. This experience brought home to my students and others the idea that profit maximization, or any other measure of financial success, does not by itself adequately capture the purpose of business. It is more accurate to say that the purpose or function of any business is to contribute to the effective functioning and development of the patterns of cooperation in which it participates. That is what the aluminum smelter did. The fact that it failed to achieve a sufficient level of profit proves not that profit was the smelter's purpose, but only that profit was a necessary means for achieving its purposes of producing aluminum, providing wages to its employees, and generally raising the community's standard of living.

Just to be clear: I am not denigrating profit. I myself am an investor and have been a small business owner. If a business fails to reach a sufficient level of profit, it dies. Nor am I saying that owners or shareholders are just one more stakeholder group whose interests should carry no greater weight than those of any other constituency. The only claim I am making here is that even if the owners or investors are motivated solely by the desire to make as much money as they can, the primary function of their business extends much farther than that. Engaging in any kind of transaction—such as taking out a loan, renting office space, designing and manufacturing a product, buying parts or supplies or advertising, hiring an employee, or selling to a customer—immediately pulls the business into the network of patterns of cooperation that we call the economy. The business is part of that larger, dynamic whole that exists in order to produce an appropriate standard of living for society.[6] To define the purpose of business without considering this broader context is a mistake, one that makes it easier for business people to overlook the ethical obligations that flow naturally from the various cooperative roles they and their businesses play.

In the early 1940s and again in the 1970s Lonergan devoted a great deal of effort to the study of economic theory. His experience of the Great Depression, which he had lived through partly in Canada and partly in Rome, led him to wonder about the causes of booms and slumps in the economy. He soon became convinced that the various schools of macroeconomic theory had not yet produced a fully adequate account of the economy—that is, an account that, in making a clean break from descriptive categories, succeeds in identifying the interrelated, explanatory variables that reveal the underlying intelligibility of economic activity, including the causes of the business cycle.[7] In response to this need, Lonergan worked out and kept refining the main lines of what he thought of as a new paradigm for understanding the economy.[8] The work he produced is quite technical, and attempting even a brief explanation of it here would go too far afield for the purposes of this chapter. But it is worth noting that Lonergan concluded that the economy has as its "natural goal" what he termed a "major basic expansion" leading to progress in the standard of living of an entire society.[9] For that goal to be reached, however, those who participate in the economy as producers and consumers need both to understand how their actions affect the economy and to make intelligent, responsible choices about those actions.[10]

From an Ethics of Compliance to an Ethics of Achievement

I cannot count the number of times when, after introducing myself as someone who works in the field of business ethics, I have been met with the rejoinder, "Business ethics—isn't that an oxymoron?" There is some justification for that remark, of course. Individuals sometimes encounter unfair or dishonest practices in the businesses they deal with or work for, and we are treated to a steady stream of publicity about scandals in large corporations and ethical violations on the part of their executives. When this large-scale misbehavior is sufficiently egregious, it tends to inspire calls for more regulation and stricter oversight, as when the US Congress enacted the Sarbanes-Oxley Act in the wake of the Enron debacle. In general such laws and rules identify undesirable types of business practice, mandate various procedures aimed at preventing the occurrence of those practices, and specify the punishments that will be meted out to those who fail to comply. As a result, in the current business environment most ethics programs focus on ensuring compliance with the law. "Being ethical" tends to get reduced to "not being unethical."

I do not believe that this is an adequate standard for business ethics, especially if the purpose of business is defined in terms of its contribution to maintaining and developing patterns of cooperation. To help business people think about a more adequate ethical standard, I share with them the following analysis.

The standard approach to business ethics can be termed an "ethics of compliance." When ethics is seen in this light, developing an ethics program for a company means clearly stating the relevant rules and laws, telling people to obey them, and punishing those who do not. How does this approach motivate people to comply? It does so by making them fear the punishment that would result from noncompliance. The need for this type of ethics will never be entirely eliminated, since some people need the threat of punishment hanging over their head to keep them from acting in an unethical way. And for habitually ethical people who are under pressure or tempted to act contrary to their character, rules and sanctions can be helpful reminders of where the boundaries of permissible behavior lie.

Many business people, however, hold themselves to a standard higher than mere compliance. They practice what might be called an "ethics of surplus." Besides obeying laws and rules, they go a step further and find ways for the company to share some of its extra resources from time to time. This can take the form of philanthropy, such as donating money to nonprofit organizations or giving employees time off to work for local charities. Often this is spoken of as "giving back"—sharing some of the company's surplus with those in need. The ethics of surplus is certainly a praiseworthy approach. It involves not just staying out of trouble and avoiding obvious harm, but also serving the community, even if in only limited ways and when financial circumstances permit. Nonetheless, in this approach ethics is viewed not as something intrinsically related to the business and its operations, but instead as something extra that does not affect the underlying business as such. Business is business, and philanthropy is sometimes layered on top of it.

There is a still higher standard that Lonergan terms the "ethics of achievement."[11] According to this approach—one to which I believe some business people adhere, even if they don't explicitly think of it in those terms—the goal of human living in general is to live a life fully committed to the good. Business is a part of human living, not an activity existing in an imaginary separate sphere where people play by different rules. The ethics of achievement does not restrict ethical business performance to compliance augmented by occasional gestures of generosity. Instead, it encourages a sort of restlessness, a desire to keep developing the organization's capacity to add greater value to human living. The kind of good that the ethics of achievement envisions isn't usually spectacular or newsworthy, and it doesn't try to reach some lofty state of ethical perfection. Nor does it renounce the solid, intelligent, innovative practices that make a business successful, including an adequate level of profit. In other words, it does not ask the business to not be a business. But in a business that tries to practice the ethics of achievement, people are encouraged to ask such questions as, How can we make this a better place to work? How can we better meet the needs of our customers? How can we operate in a way that promotes the good of the community over the long term? How can we communicate more effectively with each other so we accomplish more of the good we're capable of? In short, the ethics of achievement is an ethics that takes seriously the multiple, concrete interdependencies and obligations that come with participation in patterns of cooperation.[12] It views a business as a reservoir of potential for doing good, both for itself and beyond itself, and it searches out creative, intelligent ways of incrementally realizing that potential. From the standpoint of the ethics of achievement, one is never satisfied that a company's performance, or one's own performance, is ethical enough. It means never thinking that one has arrived; there is always more good that can be done.

The Need for Authentic Performance

From the standpoint of the individual business person, of any particular business, or of the business community as a whole, the key to operating in a manner consonant with the ethics of achievement is committing oneself to a life of what Lonergan termed "authenticity," which others in this volume describe. Sustained progress on any scale is possible only to the extent that people pay attention, make the effort to understand thoroughly, verify the correctness of their insights, deliberate and decide responsibly, and then repeat the cycle—again and again and again, correcting their mistakes, revising their actions, and enlarging their understanding over time. This is *the* fundamental human method for achieving the good. If we live authentically, then we approach our work with a desire not simply to maintain the status quo effectively, but also to improve ourselves, our organization's products and systems, and the relationships among the people we work with; and we do so not for the sake of self-aggrandizement but out of a desire to promote whatever good we can in our corner of the world.

One of the aspects of Lonergan's thought that needs further investigation and development is his notion that authentic decision making requires having values (that is, concrete instances of what is truly good) rather than mere satisfactions as one's goal.[13] According to Lonergan a fully authentic person recognizes that values are related to each other according to a particular scale of preference.[14] At the lowest level are vital values, such as health and physical grace. Above these are social values (technological, economic, political) followed by cultural values, such as love of family and country, which provide a higher context of meaning in which vital and social values find their significance. Higher yet are personal values, which are constituted by human beings who are attempting to live authentically; and at the pinnacle are religious values, which are constituted by human beings whose efforts at authentic living are a response to their experience of grace, which Lonergan describes as "being in love with God."[15] The scale implies that among the many good things that do or could exist, some are more worthwhile than others, and each lower level is to be pursued not only for its own sake but also for the sake of the levels above it. Consequently, in an authentic person the drive toward responsible decisions and actions is expressed in a spontaneous willingness to pursue values in accordance with the priorities reflected in the scale. For instance, a salesperson strives to sell goods and services (on the level of social values) in ways that respect the dignity of his or her customers (on the level of personal values). Conversely, inauthenticity shows itself in decisions and actions that invert the priorities of the value scale, so that lower values are pursued in preference to higher.

Connecting Faith and Work

What does any of this have to do with systematic theology? When I speak as an ethicist, and do so with groups of people who do not all share the same (or perhaps any) religious commitment, I usually have to keep the issue of faith on the periphery, if I mention it at all. But when I do have an opportunity to discuss ethics, and especially business ethics, in the context of Christian faith, I usually emphasize three points.

The first point is that from the Christian perspective, the human race—contrary to the view that underlies much of classical and contemporary economic theory—is not a collection of essentially selfish individuals engaged in competition for the scarce goods of the world. There is selfishness and competition aplenty, to be sure, but Christians believe that God created human beings as a family and gives them the help (grace) to choose and do what is good. The view of business that I have been outlining incorporates this view of humanity. Whether Christian or not, many people share the sense that we human beings are meant to live together, to share each other's concerns, and to find our happiness in working not just for ourselves but for the good of all. Although we frequently fail to live up to this standard, it remains the criterion by which we ought to judge ourselves.

The second point has to do with God's response to human sin. According to Christian teaching, the Son (Jesus) and the Holy Spirit have become participants in human history: the Son by being born, living, teaching, healing, dying, rising from the dead, and leaving behind a community of disciples; and the Spirit by being sent into human minds and hearts to turn people from sin and self-centeredness and empower them to become friends of God and ever greater sources of good in the world. To live authentically, I believe, is to participate in, or carry on, the missions of the Son and the Spirit.

The third and final point is that living one's faith in the world of business does not primarily mean praying at work, although that is a good thing. Primarily it means doing business well in the ways I have described above —intelligently, responsibly, with a view to serving the greater good—because that is how God intends us to live, and because that way of living ultimately leads to happiness. It is a matter not so much of bringing one's faith into work, but rather of recognizing that there is only one "real world"—this world, which God has created— and that business, along with every other part of our lives, belongs to it and is called to operate accordingly. This is the kind of wholeness that I challenge myself and others to pursue.

Notes

The author retains copyright for this chapter.

1. On Bernard Lonergan's ethics, see, e.g., Kenneth R. Melchin, *Living with Other People: An Introduction to Christian Ethics Based on Lonergan* (Collegeville, MN: The Liturgical Press, 1998); Mark J. Doorley, *The Place of the Heart in Lonergan's Ethics* (Lanham, MD: University Press of America, 1996); and William F. Sullivan, *Eye of the Heart: Knowing the Human Good in the Euthanasia Debate* (Toronto: University of Toronto Press, 2005). Lonergan's writings on economics include *Macroeconomic Dynamics: An Essay in Circulation Analysis*, ed. Frederick G. Lawrence, Patrick H. Byrne, and Charles C. Hefling Jr., Collected Works of Bernard Lonergan 15 (Toronto: University of Toronto Press, 1999); and *For a New Political Economy*, ed. Philip J. McShane, Collected Works of Bernard Lonergan 21 (Toronto: University of Toronto Press, 1998). For secondary works on Lonergan's economics, see, among others, Philip McShane, *Economics for Everyone* (Halifax, Nova Scotia: Axial Press, 1998); Stephen L. Martin, *Healing and Creativity in Economic Ethics: The Contribution of Bernard Lonergan's Thought to Catholic Social Teaching* (Lanham, MD: University Press of America, 2008); and Eileen de Neeve, *Decoding the Economy: Understanding Change with Bernard Lonergan* (Montreal: Thomas More Institute, 2008).

2. In trying to work out the implications of Lonergan's thought for the specific field of business ethics, I have been helped especially by the insights of Mark Nielsen, Kenneth Melchin, Morag McConville, and Patrick Byrne.

3. "Patterns of cooperation" is a term I use in place of, but with the same meaning as, Lonergan's "good of order." For discussions of that notion, see Bernard Lonergan, *Insight: A Study of Human Understanding*, ed. Frederick E. Crowe and Robert M. Doran, Collected Works of Bernard Lonergan 3 (Toronto: University of Toronto Press, 1992),

238–39, 619–20, 628–30; and Lonergan, *Method in Theology* (Toronto: University of Toronto Press, 1990), 48–50.

4. John Paul II, *Sollicitudo rei socialis*, sec. 38, www.vatican.va/edocs/ENG0223/_ INDEX.HTM. See J. Michael Stebbins, "The Meaning of Solidarity," in *Labor, Solidarity and the Common Good: Essays on the Ethical Foundations of Management*, ed. S. A. Cortright (Durham, NC: Carolina Academic Press, 2001), 61–74.

5. Peter Drucker gives one critique of the notion that the purpose of business is to make as much money as possible: "Asked what a business is, the typical businessman is likely to answer, 'An organization to make a profit.' The typical economist is likely to give the same answer. This answer is not only false, it is irrelevant. The prevailing economic theory of business enterprise and behavior, the maximization of profit . . . may adequately explain how Richard Sears operated. But it cannot explain how Sears, Roebuck or any other business enterprise operates, nor how it should operate. The concept of profit maximization is, in fact, meaningless." Peter F. Drucker, *Management: Tasks, Responsibilities, Practices* (New York: HarperBusiness, 1993), 59.

6. The precise meaning of "suitable" is, of course, open to a good deal of debate. The point is that what one conceives of as an adequate, humane, or just standard of living will differ in different places and at different times.

7. "The facts of the macroeconomy are already well known. What is lacking is a clear and precise understanding of the mechanism behind such obvious facts as the relations between expansion and contraction of the economy, employment and unemployment, inflation and deflation, and many other things that are just common knowledge." Lonergan, *Macroeconomic Dynamics*, 12.

8. See ibid., lviii-lix.

9. Ibid., 77.

10. "What is needed is a new political economy that is free from the mistakes of the old, a democratic economics that can issue practical imperatives to plain men." Lonergan, *For a New Political Economy*, 5.

11. Bernard Lonergan, *Topics in Education*, ed. Robert M. Doran and Frederick E. Crowe, Collected Works of Bernard Lonergan 10 (Toronto: University of Toronto Press, 1993), 103, 106. What I have called the "ethics of compliance" Lonergan terms the "ethics of law." The term "ethics of surplus" and its analysis I owe to Mark Nielsen.

12. As Abraham Maslow puts it, "Good management and good workers and good enterprises and good products and good communities and good states are all conditions of one another and of good mutual relations." Abraham Maslow, with Deborah C. Stephens and Gary Heil, *Maslow on Management* (New York: John Wiley & Sons, 1998), 141.

13. See Lonergan, *Method in Theology*, 50–52, 240.

14. Ibid., 31–32, 39.

15. E.g., ibid., 105. Lonergan, in keeping with Catholic teaching, would maintain that it is entirely possible that many people experience the reality of grace or being in love with God even though they are not Christian (or even explicitly religious) and would not describe the experience in those terms.

PART TWO

Whole as Identity

CHAPTER 7

Attaining Harmony as a Hindu-Christian

Michael Amaladoss

I am an Indian Christian and a Jesuit. I was born and grew up as an Indian. My priestly formation has been in traditional scholastic philosophy and in a theology in transformation after the Second Vatican Council. I have been a student also of Hindu philosophy, theology, and spirituality. I have lived through the aftermath of the Second Vatican Council. I have been involved in interreligious dialogue between Hindus, Christians, and an occasional Muslim for thirty-five years. All this has led me to an awareness today of being a Hindu-Christian. I am encouraged by the thought that my guru, Jesuit Father Ignatius Hirudayam, and Swami Abhishiktananda (Henri Le Saux), whom I was privileged to know in his last years, were both Hindu-Christians according to my understanding. I think that Mahatma Gandhi was also a Christian-Hindu, perhaps the best Indian Christian of the twentieth century, if a Christian is someone who follows the teachings and example of Christ. At an international conference on "Double Belongingness in Religion" in Brussels, Belgium, in 1999, I felt at home in a group of about forty people who felt themselves to be Hindu-, Buddhist-, or Taoist-Christian.[1] Such a double identity will seem confusing to many. Some will cry, "Syncretism!" In this chapter I therefore try to explain how I arrived at this point and how I feel and live such a liminal identity. At the end I also clarify my position by referring briefly to the experience of Swami Abhishiktananda, among others.

My Story

I was born in 1936 into a family that has been Christian for five generations. But my parents were teachers working in government schools in largely Hindu villages. So from the age of three I grew up in a large Hindu village with about five hundred families, of whom only three families (all teachers) were Christian. The village had a big temple to the goddess Mariamman. I was familiar with the temple's rituals and festivals, observing them with my Hindu friends. On Sundays we had to walk three miles to go to our church. So I grew up surrounded by Hindus. Our different identities were clear, but we were friends and playmates, not enemies. At the age of eleven I went to a Jesuit boarding school. There, too, the majority of the students and many of the teachers were Hindu. In the morning and in the evening the sounds of the bells from the nearby Hindu temple and the Christian church used to mingle harmoniously. The Christian atmosphere in the school and in the boarding school was clear and dominant, but not aggressive or offensive. I went to nearby parish centers on Sundays to teach the catechism to children.

I joined the Society of Jesus in 1953, at the age of seventeen. During the novitiate I spent two weeks with Father Hirudayam in a parish. He was a pioneer of inculturation and interreligious dialogue, born a little ahead of his time. In that period, because of his theology, he was living in some sort of exile in a small parish after teaching for a couple of years in the seminary. I imbibed from him his love for Hinduism, Indian culture, and music. He was an expert in Shaiva Siddhanta, one of the branches of Hinduism. Fifteen years later, after the Second Vatican Council, he was allowed to start an ashram in Chennai devoted to inculturation, interreligious dialogue, and Indian Christian spirituality.

When I was student of philosophy, there was a growing interest in Indian culture among the students. A small group of us joined together to study various dimensions of Indian arts and culture, the aim being to understand better our own Indian identity and also use these dimensions to proclaim the good news in India. During my philosophical studies I read the *Summa theologica* of Saint Thomas Aquinas in the original Latin, as well as the works of other European Thomists, like Jacques Maritain and Etienne Gilson. I also read the five-volume history of Indian philosophy by S. N. Dasgupta and the writings of other Hindu philosophers, like S. Radhakrishnan and Ananda Coomarswamy, who was also an art historian. My paper at the end of the philosophy course compared C. G. Jung and Yoga. One consequence of this plunge into Hinduism was the slow realization that there are many good and holy elements in Hinduism that should provoke appreciation and even admiration.

After studying philosophy I spent two years studying south Indian classical music in Chennai. I was the only Christian among about one hundred students. The experience was another immersion into Hinduism. Many of my masters were not only musicians but devotees of Hindu gods. The compositions they taught us were devotional songs. Music was for them a means of *sadhana* (spiritual practice), searching for God-experience. I was also shocked when my Hindu companions wondered why I, a Christian, was interested in "their" music—a subtle hint that I was not considered Indian culturally, that Christianity was a foreign religion.

In 1965 I went to Kurseong, in the Himalayas, for my studies in theology. My interest in Hinduism continued. My first major paper published at this time was a comparison between Indian and Ignatian spiritualities. My second was on Gandhian spirituality. After my first year three of us students went on a pilgrimage to Hindu centers in north India to experience Hinduism at close quarters, so to speak. We traveled as Hindus (that is, not revealing our Christian identity), visited their temples, spoke to the sannyasis, stayed in their ashrams meant for pilgrims. We went to Haridwar and Rishikesh in the Himalayas, Brindavan and Mathura sacred to Krishna (a Hindu avatar, or divine manifestation in human form), and Varanasi and Bodhgaya. Two memories remain engraved in my memory. At Brindavan, the birthplace of Krishna, his life story was reenacted in the evenings as a dance drama. The emotional involvement of the audience, transforming drama into a lived experience of contemplation and prayer, was remarkable and touching. Near Mathura we met a Hindu sannyasi who had just emerged from a two-year period of total silence. I have never seen such brightness on a face anywhere, either before or since. I felt humble in the presence of a person who certainly had experienced the divine. Translated into theological terms, this indicated my recognition of God's action in and through another religious tradition. At this time I was also in contact with leaders of Christian-Hindu dialogue like Raimon Panikkar, Swami Abhishiktananda, and Bede Griffiths. When I finished my theology studies, I wanted to study Hinduism more deeply. But my superiors did not favor the idea. So from 1969 to 1972 I finished a research degree in Paris on inculturation in the sacraments. My focus subsequently has been the development of an Indian Christian theology and spirituality. But let me note in passing that in 1975 I published an article in French titled "Qui suis-je? un catholique-hindou"—Who Am I? A Catholic-Hindu.[2]

Research and Reflection

When I came back to India and started teaching in 1973, the orientations of the Second Vatican Council had already begun to take effect. In 1973 a seminar in Bangalore explored the question, Can we consider the scriptures of other religions as inspired? The answer of the theologians was affirmative. They saw the history of salvation as a progression of three covenants: a cosmic or natural one with all human beings, illustrated for example by God's covenant with Noah; then God's covenant with Israel; and finally the new covenant in Jesus Christ. The other religions and their scriptures belong to the cosmic covenant and can therefore be considered inspired analogically. This means that though God is not directly speaking to us through them, what God tells the members of other religions is of interest to us, just as we acknowledge God speaking to us through the Old Testament. The theologians concluded that we can draw spiritual nourishment from the other religious scriptures. More concretely they suggested that, on a Sunday, we could have a first reading from the scripture of another religion, followed by readings from the Old and the New Testaments. The readings would center on the same theme. The theological paradigm is one of preparation-fulfillment. The Vatican disallowed this proposal even before being formally asked. Nonetheless, the use of other religious scriptures continues in private devotion and in the ashrams. Collections of passages from other religious scriptures, mostly Hindu, exist and are occasionally used in prayer services in India or for personal devotion and reflection. A couple of Jesuits, Sebastian Painadath and Francis D'Sa, guide retreats based on the *Bhagavad Gita* even today.

Now there is a general acknowledgment that the Spirit and the Word of God are also present and active in other cultures and religions.[3] This acknowledgment includes their scriptures, too. This recognition has led to a change of paradigm in the theology of religions. The preparation-fulfillment paradigm sees other religions as pre-Judaic. "Preparation-fulfillment" also supposes "partial-full." The consequence is that, if we have the fullness of truth in Jesus Christ, we do not have to worry about the partial truths available in Judaism and other religions. But historically and experientially it is difficult to see how the New Testament fulfills, say, Hinduism as it docs the Old Testament. As I come to understand these things, I have concluded that if God is really speaking through the other religious scriptures, God seems to be speaking in a different way. We must respect God's freedom in self-revelation. God is not bound to our paradigms. So we may have something to learn from what God is saying to the others. Interreligious dialogue then becomes mutual and not unidirectional. I will not go into the theological implications of all this here.[4]

In 1973 I began teaching theology part-time at Vidyajyoti College of Theology in Delhi and part-time also in St. Paul's Seminary in Tiruchirapalli in south India. In Tiruchirapalli, with the collaboration of Bede Griffiths, a British Benedictine monk who had his ashram nearby, I launched an interreligious group. About twenty Hindus and Christians came together every month to reflect on themes like God, prayer, and salvation in Hinduism and Christianity. Once we went to Griffiths's ashram, about twenty miles away, for a whole day of reflection and prayer. We joined the midday prayer at the ashram, read from Hindu and Christian scriptures, and sang hymns (*bhajans*) addressed to God. When a prayer ended with a gesture of honoring the Blessed Sacrament, a Hindu monk was the first to fall prostrate in adoration, followed by other Hindus and, of course, by us, the Catholics. Praying together has not been a problem for us then or later. It seems even more easy and relevant when we come together on special occasions such as natural disasters, like the tsunami and earthquakes, or human-caused destructions, like violence and wars. Sitting together in silence before the Absolute has been a powerful experience, especially at such times.

A Shift in Approach and Identity

What led to a community shift in experience and reflection on identity, at least as far as I was concerned, was the use of some symbols like *Om,* and gestures like *arathi* (waving of lights or flowers as a gesture of paying homage), in Christian worship as a consequence of attempts at inculturation.[5] A few Christians and Hindus objected to such use. At the ashram our response to the Christians was that these symbols were not basically religious, but cultural. They were not Hindu, but Indian. So the Indian Christians are entitled to use them and can do so profitably by reinterpreting them in the Christian context, like the symbol *Om*. This was what happened in ancient Roman times in the liturgy. The response to the Hindus was similar: These symbols were not Hindu, though they were used in Hindu ritual, but Indian, and as Indians we had a right to use them, reinterpreting them in a Christian context.

The next step in our ongoing reflection went this way: Even if these symbols were not purely cultural but also religious, there is still no problem with using them, because Hinduism as such is not evil. The Spirit of God is present and active in it. Of course we avoid symbols that look superstitious. We also keep away from mythico-historical symbols like Krishna or the Nataraja (the dancing shiva) that belong to the Hindu tradition. Using them can lead to a misunderstanding with a living religion like Hinduism and can give scandal to the Christians and can end up as syncretism. But there should be no problem in using general cultural symbols, linguistic and iconic, even integrating some of the general religious meaning which they may have acquired in Hinduism.

The response to the Hindus' objection took another turn, at least in the minds of some of us. This has not been spelled out too openly yet in the community. I am not only Indian, ethnically and culturally. My heritage is also Hindu. My ancestors were Hindu. If God has spoken to my ancestors, and if the Spirit of God has been present and active in their religion, there is no reason why I should not reclaim my Hindu spiritual heritage and integrate it with my Christian heritage. I am heir to two traditions, namely Hinduism and Christianity. I feel proud of both of them and seek to integrate them in myself. This is how I become Hindu-Christian. What are the implications of this?

A Hindu-Christian

Hinduism and Christianity are also social institutions. I do not claim nor seek to belong to two social institutions. I am a Christian. I do not have a hybrid identity, one that is both Hindu and Christian in a social, communitarian sense. Am I an interfaith person? Am I doing interfaith theology or practicing interfaith spirituality? I do not think so. I think that paradigms like "exclusivism-inclusivism-pluralism" and "interfaith theology" are abstract. They look at religions from the outside, as it were, disconnected from them as lived by the members of other religions. There is no interfaith or universal theology. Theologians of different religions can engage in dialogue and move toward a consensus on the defense and promotion of common human and spiritual values. Today they need to do so.[6] I would then speak of dialogical theology and, even more especially, of dialogical spirituality. Being a Hindu-Christian is therefore an ongoing intrapersonal dialogue between two poles of a complex identity within me as a person. It has more to do with attitudes and ideas than with ritual practices, which have a social focus. Such an intrapersonal dialogue seems a crucial preparation for an interpersonal dialogue with Hindus at a sociocultural, even political level.

When I am actually in dialogue with a Hindu in the contemporary sociopolitical context in India, what seems crucial is the recognition of and respect for identities based on difference. Dialogue consists not in looking for a common denominator but in developing an overlapping consensus that can animate not only a search for God or the Absolute, but also common sociopolitical action. Religions are not something that we humans create and can play with. For a Hindu or a Christian, his or her religion is a particular way through which God has reached out to him or her. It is a personal relationship. One does not compare personal relationships. They have a certain uniqueness about them. One does not seek to merge them in some way. Rather, one celebrates their difference. Learning from the other, being challenged and transformed by the other, integrating the other is different from a sort of syncretism that easily mixes up symbolic worlds. I would be justified in reinterpreting a symbol like *Om* in a Christian context, because it is a sound symbol, more basic than even language. But I cannot borrow Hindu mythological symbols like Rama, Krishna, or Shiva. These are the Hindus' symbols, and Hindus will use them to define, defend, and celebrate their identity. I relate to God through Christ, and my Hindu friend relates to God through Krishna or Shiva. We may compare these ways. We may even consider them homologous. We may say something about the transcendent God whom both of us are trying to reach in and through our respective real-symbols. We do not experience God in some nonsymbolic way in Godself. Christ and Krishna are not mere symbols for us that can be easily exchanged. They are mediations. They represent a history. We cannot mix them to produce an interfaith Krishna-Christ.

In my research and writing I have explored these questions at two levels. I develop my reflections on pluralism in *Making Harmony: Living in a Pluralist World*. In that book I write of perspectives like a pluralist social democracy, multiculturalism, and pluralism of truths and religions. I discuss the more theological issues in *Walking Together: The Practice of Inter-religious Dialogue* and *Beyond Dialogue: Pilgrims to the Absolute*.[7]

An Indian Hindu-Christian

At the cultural level I am an Indian. I constantly interact with Euro-American culture, and this encounter also shapes my thinking. But I try to keep my Indianness in the way I approach persons and things. I do not think I will ever be at home totally in Euro-America, even though Indian culture is

Indo-European. Because of my ongoing dialogue with Hinduism and Indian culture, my philosophical and theological approaches have changed over the years. I have moved away from a Greek, rational, conceptual, logical, object-focused, dichotomous (either-or) theory of knowledge and toward an Indian (Asian), symbolic, interpretative, narrative, subject-focused, inclusive (both-and) theory. In this I have also been helped by contemporary European philosophy, with its turn to the "subject" and to language. I have also abandoned a physics-based Aristotelian metaphysics in favor of a person-based, nondual, relational ontology. To "be" is to "inter-be." I speak no longer of things and causes, but instead of persons and transforming, empowering relationships. With these new approaches I find it easier not only to be in dialogue with the Asian Hindu, Buddhist, and Taoist others, but also to be an Indian (Asian) Christian. In my latest book, *The Asian Jesus*, I attempt to understand the meaningfulness of Jesus using Asian cultural and religious symbols like the Way, the Sage, the Avatar, the Satyagrahi, the Guru, the Dancer, and so on, just as the Europeans saw him as shepherd and king.[8] Of course, this is not making my work as a theologian easy, since the official Church is all too often tied to neoscholastic epistemology and metaphysics.[9]

Starting with a positive approach to other religions as participants in God's plan of salvation, I have a new theology of history focused on the Kingdom of God, which embraces also other religions, with the Church becoming the symbol and servant of the Kingdom, called and challenged to collaborate with the other religions and righteous causes in realizing it in history. The real enemies of the Kingdom are Satan, as the personal principle of evil, and Mammon, as the power of money—not the other religions, who also struggle against these evil principles. I also have a new spiritual vision that searches for a personal and cosmic integration. In this vision God, the Spirit, the Word, and Jesus are experienced and seen in new ways. I believe that it is at the level of divine-human relationship (spirituality) and my reflection on it (theology) that I am a Hindu-Christian. Here too I am basically Christian but am in interaction with Hindu theological and spiritual perspectives. For me this is a personal identity. But I can and do see it as a group identity in some of the ashrams.

Being Hindu-Christian, what do I seek to integrate from Hinduism into my Christianity? I think that this integration involves four basic things.

First, through the principle of *advaita*, or nonduality, I seek to overcome the dichotomous perspective that separates the divine and creation, the humans and the cosmos, the body and the spirit. God and the world, the spirit and the body, in us humans do not represent two distinct realities. They are not one reality either. They are two-in-one, or nondual. At the same time, one (the body, the world) is dependent on the other (the spirit, God). But the dependence is not separation. The *advaita* takes a middle position between monism/pantheism and dualism.

Second, this integration includes a pluralistic perspective that is respectful of difference and is inclusive, as opposed to the either-or logic of the Greek-scholastic tradition. In the official circles of the Church, theological or religious pluralism is too often considered suspect or is decried as relativism or subjectivism. The possibility of different perceptions of the real is not admitted. Reality is one. But perceptions of reality are conditioned by culture and history and personal perspectives and limitations. There is no reason to assert that the truth of one's own perception negates the truth of others. What I perceive to be true is not asserted as the whole truth. Other perceptions and affirmations of the same reality remain possible.

Third, integration also involves an emphasis on experience and praxis, with their complexities—an emphasis that challenges the conceptual, abstract, and objective metaphysics. Our experience is complex. In order to understand it, we abstract various concepts from it. These concepts are limited, abstract, and partial perceptions. But our tendency is to universalize and objectify these concepts, while reality and its experience are forgotten. I have discovered recently that the Spanish philosopher Xavier Zubiri has protested against such abstraction and has proposed a more concrete theory of knowledge.[10]

Finally, I seek an integration of the energy field that mediates between the spirit and the body, that also links the humans to the universe. This is the field of Yoga in the Indian, Hindu, but also Buddhist traditions. The Greeks dichotomized the spirit from the body. Contemporary science tends to forget the spirit and focuses on the body, because only that which is of the body can be touched, measured, and scientifically experimented upon. But the energy field is neither spiritual nor corporal, yet it can be experienced. One can get in touch with it through breathing and concentration. It can both heal and cause harm in the psychosomatic area of human experience. Alternative healing techniques make use of this, as do Hindu and Buddhist meditation techniques to promote inner healing and wholeness. Taken seriously and systematically, these four orientations would transform Indian Christian theology and spirituality.[11]

Some Questions

In this process of integration, how do I judge what is true and proper? Does this process promote a relativistic attitude of "anything goes," provided one feels helped? In the area of religion and spirituality, the real criterion is not orthodoxy but orthopraxis (see Matt. 25:31–45). In our approach to God, even our true affirmations, though being true, cannot claim to be the absolute truth—the last word. All that we can really say about God is *neti, neti*—not this, not that. It is not that we cannot say anything about God, but rather that all our affirmations are limited and have to be transcended. Therefore, what we have to look for is not that all our affirmations about God say the same thing in different words, but that they do not contradict each other. It is convergence that leads to greater truth.[12] In the process of divine-human encounter, both God and the humans are free. They need not repeat themselves. This is a source of a legitimate pluralism that is not relativistic. It is relativism if I create my truth. It is not relativism if I accept that my own experience, perception, and expression of the Ultimate are conditioned by the limitations of my situation. Even God's self-revelation is conditioned by my historical circumstances and the limitations of my language.

So what we need is mutually challenging dialogue and not the pretention of any one group to possess the absolute truth. Only the Ultimate Reality is normative, not anyone's perception of it. Even Jesus's manifestation of God was kenotic and eschatological. The One we all pursue can only be the convergent horizon of the many paths that people follow inspired by the Spirit. In the process of cosmic harmony, my Hindu-Christian integration is only one step. Asian bishops and theologians speak of the people of different religions as "co-pilgrims" toward the reign of God. The Office of Theological Concerns of the Federation of Asian Bishops' Conferences, in its document on *Asian Christian Perspectives on Harmony*, recognizes "in all sisters and brothers, of whatever faith-conviction and culture, fellow way-farers to God's Reign."[13] On the occasion of the Church's Asian synod, the Indian bishops said: "God's dialogue with Asian peoples through their religious experiences is a great mystery. We as Church enter into this mystery by dialogue through sharing and listening to the Spirit in others. Dialogue, then, becomes an experience of God's Kingdom."[14] The bishops from the Philippines said, "In the social context of the great majority of Asian peoples, even more use should be made of the model of the Church as servant, a co-pilgrim in the journey to the Kingdom of God where fullness of life is given as a gift."[15]

A certain perspective on inculturation pretends to already have the One, which only needs to be translated into many cultures. The One that we seek to reach, however, is not in the past but in the transcendent future. God's Word has challenged us to respond to it. What we should do is to let this Word and the other words of God challenge other people to respond in their own way and look for a convergence. Inculturation is not a move from the center to the periphery. Rather it is a movement from the periphery to the transcendent center that will be manifest only on the last day, when God will be "all in all" (1 Cor. 15:28, NRSV).[16]

Models

Is being a Hindu-Christian simply idiosyncratic? My contacts in Asia and Europe show that it is not unusual. I do not think that everyone is called to live it. It may be intended only for a few. But I think that these contacts are liminal people who are called to, or given the grace to attempt, such a way of life that may lead to a deeper dialogue between religions. Today interreligious dialogue seems to be in crisis because of the many religious fundamentalist conflicts going on all around the world. In such a situation liminal people witness to challenges and possibilities. I would even say that they follow a special call of God.

Just as I am Hindu-Christian, some Hindus, like Keshub Chandra Sen (1858–84) and Mahatma Gandhi (1869–1948) have been Christian-Hindus, deeply influenced by the example and teachings of Christ. Gandhi said that if a Christian is someone who follows the teachings of Christ, then he was a Christian. But he clearly distanced himself from the Christian community in a social sense. There are similar Christian-Hindus even today who consider Jesus their guru. To respect religions and their believers is also to respect their sociocultural-political identities and differences.

I think that Hindu-Christians like me and Christian-Hindus like Gandhi are liminal people. We are people on the borders, staying within our boundaries and yet open to the others, reaching out to them. We can be models and animators of dialogue in a special way. But any effort to stand with one leg on each side of the border will be a disaster. Brahmabandab Upadyaya (1861–1907) called himself a Hindu-Christian—Hindu socially and Christian religiously. But his later efforts to become religiously Hindu-Christian ended up as a disaster because he transgressed the social borders.

It is from this point of view that Swami Abhishiktananda offers us a model. He was a French Benedictine monk, Henri Le Saux, who came to India with the aim of witnessing to Christian mysticism in order to attract Hindu mystics. During his visit to the Hindu ashrams, he was attracted by a Hindu advaitic mystic, Ramana Maharishi. So in a first book, *Saccidananda*, Swami Abhishiktananda tried to show how the mysticism of Ramana will find fulfillment in the Christian mysticism of the Trinity. But then he himself began following the advaitic path. After many years of intense practice he claimed to have achieved the advaitic (nondual) experience. To the end of his life he was faithful to the Eucharist and to the praying of the psalms. He tried all through his life to intellectually integrate his Christian and his Hindu experience, but without success. His logical (French) rationality and his neoscholastic theological background may have been a problem. His only disciple, Marc, was jointly initiated as a sannyasi by him and a Hindu, Swami Chidananda of Rishikesh. In the last few years of his life he often said that he had gone beyond the symbols and rituals of any religion. Accordingly, his experience of the *advaita* or nonduality was beyond all religions, all names and forms (*namarupa*).

Maybe he was making a mistake by seeing his experience as Hindu and seeking to integrate it with his Christian *namarupa*. At the same time he felt free to experience the Absolute through the Christian *namarupa*—the

Eucharist. I do not think that at any time he was practicing any Hindu ritual (*namarupa*). He must have realized in his last days that he was experiencing God—the Absolute—in two different ways, and he did not have to integrate them rationally, but just enjoy the diversity. In fact there is nothing Hindu about the advaitic experience, socially, ritually, and institutionally, though it cannot be totally detached from the Hindu spiritual tradition either. Swami Abhishiktananda's intellectual tension seems to have disappeared after he experienced a heart attack some months before his death. My own understanding is that he accepted both experiences as valid without trying to artificially integrate them.[17] Not everyone can lay claim to such mystical experiences. But they might be able to follow a similar path of a tensive integration.

God alone is absolute. I think that God is calling us not to make absolute the paths that God has indicated to us to seek the experience of God. Ultimately it is in the world and in humans that we encounter God. This is the lesson of Jesus and of the *advaita*. In this quest cultural and religious boundaries are not sacrosanct.

Postscript

At present my assertions about being a Hindu-Christian can seem naive. What happens to such an identity when Hindu mobs are attacking and killing Christians, burning their houses and churches, and driving them into the forest? It is true that only a small minority of Hindus indulge in violent action. But apart from another small minority of "secular" Hindus that support the Christians, the majority seem to be silent, perhaps embarrassed, spectators. It is obvious that it is not Hinduism and Christianity that are in conflict, but rather communal groups that are using religion as a political weapon. A Hindu-Christian will be attacked by fundamentalists from both sides. But the dialogue between Hindus and Christians has to continue, and the few Hindu-Christians have an important role in its continuance. They are not playing politics but following God's call. They can be witnesses for peace and communion. The Hindu-Christian conflicts in India are not merely religious. They also have economic, political, and social causes. When the overall economic level in the country rises and there is social progress, the communal clashes in the name of religion will probably subside. But God, religions, and spirituality will and should continue to bring people together.

Notes

1. For some of the papers read at the seminar, see Dennis Gira and Jacques Scheuer, eds., *Vivre de plusieurs religions. Promesse ou illusion?* (Paris: L'Atelier, 2000). My own contribution was "La double appartenance religieuse," 44–53. For an English version of my paper, see Michael Amaladoss, "Double Religious Belonging and Liminality," *Vidyajyoti*

Journal of Theological Reflection 66 (2002): 21–34; also Amaladoss, "Double Religious Belonging and Liminality," *East Asian Pastoral Review* 39 (2002): 297–312.

2. Michael Amaladoss, "Qui suis-je? un catholique-hindou," *Christus* 86 (1975): 159–71.

3. See John Paul II, *Redemptoris missio*, secs. 28–29, www.vatican.va/edocs/ENG 0219/_INDEX.HTM.

4. See Michael Amaladoss, "Other Scriptures and the Christian," *Vidyajyoti Journal of Theological Reflection* 49 (1985): 6–15; Amaladoss, "Other Religions and the Salvific Mystery of Christ," *Vidyajyoti Journal of Theological Reflection* 70 (2006): 8–23.

5. The first stage of evolution of the Absolute is said to be sound. *Om*, when sung, is a symbol of this sound manifestation. Some Christians reinterpret it as a noniconic Trinitarian symbol of God: *Om*, or *A* plus *U* plus *M*.

6. I have explored this in *Life in Freedom: Liberation Theologies in Asia* (Maryknoll, NY: Orbis, 1997). It presents liberation theologies from various Asian religions.

7. See Michael Amaladoss, *Making Harmony: Living in a Pluralist World* (Chennai, India: Institute of Dialogue with Cultures and Religions, 2003); Amaladoss, *Walking Together: The Practice of Inter-religious Dialogue* (Anand, India: Gujarat Sahitya Prakash, 1992); and Amaladoss, *Beyond Dialogue: Pilgrims to the Absolute* (Bangalore, India: Asian Trading Corporation, 2008).

8. Michael Amaladoss, *The Asian Jesus* (Maryknoll, NY: Orbis, 2006).

9. For a discussion on the challenges of inculturation see my book *Beyond Inculturation: Can the Many Be One?* (Delhi: Indian Society for Promoting Christian Knowledge, 1998).

10. See Kevin F. Burke, *The Ground beneath the Cross: Theology of Ignacio Ellacuria* (Washington, DC: Georgetown University Press, 2000).

11. I have made a small attempt at developing such a spirituality in *The Dancing Cosmos: A Way to Harmony* (Anand, India: Gujarat Sahitya Prakash, 2003).

12. See Michael Amaladoss, "Which Is the True Religion? Searching for Criteria," in *Co-worker for Your Joy: Festschrift in Honour of George Gispert-Sauch, S.J.*, ed. S. Painadath and Leonard Fernando (Delhi, India: Vidyajyoti/Indian Society for Promoting Christian Knowledge, 2006), 45–60.

13. Josef Eilers, ed., *For All the Peoples of Asia*, vol. 2 (Manila, Philippines: Claretian Press, 1997), 285.

14. Bishops of India, quoted in Peter C. Phan, ed., *The Asian Synod: Texts and Commentaries* (Maryknoll, NY: Orbis, 2002), 20–21.

15. Bishops of the Philippines, quoted in Phan, *Asian Synod*, 39.

16. *New Revised Standard Version* (London: Harper Collins Publishers, 1993).

17. Henri Le Saux, *La montée au fond du coeur* (Paris: OEIL, 1986).

CHAPTER 8

Arriving at a Christocentric Universe

Ilia Delio

Faith Seeks Understanding

From where does a theological vision begin? What gives rise to theological insight and, in particular, to my insight? I ask these questions not only as a matter of self-reflection but out of wondrous surprise that I am a theologian because, truth be told, I never intended to be one. Unlike the typical theology student finely tuned in philosophy, theology, and classical languages, I was a hard-core student of science who took only the necessary courses in theology and philosophy to meet the requirements of my undergraduate institution. As a science major I believed that science held the key to unlocking the secrets of life. I pursued graduate work in neuroscience, initially studying the pharmacological basis of schizophrenia and eventually publishing studies on neuronal dysfunction in a model of amyotrophic lateral sclerosis. I reveled in the discoveries of science and clearly remember the day I made my own original discovery in the lab, as if I had become privy to divine secrets hidden in the human brain. There was a lure to science that captivated me, the intricate mechanisms of the nervous system, the precise functioning of multiple neural circuits. How could this come to be, this incredible mass of neurons entangled with one another in the most elaborate loops and patterns, firing electrical potentials into a self-reflective "I"?

I discovered God in the lab. It was not a God I sought; rather it was a God who emerged from the mysterious and incredible formation of organs, neurons, and chemicals that compose the human brain (and person) beyond what any human could invent and much more than the blind chance of evolution. From the single living cell to the mammalian neocortex, human life, indeed all life, is a magnificent work of art. It was scientific research that impelled me to seek the artist. Thus, I made a dramatic leap from the world of scientific research into the silence of a Discalced Carmelite cloister, believing that the God hidden in the details of the cell would be found more fully in the details of the soul. Although my time with the Carmelites lasted only a few years, I gained a foundation in prayer and mystical theology that has endured. Upon leaving the Carmelites, I entered the order of Franciscans, where I was offered the opportunity to study theology. I began my studies in theology at Fordham University with an eclectic background in science and philosophy. However, I appreciated the Jesuit approach to study and found the intellectual rigor of theological study exhilarating. Studying theology was a coming-home experience for me, and each new discovery in the rich Christian tradition was an expansion of being.

If I had to identify one central element that has governed my journey from science to theology, it is the meaning of Christ. What does it mean to say "God Incarnate" in a world of science and creativity? In this new world of technology and globalization, who is Christ for us today? The relentless pursuit of these questions lured me to the Franciscan intellectual tradition, especially through the influence of Ewert Cousins and his insightful interpretation of Bonaventure's Christ mysticism. What drew me to Bonaventure was the depth and breadth of his thought and its integral unity in Christ the center. Cousins was also a Teilhardian scholar who introduced me to the works of this Jesuit scientist, Pierre Teilhard de Chardin, whose rich evolutionary Christology complemented the dynamism of Bonaventure's thought. These two great spiritual masters, Bonaventure and Teilhard de Chardin, have become the two principal lenses through which I view the meaning of Christ and Christian life. Here I explore the influence of Bonaventure and Teilhard on my thought, first by examining Bonaventure's contribution to the meaning of Christ in the cosmos, and then by showing how Teilhard's insights have shaped the horizon of my theology in this new millennium.

Bonaventure's Theology: Trinity and Christ

Bonaventure's theology is like a rich tapestry woven with a single thread. It has been said of Bonaventure that his thought is such an integral synthesis that one sees either the whole or nothing. Although Bonaventure's theology is dense, I found a pattern to his thought reflected in his consistent themes of the Trinity, Jesus Christ, creation, the human person, and metaphysics. The medievalist Etienne Gilson wrote that Bonaventure "appeared bent towards the creation of a new synthesis wherein he should find a place for all the philosophical and religious values of which he had a living experience."[1]

What drew me to Bonaventure was his own search for meaning and purpose, not simply as an academician but as a Friar Minor. He was constantly asking the questions, Where did we come from? What are we doing here? Where are we going? Just as I was trying to find my way to God through the path of religious life, so too was Bonaventure. He had been elected minister general of the Franciscan order at a time when the order was deeply divided over issues of poverty, learning, and Franciscan identity. Although he was a beloved student of Alexander of Hales, from whom he inherited the wealth of patristic and medieval theology, his original insights came from his own internal struggles to lead the order in the footprints of Francis of Assisi. Bonaventure became a theological and spiritual guide for me as he held together the mystery of God and the centrality of Jesus Christ. He wrote from a depth of insight, deeply immersed in the mystery of God. Through Bonaventure I began to find theological language to describe my own experience of God.

Bonaventure's theology rests on two fundamental beliefs: the Trinity and Christ. His originality lies in the way he explored the relationship between the Trinity and Christ. Although his commentary on the first book of the *Sentences* provides his fundamental understanding of the Trinity, it shows up in all of his spiritual writings as well, especially because it is key to understanding the meaning of Christ. There is such an inextricable relationship between these two mysteries that one cannot be thought of without the other: The Trinity is incomprehensible without Christ, and Christ is incomprehensible without the Trinity. Christology begins with the Trinity because it begins with the divine Word of the Father breathed forth by the Spirit. I believe Bonaventure wrestled with this inextricable relationship between the Trinity and Christ throughout his lifetime. Even in his final lectures at the University of Paris, he tried to explain how Christ is the metaphysical center. For Bonaventure, Christ is not only the center of theology but the center of philosophy. I am sure the students did not fully understand his lectures (neither do we, since we have at least two different versions of the lectures), and Bonaventure died before completing his lecture series, leaving his theological metaphysics unfinished and incomplete.

To understand Bonaventure's trinitarian theology, one must reach into the patristic tradition, especially Cappadocian theology and Pseudo-Dionysius. Following Dionysius, Bonaventure considers the primary name of God as goodness and explores the Dionysian good as self-diffusive.[2] Bonaventure also looks to the canon Richard of St. Victor, who claimed that the highest good is love, which is personal and communicative.[3] The perfect communication of love, according to Richard, must involve no fewer than three persons. Bonaventure brings together the impersonal Dionysian good with Richard's mysticism of ecstatic love to produce his own trinitarian metaphysics of love. His Cappadocian influence appears in the way he understood the trinitarian persons as related by the origin of the good.

Bonaventure uses the concepts of self-diffusive goodness and personal love to distinguish the persons of the Trinity as a communion of persons-in-love based on three closely related terms: primacy, fecundity, and communicability. The Father is without origin and is primal and self-diffusive, the fountain fullness (*fontalis plenitudo*) of goodness.[4] The Son is that person eternally generated by the Father's self-diffusive goodness (*per modum naturae*); that is, the Father naturally and necessarily communicates goodness out of the fountain fullness of goodness. As the total personal expression of the Father, the Son is Word; and as ultimate likeness to the Father, the Son is Image.[5] The Son-Word is generated by the Father and with the Father breathes forth the Spirit, who is that eternal bond of love between the Father and the Son. The Spirit proceeds from the Father and the Son in an act of full freedom (*per modum voluntatis*) and from a clear and determinate loving volition between them.[6]

It is in the relationship between the Father and Son that I began to understand Bonaventure's doctrine of creation, for just as the Word is the inner self-expression of God, the created order is the external expression of the inner Word. The dialectical nature of the Father marked by unbegottenness and self-diffusive goodness is the dynamism of love that expresses itself in the Word, or second divine person. The Word is the openness of the Father to the other in all its forms. God's being is self-expressive, and this self-expressiveness is the Word of God, the Son of the Father, in whom the Father speaks himself. God's being as self-communicative love gives expression to its entire fruitfulness in the generation of the Son, so that in the Son, the Father speaks one Word immanent to himself, in which is expressed the possibility of creation. Because there is a Word in God, creation can exist as an external word. Because there is an Absolute Otherness, there can be a relative otherness.[7] The possibility of God's creative activity rests in his triune being, which is to say God could not communicate being to the finite if God were not supremely communicative in Godself. God's creative activity is the pure, essential dynamism of love. To say that God is love means that love is not a quality of God's being; rather love *is* God's being, and this love is the ground of creation. It is precisely on this note that I see a confluence of thought between Bonaventure and Pierre Teilhard de Chardin, whom I discuss below. Bonaventure provides a trinitarian ground to Teilhard's Christocentric universe by centering creation in the divine Word or the self-expression of divine love.

The whole process of creation is really one divine act of love between the Father and Son unified in the love of the Spirit. That is, there is really only one act of creation: the love of the Father for the Son in the Spirit or, we might say, one self-expressive Word of divine love. In a sense this is why the fullness of unity is already within creation, because it is the one Word of God expressed in time and space. The primal relationship between the Father and the Son, from which creation originates, is consonant with Bonaventure's theology of creation *ex amore*. Bonaventure indicates that what characterizes the inner life of God takes place in creation as well, although the exemplary character of the Word does not make the act of creation necessary (though one could argue in favor of a necessary creation). As a good medieval theologian, he maintains that the act of creation is a free act of God, but it is the free overflow of his necessary, inner-divine fruitfulness.

Bonaventure's preference for the title of the second divine person as "Word" is rooted in the Gospel of John. "In the beginning was the Word," John writes, and "all things were made through him, and without him was not anything made that was made" (John 1:1–3, RSV).[8] He indicates that to speak of the Word as center of creation is also to speak of God as gift, since the Word spoken cannot be adequately expressed unless it is also received. Thus the total self-expression of God is the total gift of God. Bonaventure points to the poverty of creation as its capacity to receive the divine within it. Creation is both divine self-expressiveness and self-gift. All that God is, is given in the act of creation. Creation is more than sheer divine will. It expresses the self-communicative love of God and is an outward expression of love insofar as it is an external embodiment of the divine Word.

I think the only way to know creation as gift, and myself within the gift, is to rediscover the Incarnation. For too long the meaning of Jesus Christ has been cut off from the natural world: an otherworldly Savior in an otherworldly heaven. As I ponder the deep relationship between creation and Incarnation in Bonaventure's writings, I see more and more that they are not two different mysteries but rather two aspects of the same mystery. I think it is time to rediscover the Incarnation not as an event over and above creation but as the inner meaning of creation itself, to realize that God's incarnation is God's creation.

The Primacy of Christ

According to Bonaventure, Incarnation is primarily a mystery of relation, which means that whenever the word "Incarnation" appears, "relationship" must appear as well. Incarnation is another way of talking about the plurality of God, God's involved otherness. God's creative action places the created human nature of Jesus in a unique relation to the divine. Bonaventure says that the humanity of Jesus is the fullest and most perfect external Word that gives expression to the inner, eternal Word as its perfect content. There is only one Word of God, and creation expresses that Word in a finite way. Jesus humanizes the Word, in that Jesus is the divine Word Incarnate come to explicit consciousness.

In reading Bonaventure's texts I see the intrinsic relationship between Incarnation and creation, which he formulated in the doctrine of cosmic Christology. Like other theologians of his time, Bonaventure perceives the possible relations between the story of Jesus and the larger picture of the world. The Incarnation is not an isolated event but is integral to the possibility of creation itself; one is inconceivable without the other. Because of the relationship between creation and Incarnation, Bonaventure holds that a world without Christ is an incomplete world; that is, the *whole world* is structured Christologically. Today we might take offense with such an idea in light of religious pluralism, but what Bonaventure had in mind was the unity of creation. Christ is not accidental to creation; he is not an intrusion into the universe but rather the inner ground of creation and its goal. John Duns Scotus claimed that the Incarnation is due not to sin but to the free, absolute love of God. Since perfect love cannot will anything less than the perfection of love, Christ would have come as the highest glory in creation even if there were no sin and thus no need for redemption.[9]

Bonaventure sees the Incarnation as the highest work of creation, while carefully refraining from any necessity on the part of God. He views sin as embedded in historical reality. However, he does not confine the mystery of Christ to sin.[10] He indicates that the Incarnation cannot be willed by God simply because of sin.[11] The Incarnation is not a sort of afterthought on the part of God. Rather, from eternity God included the possibility of a fall of the human race and therefore structured the human person with a view to redemption. As the consummation of the created order, the Incarnation is willed for its own sake, not for a lesser good such as sin. It is not sin that is the cause of the Incarnation, but simply the excess love and mercy of God.[12] By reversing the order of sin and Incarnation, Bonaventure shifts the order of salvation and creation. Salvation does not flow from a sinful creation; rather salvation is the reason for creation. I find this insight helpful, as it gives salvation a positive role in the economy of creation. Creation is not a backdrop to an otherworldly salvation; rather salvation is the basis of new creation. The overcoming of separateness and the movement toward greater unity of life *is* new creation. What God intends first in every act of creation is wholeness and unity in love, and this unity is Christ. Christ is not ordered to us, Bonaventure says, but we to Christ.[13] Thus, Christ does not save me from the world; rather Christ is my reason for being in the world. All of creation has a source and goal in the fruitful, creative love of God. Thus all of creation has the potential to become, through God's grace, something of what has already come to be in the mystery of Christ.

Teilhard de Chardin and Christogenesis

Bonaventure's rich dynamic Christology locates Christ as center of the cosmos and hence as center of life in the universe. By "center" I understand him to mean *theological* center and hence the mediating unity between God and created reality. In this respect Bonaventure's Christocentrism makes sense only in light of a triune God who is fecund, personal, relational, and communicative love. The overflowing love of God expressed in time and history as Word is vivified through the life-giving breath of the Spirit. The Trinity of personal relations of love is personalized in the universe through the Spirit-filled Christ. I believe that this relationship between Trinity and Incarnation is what Teilhard de Chardin tried to articulate in his time. It is unfortunate that the Teilhard de Chardin did not know Bonaventure's writings, for his thought is deeply compatible to the Franciscan's. Whereas Bonaventure wrote within a patristic-medieval worldview, Teilhard was deeply immersed in the science of evolution. It is Teilhard's evolutionary Christology that has helped me further Bonaventure's dynamic Christocentrism, or at least identify the limits of it in light of evolution.

Teilhard understands the science of evolution as the explanation for the physical world and views Christian life within the context of evolution. Evolution, he claims, is ultimately a progression toward consciousness; the material world contains within it a dynamism toward spirit. His thought can be described in terms of three stages of evolution. In the first stage, evolution follows an axis of increasing organization. In view of the ancient history of the universe (13.7 billion years), Teilhard says there came a point where inert elements came together and formed the first living cell. All of the separate elements were there before the cell appeared, but the union of these elements caused a new entity to emerge that was more than the sum of its parts. To form this complex union, the cell continued to reach beyond itself to find new elements and incorporate them into its unity. To describe this process Teilhard uses the word "groping," an unscientific yet practical word to make sense of how things grow; for example, a cell gropes or feels beyond itself for what it can use. By using the word "groping," Teilhard acknowledges a dependence on chance but also affirms that life has direction, orientation, and preference. Groping is "directed chance."[14] The second stage he describes is one of convergent evolution, whereby the groping of matter is directed toward a point of maximum human organization and consciousness—the human person. Following Julian Huxley, Teilhard says, "The consciousness of each of us is evolution looking at itself and reflecting upon itself."[15] I find this idea to be a powerful insight. Not only do I emerge from the process of evolution, but I give meaning to the process from which I come. I give meaning to this process not only as my history but as my future; that is, my decisions or my groping determines the direction of my ongoing evolution. At a third level of evolution, Teilhard constructed a spirituality based on his understanding of Christ, a spirituality of union with God through the world. This forms his Christocentric vision of reality, which I explore further on.

I find Bonaventure and Teilhard different but complementary. Bonaventure was a trained theologian, and his dynamic Christocentrism arose out of his personalist trinitarian theology. Teilhard was a scientist, and his Christocentrism emerged out of his relation to God in a dynamic evolutionary universe. It is in view of evolution toward greater complexity and consciousness that Teilhard reflected on the meaning of Christ and Christian life. Although I find his theology of creation weak, insofar as he does not provide a clear theological ground of creation, he goes through detailed explanations to show how the physical processes of cosmogenesis and biogenesis are from the point of Christian faith Christogenesis, or a "coming-to-be" of Christ.[16] What attracts me to Teilhard is what attracts me to Bonaventure: a deep union between God and creation through Christ the center. Both thinkers see Christ as the personal center of unity in the cosmos. Teilhard recognizes a unifying influence in the whole evolutionary process, a "centrating" factor that continues to hold the entire process together and move it forward toward greater complexity and unity. His faith in Christ leads him to posit Christ, the future fullness of the whole evolutionary process, as the "centrating principle," the "pleroma," and "Omega point" where the individual and collective adventure of humanity finds its end and fulfillment.[17] Through his penetrating view of the universe, Teilhard sees Christ present in the entire cosmos, from the least particle of matter to the convergent human community. The whole cosmos is incarnational. The heart of God is the heart of the world. Christ invests himself organically with all of creation, immersing himself in things, in the heart of matter, and thus unifying the world.[18] By taking on human form Christ has given the world its definitive form: He has been consecrated for a cosmic function. As I reflect on these profound insights into Christ, I wonder what Christian life would be like if it took seriously the genesis of Christ in evolution.

The Evolutive Christ

It became increasingly evident to Teilhard that if Christ is to remain at the center of our faith in an evolutionary universe, then this cosmic Christ must begin to offer himself for our adoration as the "evolutive" Christ—Christ the Evolver.[19] What Teilhard sought to show was that the cosmic function of Christ was not only moral but physical. The Pauline phrase *Omnia in ipso constant* (In him all things consist) (Col. 1:17) dominated Teilhard's thought. "I find it quite impossible," he wrote in 1924, "to read St. Paul without being dazzled by the vision under his words of the universal and cosmic dominance of the incarnate word."[20] In the words of his biographer Henri de Lubac, "The *one who is in evolution* is himself the *cause and center* of evolution and its goal" (his emphasis). This evolutive Christ is not distinct from Jesus but indeed is "Jesus, the center towards whom all moves."[21] It was the humanity of Jesus Christ—his life, death, and resurrection—that spoke to Teilhard of the evolutive Christ. Because Christ is both the center and goal of an evolutionary creation, Teilhard views Christ as a dynamic impulse within humanity (and nonhumanity) that is moving toward greater complexity and unity, from biogenesis to noogenesis, from simple biological structures to the emergence of mind. Christ is not a static idea, Teilhard indicates, but a living person, the personal center of the universe. He posits a dynamic view of God and the world in the process of becoming something more than what it is because the universe is grounded in the personal center of Christ.

Teilhard's notion of a Christic universe cannot be understood apart from his own spirituality, especially his devotion to the Sacred Heart. The Sacred

Heart was the heart of matter. It was here that God's love for the whole of the universe was revealed. Teilhard's response to the Sacred Heart was one of love, action, and will, since this Heart is the very wellspring of life. He wrote: "The Sacred Heart has been good to me in giving me the single desire to be united with him in the totality of my life."[22] The personal love of God poured out in the crucified Christ seized the heart of Teilhard. He saw this love as passionate love, a fire of divine love that energized and propelled this evolutionary universe toward the fullness of Christ-Omega. God, who is love, is dynamically in love with creation in the most intense and personal way. Only by coming to know this God within my own life can I know this God at the heart of the universe.

The stories of the Gospels form the basic knowledge of Jesus upon which the Church has constructed the doctrine of Jesus Christ as two natures united in one person—without confusion, change, separation, or division. Though Teilhard knew the formula of Chalcedon, he did not refrain from suggesting a third nature of Christ based on spiritual insight and contemplation of the world. By positing a third nature, he indicates that the whole physical world has a spiritual nature that attains its full consciousness and openness to God in the person of Jesus Christ. Thus, Christ is related organically, not juridically, to the whole cosmos. It is a nature contingent on the humanity of Christ, but not subordinate to his divinity. Since the cosmic Christ is the resurrected Christ, this third nature or cosmic nature emerges from the union of divine and human natures, so that it is neither one nor the other but the union of both, although it exists on the side of creation. This third nature means that Christ the Redeemer *is* Christ the Evolver. That is, the Savior is the evolver; cosmogenesis is Christogenesis.[23] The evolutionary progression toward greater complexity in creation is Christ in the making. Every bacterium, blood cell, plant, tree, animal, prehuman, or human, whether black or white, Hindu or Muslim or Jew, atheist or deist—every single aspect of creation is integral to Christogenesis. In short Christ is the fullness of nature's evolving unity in God.

The Organic Nature of Christ

Teilhard insists that it is time to return to a form of Christology that is more organic and takes account of physics. We need a Christ "who is no longer master of the world solely because he has been *proclaimed to* be such," he writes, "but because he animates the whole range of things from top to bottom" (his emphasis). The greatness of Teilhard's insight lies in the organic nature of Christ as the heart of change in the universe. "If we are to remain faithful to the gospel," he says, "we have to adjust its spiritual code to the new shape of the universe. It has ceased to be the formal garden from which we are temporarily banished by a whim of the Creator. It has become the great work in the process of completion which we have to save by saving ourselves."[24]

I think Teilhard highlights a problem that persists in our own time. The person of Jesus Christ is constrained by dogma, unrelated to the universe as we now know it, and unable to grow. Teilhard complains that we are stuck with an outmoded Christology formulated many centuries ago. He writes: "Our Christology is still expressed in exactly the same terms as those which three centuries ago could satisfy men whose outlook on the cosmos it is now physically impossible for us to accept. . . . What we now have to do without delay is to modify the position occupied by the central core of Christianity—and this precisely in order that it may not lose its illuminative value."[25] I think what impelled Teilhard to keep writing, despite alienation by his Jesuit superiors and Vatican authorities, was his inner conviction that Christ is the meaning of evolution. Spirituality drove Teilhard's theological quest. I do not think he sought to unite science and religion as an academic exercise. Rather, he was a scientist whose love of the material world was his love of God—a wellspring of love deep in the heart of Teilhard sprang up in the heart of creation. As Teilhard says, religion and science are two sides of the same conjugate. The Spirit that animates the human heart animates the universe.

Teilhard struggled to bring to birth the essential relationship between Christ and a cosmos in evolution. What he recognized is that every act of evolving nature is the self-expression of God, because the very act of nature's transcendence is the energy of divine love. God unfolds in the details of nature. Thus, evolution is not only *of* God but *is* God Incarnate. In his *Phenomenon of Man* Teilhard describes evolution as an unfolding process of withinness and withoutness. The within is the mental aspect, and the without is the physical aspect of the same stuff. I understand this insight as the unfolding simultaneity of God and world: God is the withinness of the withoutness of matter in evolution.[26] This is an incredible insight, one that challenges classical theology and the causal God-world relationship. However, Teilhard does not clearly explain the theological ground of Christogenesis, and thus many theologians dismiss his ideas. Here is where I believe Bonaventure can be helpful, because he grounds the universe in a metaphysics of trinitarian love.

When we say God is love, we are also confessing that God is eternal newness, because love is dynamic, and dynamic love is never the same from moment to moment. If love did remain the same, would it really be true love? Somehow we have accepted the incompatible if not outright contradiction between divine immutability and the dynamism of God's love. I think what Teilhard points to is that divine love is evolutionary—it grows and complexifies—and this growth and complexification expressed in trinitarian relations is the basis of unity. God is not the source of love, that is, love is not a relation to God. Rather, love is the source of God, that is, God emerges out of re-lationships of love. Where there is love, there is God. Even in human rela-tions, the perfection of love comes at the end of a long, loving relationship, not at the beginning. In this respect it is reasonable for Teilhard to say that God is up ahead, the future in which we have our being and in which we are coming to be. Creation is the self-expressiveness of divine love—the Word of God—to use Bonaventure's language. God is the dynamism of love—divine energy—at the heart of matter itself. This God-filled matter in evolution is Christ in evolution. This is certainly a radical departure from understanding Jesus Christ as an absolute, single, salvific figure. Jesus is the Christ, the one in whom and through whom divine love comes to explicit consciousness. If the humanity of Jesus emerges out of an evolutionary process, then I see in the humanity of Jesus the explosive love of God, the pattern of what the Christ is about in creation. Jesus ushers in a new level of consciousness and a new future, because Jesus returns love for love unconditionally.

When Teilhard speaks of Christ the Redeemer as Christ the Evolver, I think what he is saying is that divine love is at the heart of creation, and the movement toward the fullness of love incarnate is the Christ who is com-ing to be. This is the very process of creation itself in evolution. As I read Teilhard and reflect on the meaning of Christ-Omega, it seems to me that Incarnation does not take place in evolution. Christ does not intervene in creation and then become its goal. Rather, the whole evolutionary process is incarnational. The process of evolution *is* Christogenesis, or God coming to be at the heart of matter. Hence, a Christocentric universe is not only pos-sible; for Teilhard it is the only universe that makes sense if God is love.

The Emergent Christ

I sympathize with Teilhard when he laments that Christianity does not yet embrace the world in its spiritual power or consider evolution as a means of sanctification. Christians are not conscious of their divine responsibilities within evolution, he claims. Rather, they see Christian life as a series of ob-servances and obligations, not the realization of the soul's immense power. I could not agree more. If Christians are to remain faithful to the Gospel, Teilhard writes, "we have to adjust its spiritual code to the new shape of the universe. . . . [The Christian] is now discovering that he [or she] cannot be saved except through the universe and as a continuation of the universe."[27]

Teilhard's Christogenic universe invites us to broaden our understanding of Christ—not to abandon what we profess or proclaim in word and prac-tice, but rather to allow our beliefs to open us up to a world of evolution of which we are vital members. The openness of the cosmos to what is new, its capacity to leap forward, is what leads to the emergence of intelligent be-ings. Every human person, Teilhard claims, is the cosmos itself come to self-consciousness. Each of us represents a higher shoot of the upper thrust of this evolution. Each human person is a microcosm, a total of the universe, in the same way that the human nature assumed by Christ effects the ultimate totalization of the universe in the mysteries of creation, Incarnation, and redemption. Christ is the whole, and the whole is to be gathered by and into each of us. My task, therefore, is to build my soul by gathering the widely scattered elements of my experience into a unified whole.

As I ponder Teilhard's Christogenic universe, I do not think it is simply poetic. Rather, he explores the profound task of being human and created. Bonaventure believed that the salvation of the cosmos is mediated through the salvation of humanity. So too did Teilhard. In other words, the healing and wholeness of the human person is the healing and wholeness of the cosmos itself. Salvation may come through Jesus, but salvation is more than Jesus. To be saved is to be made whole, following the pattern of Jesus's life. What took place in the life of Jesus must take place in my life as well if I am to help creation move toward its transformation in God. I am called to give myself to Jesus Christ and to his values, which means not losing the world but finding the world in its deepest relation to God.[28] By living from an inner depth of knowledge and love, I fill the Christ-form with the elements of my personal life, embodying something of the Word in myself in a distinct and personal way. I, like every person of every race, religion, or creed, have a unique role in the genesis of Christ. I know that without my participation, Christ ceases to exist insofar as Christ ceases to exist in me. Thus I can say my active participation in the Christ mystery is necessary for the fullness of Christ.

At the level of the human person, evolution is a cocreative process, according to Teilhard. My participation in the mystery of Christ, like that of every person, lies at the basis of a healing world aimed toward the fullness of God. Thus I must continuously strive to live from a deeper center within, one that sees God shining through the world. I must seek a new depth of vision. I need to be awakened to a new consciousness of Christ's universal presence by discovering my own self-realization in "being-with-Christ." When Christ becomes the unifying and integrating center of my own being, then I will encounter Christ as being in the world. Therefore, it does matter what I do and how I go about this world, for only through my actions can I encounter God. I am created to help transform this universe in Christ by seeing Christ in the universe and loving Christ in the heart of the universe.

The Future of Christianity

As I continue to reflect on the writings of Bonaventure and Teilhard, I see paths to a Christocentric universe not yet traveled. Evolution offers a new understanding of creation that liberates theology from a static past. However, I must continuously strive for an openness of heart and a poverty of being to embrace this new paradigm. Teilhard trusted his insights sufficiently to transcend ecclesial opposition to his work, although he suffered from loneliness and isolation.

Courage is needed to think anew in our time. And although Bonaventure's Christology bears its medieval context, his cosmic Christology reaches to the farthest ends of the universe. Jesus is the most explicit statement of what God is like in the universe, the form of divine wisdom that structures reality. Jesus is the Christ, but Christ is more than Jesus. Bonaventure's logic of the Word, read in the context of religious pluralism, suggests that Christ is the personal center of the universe, what holds it together and unifies it. This too is what Teilhard arrived at—not just something but Someone holds together the plurality of elements in a personalizing center, and this is Christ. Hence Christ does not belong to Christians; rather Christians and all people, whatever their religion or no religion, belong to Christ. Bonaventure and Teilhard profess a "deep Incarnation," which means God is intimately involved with creation, from the spiritual consciousness of primal matter to the human person as image of God. Every created thing—quark, leaf, tree, worm, spider, frog, flower, stream, lake, ocean, mountain, person—shares in the Christ mystery, because everything proclaims the Word of Love and is Love Incarnate. In one of his sermons Bonaventure says: "As a human being, Christ has something in common with all creatures. With the stone he shares existence; with plants he shares life; with animals he shares sensation; and with the angels he shares intelligence. Therefore, all things are said to be transformed in Christ since—in his human nature—he embraces something of every creature in himself when he is transfigured."[29]

Although I have spent the past twelve years focusing on Bonaventure's cosmic Christology and its implications for today, I am deeply invested in Teilhard and the historical process of evolution itself. Evolution not only tells me who I am, where I come from, and where I stand in the creation story; evolution also tells me about God. What Teilhard tried to articulate is that evolution is not only the universe coming to be but is God who is coming to be. The God of evolution is in evolution. Teilhard indicates that we need a radical paradigm shift in our fundamental understanding of God. We cannot understand Christogenesis unless we dare to think about theogenesis. I believe our greatest religious challenge in the twenty-first century will be to revolutionize our understanding of God, that is, to grapple with the historicity of God. In *Christianity and Evolution*, Teilhard writes:

> In the case of a world which is by nature evolutive . . . God is not conceivable (either structurally or dynamically) except in so far as he coincides with (as a sort of "formal" cause) but without being lost in, the centre of convergence of cosmogenesis. . . . Ever since Aristotle there have been almost continual attempts to construct models of God on the lines of an outside Prime Mover,

acting *a retro*. Since the emergence in our consciousness of the "sense of evolution" it has become physically impossible for us to conceive or worship anything but an organic Prime-Mover God, *ab ante*. Only a God who is functionally and totally "Omega" can satisfy us. Who will at last give evolution *its own* God?[30]

This coming-to-be of God in evolution is Christ. Teilhard encourages us to participate in the process of Christogenesis—to risk, get involved, aim toward union with others—for the entire creation is waiting to give birth to God's promise, the fullness of love (Rom. 8:19–20). I must strive daily to recognize my life in evolution and to nurture the growth of my life as an evolutionary process of development and change. I believe this is what it means to be a Christian: not to live in some glorious past or with an ahistorical consciousness, but to be engaged in an evolutionary universe. Teilhard sees a particular role for Christianity in the universe, to divinize creation by energizing it through love. Christianity is an emergent religion. It is intended to become something more than what it already is because it is an organic religion, symbolized by the elements of bread and wine. The body of Christ grows by the flourishing of personalities. In *Phenomenon of Man* Teilhard writes: "Union differentiates. . . . The more 'other' they become in conjunction, the more they find themselves as 'self.'"[31] To believe in the organic body of Christ, therefore, is to believe in all humans (and creation itself) as bearers of the Word—to listen, contemplate, comprehend the language of universal love in each particular created being who utters the Word Incarnate. In view of religious pluralism I believe a diversity of religions contribute to the fullness of Christ.

Christology after Darwin

Teilhard recognizes that the God of evolution must be a God who is "less Alpha than Omega." He says that the traditional view of God and creation, the metaphysics of the eternally present, is inadequate for the reality of evolution. Evolution, he claims, requires a divine source located not in the past or "up above" in a timeless present but rather "up ahead" in the future.[32] He describes the God of the future, the God up ahead, as the ultimate force of attraction for the universe, drawing the universe toward intensification of complexity and new creation. If the Trinity is eternally self-expressive, dynamic, overflowing love, then the future is marked by the horizon of love. To think of the triune God residing in the future is to think of God as the horizon of love. By "future" I do not mean the unknown or the not-yet. Rather "future" pertains to the *plenum* of divine energy or love, all the possibilities that can be realized through grace. As John Haught writes, God "is the transcendent future horizon that draws an entire universe, and not just human history, toward an unfathomable fulfillment yet to be realized."[33] Evolutionary creation is progress toward ultimate love in relationship to a God of ever-deepening love. If the power of divine love—which is the dynamic, emergent, triune God—is source and goal of all that is, then I believe the fidelity of divine love in an evolutionary universe is the transcendent source of change. God is ever-newness in love, eternally becoming other in love unto love.

As I read and reflect on Teilhard, my thoughts on God are challenged. I am becoming more conscious of Christ as the evolving pleroma of creation, in which I participate through my own individual creation. Teilhard calls us to be attentive to our human lives as Christ bearers in creation. Through my life and that of each person, Christ is born when we act to creatively unite. Through our lives Christ becomes the Omega of a new "centration" in the universe, that is, a new unity brought about by a deeper consciousness of divine presence; hence our lives become essential for the emerging new creation. If we truly allow our lives to be grasped by God and thus give ourselves completely to love, to be Christ in evolution, then the cross becomes our symbol of victory, because the sufferings of the present are integral to our participation in the unfolding pleroma. With Teilhard I see creation, Incarnation, and redemption not as three separate mysteries but as a single mystery of creative union. Evolution is redemptive because it is the emergence of new being, the act of making a new future. Sin is our refusal to participate in the ongoing creation of the world. It is a rejection of the future, of the call to become new being and to participate in what is coming to be.

We are called to be cocreators of this evolutionary universe, which means helping to realize this new creation, although it will always be unfinished. Every end marks a new beginning, and every arrival a new departure.[34] My ability to be a new creation in Christ will always depend on my fidelity to love as an act of the future. Christ is the future into which each of us is drawn, and the fullness of what we are coming to be.

Conclusion

My thoughts here have traveled over several centuries, from Bonaventure to Teilhard, but the course of this journey has unfolded the Christ mystery. There is a continuum of ideas between Bonaventure, Teilhard, and myself. Just as each thinker contributed insight to this God-enfleshed creation in evolution, so must I do the same if I am to be faithful to my vocation. I believe a Christocentric universe is not only possible but is the only credible one for a universe in evolution, if we believe God is dynamic, relational, and personal love. To know the meaning of Christ in an evolutionary universe requires a depth of vision and a contemplative heart. All religions are part of this unfolding Christ mystery, but Christianity plays a particular role. Christianity is a religion of unity because the love of God heals and makes whole; hence Christianity is a religion of evolution. However, Christianity will not be able to adequately engage evolution in the twenty-first century unless it undergoes a radical shift in consciousness. With Teilhard I believe it is time to rethink Christ the Redeemer as Christ the Evolver. In this regard I conclude with several points for reflection:

- To see God in evolution is to see Christ, the Word Incarnate, as an emergent person in evolution.
- Love is the reason for the Incarnation, and redemption is new being. We need to redirect our attention from an upward, heavenly Christ to a forward movement of Christ in evolution marked by novelty and future.
- We need to see ourselves and all of nature, at this moment, in the process of evolution.
- We need to see the virtues of love, mercy, compassion, forgiveness, and reconciliation, exemplified in Jesus, as the pattern that forms the emergence of Christ in each person.
- We need to participate in the emergence of Christ as a movement toward complexified bonds of relationship with one another and with the natural world.
- We need to participate in the emergence of Christ as new forms of religious consciousness and hence to realize that world religions are integral to the meaning of Christ.
- We need to live Christian life with an evolutionary spirit, letting go and flowing into new structures when the right time comes.
- We need to know the forward movement of evolutionary emergence as one of costly discipleship and therefore be willing to sacrifice structures of isolation for the sake of greater union.
- Finally, we need to trust in the future, because God is ever-newness in love.

With the world undergoing a human and ecological crisis of planetary proportions, we can no longer function with a Christology deaf to the cries of the Earth and mute to the voice of God in other religions. Either Christ is the meaning of the whole, or Christ has no meaning at all. Teilhard points out that evolution is a resilient process because the power of love triumphs over sin and death. Love is the freedom within creation to become something new. My reflections lead me to see, through Bonaventure and Teilhard, a new "big bang" in our midst, the beginning of a new universe, a new religious consciousness, a new way of Christian life. Christ is the dynamic life of God at the heart of the universe. In a universe billions of years old, with billions of years stretching before us, we are not at the end of Christianity. Rather, we have only just begun.

Notes

1. Etienne Gilson, *The Philosophy of St. Bonaventure*, trans. Dom Illtyd Trethowan (New York: Sheed and Ward, 1938), 480.

2. The comparison between John Damascene and the Pseudo-Dionysius on the names of God as being and good are discussed by Bonaventure in his classic *Itinerarium Mentis in Deum*. See Bonaventure, *Itinerarium Mentis in Deum*, 5.2 (V, 307).

3. Richard of St. Victor, *De trinitate*, 3.14–19 (PL 196, 924–27).

4. Bonaventure, I *Sentence*, d. 27, p. 1, a. un., q. 2, ad 3 (I, 470). The idea that the Father is innascible and fecund underlies the dialectical style of Bonaventure's thought. It also provides the basis of Bonaventure's metaphysics as a *coincidentia oppositorum*. The Father's innascibility and fecundity are mutually complementary opposites that cannot be formally reduced to one or the other; the Father is generative precisely because he is unbegotten. See Zachary Hayes, introduction to *Disputed Questions on the Mystery of the Trinity*, vol. 3 of *Works of Saint Bonaventure*, ed. George Marcil (New York: The Franciscan Institute, 1979), 42n51.

5. Bonaventure, I *Sentence*, d. 5, a. 1, q. 2, resp. (I, 115); I *Sentence*, d. 2, a. u., q. 4, fund 2 (I, 56); Hayes, introduction, 34n10. Bonaventure uses the terms *per modum naturae* and *per modum voluntatis* to designate the two trinitarian emanations. The terms are inspired by Aristotle's principle that there exist only two perfect modes of production: namely, natural and free.

6. Bonaventure, I *Sentence*, d. 6, a.u., q. 2, resp. (I, 128), "*Processus per modum voluntatis concomitante natura.*" Kevin P. Keane writes: "It is noteworthy that Bonaventure's reason for attributing creation to the divine will is quite different from Thomas's. Where Thomas is in the main concerned to protect the divine perfection and radically free will, Bonaventure is at pains to elucidate how only through the will can an act be truly personal—both free and expressive of the outward dynamism of goodness, an act spontaneous yet substantial." Keane, "Why Creation? Bonaventure and Thomas Aquinas on God as Creative Good," *Downside Review* 93 (1975): 15.

7. Bonaventure shows a decided preference for the term "Word." This title signifies a complex network of relations that the Son bears to the Father, to creation, to humanity, and to revelation, all of which are grounded in the fact that he who is, first of all and by reason of an act of the divine nature, the Son of the Father's love is simultaneously the Word of the Father's self-expression as loving, fruitful source of all that is. See Zachary Hayes, "Incarnation and Creation in the Theology of St. Bonaventure," in *Studies Honoring Ignatius Brady, Friar Minor*, ed. Romano Stephen Almagno and Conrad Harkins (New York: The Franciscan Institute, 1976), 314; Hayes, "The Meaning of *Convenientia* in the Metaphysics of St. Bonaventure," *Franciscan Studies* 34 (1974): 90.

8. *The New Oxford Annotated Bible with the Apocrypha, Revised Standard Version*, eds. Herbert G. May and Bruce M. Metzger (New York: Oxford University Press, 1977).

9. Mary Beth Ingham, "John Duns Scotus: An Integrated Vision," in *The History of Franciscan Theology*, ed. Kenan B. Osborne (New York: Franciscan Institute Publications, 1994), 219–22. For Scotus the mutuality between God and human persons realized in the Incarnation is grounded in the very nature of God as love. The divine initiative of love has as its primary object that creature who is capable of receiving the fullest measure of God's goodness and glory and who, in turn, could respond in the fullest measure. See Giovanni Iammarrone, "The Timeliness and Limitations of the Christology of John Duns Scotus for the Development of a Contemporary Theology of Christ," trans. Ignatius McCormick, *Greyfriars Review* 7, no. 2 (1993): 233n13.

10. Alexander Gerken, *Théologie du Verbe: la relation entre l'incarnation et la creation selon S. Bonaventure*, trans. Jacqueline Gréal (Paris: Éditions Franciscaines, 1970), 311.

11. Zachary Hayes, "Christ, Word of God and Exemplar of Humanity," *The Cord* 46, no. 1 (1996): 6.

12. Bonaventure, III *Sentence*, d. 1, a. 2, q. 2, ad 5 (III, 26–27).

13. Bonaventure, III *Sentence*, d. 32, q. 5, ad 3 (III, 706). The sentence is found within a larger passage that reads: *"Non enim Christus ad nos finaliter ordinatur, sed nos finaliter ordinamur ad ipsum"* (Christ is not ordained to us, but we are ordained to Christ).

14. Pierre Teilhard de Chardin, *Phenomenon of Man*, trans. Bernard Wall (New York: Harper & Row, 1959), 110.

15. Ibid., 221.

16. Ibid., 297–98.

17. Ibid., 262–63.

18. Ibid., 293–94; Timothy Jamison, "The Personalized Universe of Teilhard de Chardin," in *There Shall Be One Christ*, ed. Michael Meilach (New York: The Franciscan Institute, 1968), 26.

19. Pierre Teilhard de Chardin, *Christianity and Evolution*, trans. René Hague (New York: Harcourt Brace Jovanovich, 1971), 181; Henri de Lubac, *Teilhard de Chardin: The Man and His Meaning*, trans. René Hague (New York: Hawthorn Books, 1965), 37.

20. Pierre Teilhard de Chardin, "My Universe," trans. René Hague, in *Process Reality*, ed. Ewert Cousins (New York: Newman Press, 1971), 251.

21. De Lubac, *Teilhard de Chardin*, 37.

22. Pierre Teilhard de Chardin to Berthe Teilhard de Chardin, 9 February 1916, quoted in Teilhard de Chardin, *The Heart of the Matter*, trans. René Hague (New York: Harcourt Brace Jovanich, 1979), 188.

23. Teilhard de Chardin, *Christianity and Evolution*, 181.

24. Ibid., 89, 91–92.

25. Ibid., 77.

26. Teilhard de Chardin, *Phenomenon of Man*, 53–66.

27. Teilhard de Chardin, *Christianity and Evolution*, 91–92.

28. Hayes, "Christ, Word of God," 12.

29. Bonaventure, *Sermo* I, Dom. II in Quad. (IX, 215–19), cited in Hayes, "Christ, Word of God," 13.

30. Teilhard de Chardin, *Christianity and Evolution*, 239–40.

31. Teilhard de Chardin, *Phenomenon of Man*, 262.

32. John F. Haught, *Deeper Than Darwin: The Prospect for Religion in an Age of Evolution* (Cambridge, MA: Westview Press, 2003), 164.

33. Ibid., 174.

34. This idea builds on the notion of *epektasis* rooted in the Letter to the Philippians (3:13: "to reach out after") and found in the doctrine of Gregory of Nyssa, who described the movement of the soul toward God as a perpetual ascent, a movement toward the immovable. Whereas Gregory posited an eternal becoming based on the uncreated essence of God, I suggest here an eternal becoming based on the eternal future of God.

CHAPTER 9

Le Petit Philosophe

Patrick A. Heelan

My family tells me—usually with good-humored teasing—that when I was baptized, my godfather, a lawyer and a philosopher of sorts, looked bemusedly at me in the cradle and said, *"Le petit philosophe!"* Given who the *philosophes* were, it could have been an ironic lawyerly comment on the promises just made on my behalf; but in deference to the prophetic genre, this is where my story begins.

I grew up in a pretty seaside town, Dalkey, on the south side of the River Liffey in Ireland. Dalkey was once the home of George Bernard Shaw and is today the home of U2's Bono. My secondary school was Belvedere College, run by the Jesuit fathers on the north side of the River Liffey. The long commute to and from school gave me personal time, I suppose, to begin the task of growing into a philosopher. My father was a senior civil servant, an economist, who was fluent in French and German, aloof, and given to three hobbies: rose gardening, musical composition, and, after retiring, the translation of theological works from German or French into English—even some short works of Karl Rahner.

At Belvedere College I had good math teachers. I liked math because it was clear, logical, elegant, and unassailable. I liked its formal beauty. It was something one could do—or puzzle over—on the train to and from school. Mathematical physics came to me uncritically as the true and authentic model of knowledge of God's world. My attitude toward the world was that it was abstract, full of beautiful forms to contemplate and to play with. This attitude was only to be confirmed by much of my formal scientific, philosophical, and theological education in the Jesuit order. The real world, however, encroached on my life gradually and inexorably.

What follows is the story of several intellectual and spiritual conversions as I came to experience my life as a Jesuit priest and scholar. It is less the story of a career to be established, and more a story always under editorial revision and reconstruction, continuously discontinuous, as it were, yet with persistent threads leading toward unity that is both outwardly catholic toward a unified world and inwardly Catholic toward a unified spiritual life. From these beginnings I have come to be aware of myself affirmatively in a new way—choosing philosophy as a way of life in a dynamic technological Christocentric world that has eventually delivered the peace, rest, and courage promised in the Gospel.[1]

University College, Dublin, and the Dublin Institute for Advanced Studies (1944–48)

I joined the Jesuits in 1942, going directly from high school at the age of sixteen. I knew I was joining a society that respected science and mathematics, and I looked forward to a possible Jesuit career in the sciences. Spiritually I was no more than a cultural Irish Catholic who felt comfortable with the way of life of the Jesuits I knew. An eventual career in the physical sciences seemed to be confirmed by my early university studies at University College, Dublin, from which I received my BA (1947) and MA (1948) with first-class honors in mathematics and mathematical physics.

The years of my mathematics studies in Ireland coincided with the chaotic postwar years in Europe, during which the Dublin Institute for Advanced Studies offered hospitality to many émigré European scientists. I was privileged to attend courses and seminars given by very eminent theoretical physicists at the institute's School of Theoretical Physics. Among them were Erwin Schrödinger, one of the twin founders of the quantum theory with Werner Heisenberg; and John Synge, who, in addition to being a nephew of the famous Irish playwright John Millington Synge, was a very accomplished theoretical cosmologist. Cosmology is a unified physical theory, developed by Albert Einstein and a Belgian priest-cosmologist, Georges Lemaître, that explains gravitation as a warping of space-time geometry by energy stored in locally distributed force fields and physical masses, such as galaxies, stars, and planets. As a physical theory in the grand Galilean tradition, relativistic cosmology is clear, logical, and elegantly unassailable by mathematical intuition. These descriptors especially fitted Schrödinger's personal style as a teacher; he had an elegance that he expected others to cultivate. This elegance set the tone for his students, among whom I was happy to be counted.

From Schrödinger and Synge I came to understand that the general theory of relativity did not support a relativism of truth in the context of human discourse. On the contrary, the general theory of relativity was founded on the discovery of constancy, invariance, and symmetry and on the intuition of necessary mathematical truth that some scientists thought befitted the rational design of him whom Einstein called the Old One and whom Lemaître called God.

Theoretical cosmology forces one to imagine curved three- and four-dimensional spaces that are finite in size yet have no boundaries. This notion grabbed me and awoke in me a profound interest in the many ways the human imagination and human consciousness represent nature through the work of concepts, theories, and practices that shape the natural sciences, psychology, philosophy, and eventually the spiritual life.

In 1948, my final year at University College, Dublin, I won a prestigious national traveling fellowship to study for a doctorate abroad. My Jesuit superior told me that the director of the Vatican Observatory—then an Irish Jesuit, Daniel O'Connell—wanted me to prepare for and eventually take charge of the Jesuit seismological network at the Vatican Observatory. At that time this network was the only global seismological network in the world. I was sent, therefore, to the Institute for Geophysics at Saint Louis University in the United States. My assigned research project was to find a means of distinguishing between natural earthquakes and artificial seismic disturbances of (presumably) human origin. My work was to discern whether a major artificial underground explosion had a characteristic seismological signature different from that of a natural earthquake. I did not know at that time that the main purpose of the research was also connected with the monitoring of underground nuclear testing, which up to that time had not been successfully addressed.

As a theoretical physicist of the Schrödinger/Einstein variety, I converted the practical problem into a mathematical one and looked for solutions of the elastic wave equations that seemed to define the problem. I found a mathematical solution that seemed in principle to fit the case and defended my PhD dissertation in 1952, from which I was able to publish in 1954 a series of papers in the journal *Geophysics*. These papers were translated soon after into Russian and later into English. When the Russian translations were published, they were claimed to be the work of the Leningrad Acoustical Institute in St. Petersburg; but the equations had the same typographical errors that were present in my original paper, indicating that the Russian work was just a copy.

Conversion 1: Insight into "Spiritual Wisdom" and the Role of Discernment in Ignatian Prayer (1951)

The first breach in my orientation toward mathematics as my preferred instrument of human reason occurred while I was participating in the Ignatian Spiritual Exercises with other young Jesuits in the summer of 1951 at Prairie du Chien, Wisconsin. The retreat master was the Jesuit father Charles Hertzog. I began for the first time to have insight into the role of spiritual discernment in Ignatian prayer. I had made many retreats before this, but somehow I had acquired no more than a notional familiarity with the meaning of spiritual discernment. Ignatian discernment is to argumentative reason as wisdom is to mathematics. I take wisdom to be the spiritual practice of personal authenticity. It is the habit of assessing, particularly during a time of peace and recollection, the transcendent authenticity of one's interior state—the thoughts, feelings, desires, decisions, and practices that are in play—against the background of living personal memory built by faith in and love for the crucified and risen Son of Man, who was the Jesus of the gospels. At that time I must have needed such a gift, and I count it as a conversion event that breached an interior barrier and opened, as it seemed, a floodgate of insights that spoke with a new voice of reason—the voice of wisdom. I was not yet curious, however, about the cultural origins of the unconscious self, memory, and the educational environment it needed to express itself in such a way. My major insight was recognizing that pure (nonempirical) logical and mathematical reason was no more than an instrument of a higher spiritual or transcendent reason called "wisdom."[2]

I returned to Ireland in 1952. I put my science studies aside for eight years while I went through the Jesuit seminary courses of philosophy and theology preparatory to my ordination to the priesthood in Dublin in 1958. This was followed by a spiritual and pastoral year (1959–60) spent in Germany at Münster (Westphalia). In the intervening time seismology had become for the Pentagon an elaborate instrument for national defense and international peacekeeping. As a consequence the Vatican Observatory closed its global seismological network and released me for other career opportunities.

This news came to me during my theological studies in Dublin. My Jesuit superior informed me that a group of lay students at University College, Dublin, were actively promoting the need for a course in the philosophy of science, while the lay students claimed that the philosophy program, being largely for seminarians, neglected their interests. Would I be interested in eventually joining the philosophy faculty there? I replied that I would need a PhD in philosophy to teach the philosophy of science in a university setting, as well as an opportunity to refresh my scientific studies after an eight-year interval away from science. John Charles McQuaid, archbishop of Dublin, joined the discussion and advised against pursuing a higher degree, recommending instead the reading of a "good philosophy book." He did not specify what book he had in mind, but a good book was soon to find me.

Conversion 2: Lonergan's Transcendental Method of Insight (1957)

The book in question was Bernard Lonergan's Insight: A Study of Human Understanding, newly published in 1957; and it came to me while I was studying theology at the Jesuit theological institute in Milltown Park, Dublin.[3] It was this "good book" that opened for me the field of philosophy as relevant to both theology and science. Lonergan was a Canadian Jesuit professor of theology at the Gregorian University in Rome. I was later to meet him in the United States. My interest was hooked from the start, perhaps because it began with a study of mathematical insights. I found it very illuminating with respect to transcendental cognitive method, that is, the steps or processes by which insights emerge, insights from which we make meanings, test theories, and employ these theories in practical life—ultimately to grow day by day, personally and socially, toward the fullness of human life. These processes endorse the role of sensory and affective experience as foundational starting points of the greater insights from which flow conceptual, theoretical, practical, and religious cognition. This method was what was lacking in my education up to that time. I found that I had to look for the experiential foundations—those of mathematics in order to understand physics, of logic to understand philosophy, and of the interiority of human consciousness to understand theology.

The book *Insight* then introduced me to the methodical study of how we make and judge the disciplinary meanings that we use to illuminate our world of human experience, such as the natural scientific meanings that illuminate the laboratory, the social-scientific meanings that illuminate situated human conduct, and the hermeneutical sciences that illuminate texts, pictures, traces of the past, and religious practices. I make meanings from my experience through flashes of insight (founded in memory, language, mimicry, community practices, analogy, metaphor, and more). Methodologically, this meaning-making involves four steps: (1) insights lead to making concepts and categories; (2) concepts and categories lead to making theories; (3) theory making leads to testing theories; and finally (4) theory testing leads to making judgments about situated, theory-laden facts and leads to authentic decision making about how to act. According to Lonergan, these four steps are methodologically universal and transcendental and constitute the hermeneutical circle of my being in the world—my living in the world—authentically.

The emphasis on human experience opened avenues of curiosity that I had not traveled down before—curiosity about the role of subjectivity in the constitution of objectivity, about the role of the human body, about the response of the embodied world, of space and time. But fundamentally my curiosity was about the contribution of my embodied subjectivity to the making and testing of the meanings I make. Involved in these processes are brain functions and neurological activity; the use of tools and technologies, such as writing, drawing, music making, sports; the use of technologies of the arts and sciences to make present to me the shared world of everyday life and of the specialized disciplines and natural sciences. My questions were neither epistemological nor metaphysical questions. They were fundamental ontological questions about, for instance, what does it mean to see with my two eyes? What is the role of the neurological system in seeing? What is a quantum physical state? I found a pleasurable excitement in laying out the questions that Lonergan addressed in *Insight*.

After finishing the book I lent my copy to a brilliant young Jesuit priest and philosopher, Eamonn Egan, who read it through continuously—all six hundred pages from cover to cover—and it is said that he neither ate nor slept during that time and was found lying exhausted on the floor of his room three days later. Others at Milltown Park also read *Insight*, and their excitement led to the formation of a Lonergan caucus there that has continued to the present day. I thought the archbishop of Dublin was right: I needed a good book . . . and the good book had found me!

Early versions of Lonergan's course notes on method in theology were also being circulated worldwide at that time by his students at the Gregorian University in Rome.[4] I noted the coherence between Ignatian spiritual discernment—the practical art of following the Son of Man called Jesus—and Lonergan's notions of interiority and authenticity. Interiority is the awareness of the authentic processes linking subject and world in consciousness, and authenticity refers to prudential guidance of the cognitive and practical processes toward their ontological fulfillment—aimed at the practice of Christian fellowship—in human life. That summer I had my second conversion to a better understanding of Christian spirituality: that it involves not just thought and contemplation, but also the practical cooperation of authentic interior human life with the desire to follow Jesus Christ. Such an attitude was also in principle positive about the employment of science and technology in modern culture as an expression of the temporality of the personal human journey in life.

This conversion changed the emphasis of my thinking: from the abstract mathematical to the situated practical, from the world as object to the interiority of the inquiring subject's engagement with one's world, and from formal to dialogical language. I began to see these recurring interior processes as the spiritual source of the dynamism of human and cultural development in history, and to see the natural sciences as the expression of the cosmological, earthly, and biological story that gives historical meaning to the cosmos and to creation. None of this is God's direct doing, but his art of teaching creatures to be authentically themselves, learning from suffering and joy, success and failure, to realize the Kingdom of God on earth by their human activity. This became a new focus for my scholarly interest—to unify the sciences, the humanities, and religion in the spirituality of human life.

This new opportunity that I was being offered to study philosophy convinced me all the more that I needed to update my physics, learn more philosophy, and probe into a theology of the cosmos and creation. I had the chance to apply for postdoctoral Fulbright fellowships to study modern physics in the United States. I applied therefore for a two-year fellowship to Princeton University to study high-energy quantum field theory. My application was accepted.

Conversion 3: Role of Consciousness in Quantum Physics: Princeton University (1960–62)

The Princeton physics department at that time was probably the best physics department in the world. I was welcomed by Eugene Wigner, a quantum physicist, physical chemist, and chemical engineer who soon received the

Nobel Prize for his work in quantum physics. Wigner was a Hungarian, Jewish by birth and Lutheran by baptism. His family had a textile-weaving factory in Hungary. He was trained in chemical engineering at the Technische Hochschule in Berlin, Germany, and after emigrating to the United States he became the war manager of the Metallurgical Institute at the University of Chicago, where the first atomic fission was engineered. He had a very keen sense of both the empirical and the technological sides of science. Ironically Wigner occupied Einstein's old office in the original Palmer Lab, where Einstein's famous words *Herr Gott würfelt nicht*, "God does not play dice," were inscribed over the mantelpiece. Under Wigner's tutelage I switched my scientific focus from Schrödinger and Einstein to Wigner and Heisenberg, and from the general theory of relativity to quantum theory.

Einstein, like Schrödinger, loved the classical objective order of geometry, where everything in nature had its determinate time, place, and motion in space-time, guaranteed by mathematical intuition independent from any human engagement with the world. Such a view is often associated with mechanistic, materialist, and naturalistic terms, but Einstein to the contrary was closer to a pantheist than an atheist.

I was reminded then by Wigner that terms such as "space," "time," and "motion" have meanings that represent not material things but the outcomes of humanly scripted ways of engaging with the world experientially, usually by measurement. Measurements involve special laboratory setups, by human design, screened from wild nature. The output of this domesticated instrumental setup is then a number that is filtered by layers of interpretation through bodily, cultural, and linguistic filters to become a measure of a named theoretical quantity—such as mass, momentum, or charge—that is present in the act of measurement but otherwise is quite mysterious. The real number measures, as read from instruments in the laboratory, are symbolic of the real presence of the named physical quantity in the laboratory environment. The named physical quantity is known only by its name and by the coded number that the measuring process gives it.

Faced with the problem of measurement, Wigner changed the basic paradigm of questions that philosophers posed, from questions about truth (the subject's epistemology) or about nature (the object's metaphysics) to questions of ontology (the study of how a real object is present to a real subject within a real context, such as one of actual measurement).[5] Following Martin Heidegger, ontology, or *dasein* (being-in-the-world), involves a special—nonobjective—engagement within the mutual intentional presence of subject and object in the interior domain of human consciousness. Consider two people conversing with one another over the telephone. They are physically connected, but the physical connection is just the experiential medium through which they share, by means of a dialogical conversation, a common domain of meaning. This is the kind of paradigm shift that is central to Lonergan's

Insight and to the hermeneutical phenomenology of Heidegger. It was a shift also anticipated by four Nobel Prize winners in physics: John von Neumann, Erwin Schrödinger, Eugene Wigner, and Werner Heisenberg. For instance, Wigner wrote toward the end of his life: "My chief scientific interest in the last 20 years has been to somehow extend theoretical physics into the realm of consciousness. . . . Consciousness is beautifully complex. It has never been properly described, certainly not by physics or mathematics."[6] I too was soon to follow in this direction.

University of Leuven (1962–64) and Quantum Mechanics and Objectivity (1965)

At the end of my Fulbright fellowship in the fall of 1962, I went directly to the University of Leuven in Belgium to begin doctoral work in the philosophy of science at the Husserl Archives located there. My research topic focused on this question: What is "knowing the quantum world" in the practice of quantum physics? At that time Heisenberg—the twin founder with Schrödinger of quantum physics—was director of the Max-Planck Institute for Astrophysics in Munich, Germany. Since Munich was just a train ride from Leuven, I was able to visit frequently with Heisenberg to discuss the topic of my research. I found him most cordial and open, and our relationship continued after I left Leuven until his death in 1976. Eventually I wrote my dissertation on Heisenberg's philosophy of science, which had much in common with Wigner's despite the fact that their mathematical approaches to physics were quite different. Wigner's "ontology" was associated with the hands-on approach of a physical chemist—involving a subject-object sensory engagement— for which his mathematical model was an infinite-dimensional vector space called a Hilbert space. Heisenberg's approach was more like Einstein's and Schrödinger's, based on the objective intuition of their mathematical theories. My dissertation at Leuven examined Heisenberg's physical philosophy and was published under the title *Quantum Mechanics and Objectivity: A Study of the Physical Philosophy of Werner Heisenberg.*[7] Heisenberg wrote to me, in a personal letter dated November 10, 1970: "I very much enjoyed reading your book. Precisely the connection between a description of the historical development and a very careful philosophical analysis seems to me to be a felicitous foundation for the reader being able to really penetrate into quantum theory and its philosophy."

The thesis of *Quantum Mechanics and Objectivity* sustains Wigner's point that there is in quantum physics the emergence of a distinctively new and explicit nonclassical role for the physical engagement of the observer, with a specific measurement horizon within which the quantum object makes its presence known. Recall that Wigner was a physical chemist by training, though one with a strong theoretical and mathematical background. My use of the term "explicit" above refers to two types of discourse that are clearly different: theoretical discourse (about mathematical models) and empirical discourse (about facts or data). Facts in physics occur only in an appropriately chosen (and constructed) practical horizon, such as a laboratory. By a "horizon" I mean the practical situated context of, say, a measurement event. This is usually a laboratory bench prepared and supervised by an expert scientist for a measurement. In classical physics horizons are assumed to be objective and independent from the surrounding world. The independence from the surrounding world breaks down in quantum physics, where the horizon of space and time, for instance, is not independent from but complementary to the horizon of momentum and energy. They are not independent horizons of a single objective world. In discoursing about what is (in fact), the speaker has first to enact an exclusive choice between two mutually exclusive and complementary measurement horizons. Wigner saw this as evidence that human consciousness plays an essential role in the new physics, because its ontology—its performance as represented within human consciousness—explicitly involves not just theory but also the public laboratory enactment of an exclusive human choice. In short the quantum physics of nature is ontologically an enactment of human culture in the world.

Much of my later work was inspired by Wigner's measurement thesis and the desire to understand it better. I began to read deeply about the biological, neurological, historical, and cultural origins of the four meaning-making functions that—according to Lonergan's analysis—constitute the transcendental (universal and necessary) process of human intentional living that is also called a hermeneutical circle (or better, a hermeneutical spiral) of meaning-making. I asked how these functions come to be structured in the way we find them. How do they operate biologically and physiologically within the contexts of history, science, technology, culture, and religion? I began to think of the individual consciousness of a human being, an embodied being engaged with an embodied world, as a quantum macrosystem—but more about this below.

University College, Dublin (1964), and Return to the United States (1965)

When I returned to Ireland from Leuven in the midsummer of 1964, I found that my appointment had been shifted from the faculty of philosophy to the faculty of theoretical physics, and I was listed to teach the graduate course in general relativistic cosmology. It was some time before I learned that the last-minute change was due to budget considerations caused by internal political maneuvers involved in the restructuring of University College, Dublin. The students, however, thought that the clerical students were being served better than the lay students, and they showed their disapproval by briefly occupying the office of the dean of the philosophy faculty, who was a member of the Catholic clergy.

Despite *Insight*, the good book that was sent my way to clear my path to teach philosophy, *le petit philosophe* returned—for the time being at least—to be *un petit scientifique* hastily boning up on material learned sixteen years earlier from Schrödinger and Synge at the Dublin Institute for Advanced Studies. But prophetic destiny was not to be so easily frustrated.

Conversion 4: Pictorial Geometry of Van Gogh's *Bedroom at Arles*: Fordham University (1965–70)

From 1964 to 1965, while teaching relativistic cosmology at University College, Dublin, I received invitations from the United States to teach courses in the philosophy of science, and my Jesuit superior agreed to my going. I spent the following few years at Fordham University in New York City, where there was a strong, diverse, and lively department. I found my time at Fordham exciting and stimulating.

It was at Fordham that I joined a group of psychologists led by the Jesuit Richard Zegers, studying the geometrical structure of visual perception. Geometry is based on the measurement of length. In physics, surveying, and engineering, standard measurement processes give a locally Euclidean geometry. The eyes, however, measure the surrounding world differently, by a set of binocular angles; these do not in principle give a Euclidean geometry but generate families of non-Euclidean geometries. I began to ask myself, What kind of local geometry does binocular vision create? What does the local environment look like visually when represented as the visual domain of local hand-eye cooperation?

Accepting the postulate of evolutionary biology, I was able to show that the local visual world should tend to be represented by members of a family of Riemannian geometries with a variable range of curvatures to facilitate the particular needs of individual actions performed by the agent in a local neighborhood. The evidence for these claims happens to be present in everyday life. For example, there are well-known so-called perceptual illusions that stem from the difference between visual space and Euclidean space. When one drives a car, the upcoming curve of the road can be misjudged; certain drawings, such as the Müller-Lyer presentation, produce what psychologists call visual illusions; or certain art works, such as Vincent Van Gogh's paintings, appear to be both perceptually realistic and yet not in accordance with mathematical perspective. Such experiences depend, of course, on accepting as a basic premise that deliberate human action, such as looking at an object, is not like forming a mirror image but rather fulfills an intentional purpose. That is, it is open to various human purposes defined not by instrumental measurement, but by a natural focusing on what might be on that occasion something of particular interest to the viewer.

The occasion that sparked my interest in visual geometry was an invitation from Irma B. Jaffe, the chair of the Fine Arts Department at Fordham, to give a university lecture in 1968. I chose to address the role of perspective in painting. My interest in this was piqued by an experience of viewing Van Gogh's painting *Bedroom at Arles* at the Chicago Fine Art Institute. The pictorial space of the pictured bedroom seemed to me to be convincingly real, despite the fact that its representation on the canvas was not fashioned by traditional perspective. The space of the bedroom was given visually to a viewer such as me in an odd way that was not Euclidean in the anticipated traditional way. The orthogonals to the frontal plane (the perpendiculars to the canvas) obeyed classical rules for perspective, but the horizontal lines did not obey the appropriate rules. My mind went back to a seminar given by Schrödinger in 1948 on the geometry of the cosmos, in which he stressed the importance of learning how to intuit imaginatively the geometric forms of curved three- and four-dimensional geometries. In the seminar he made some remarks about the paintings of Van Gogh. I could not recall what he had said, but I remembered that he related the pictorial space of Van Gogh to curved geometry.

My puzzle about the geometry of Van Gogh's pictorial space had two parts. The first part was to relate the visual geometry of Van Gogh's paintings to the family of curved Riemannian geometries that were cosmologically important. The second part was to understand what Van Gogh meant when he spoke of a new and revolutionary art of perspective, for which he designed his own unorthodox version of a perspective frame, and about which he wrote in letters to his brother, Theo, and to his artist friends.

Regarding the first part of the puzzle, I found that the visual stability of the bedroom was anchored by the closed shutters in the painting. When I opened the bedroom shutters in the painting (using computer software), the visual shape and size of the room changed dramatically. The absence of the customary network of horizontal and vertical lines in Van Gogh's specially designed perspective frame had removed the customary depth clues, and the ambiguity that was created had to be resolved by the visual system. The work of unraveling the visual problems I was experiencing occupied several years of my life and was to influence my view profoundly about the ontology of human perception, concept formation, theory making, measurement, quantum physics, and ultimately how God is present in the world.

The second part of the puzzle asks the question, What did Van Gogh mean by his new and revolutionary art of perspective? At the time he painted the *Bedroom at Arles*, he was studying the theory and art of using a perspective frame, a technique used by artists during the high classical Renaissance. The

Vincent Van Gogh, *Bedroom at Arles*, October 1888. Oil on canvas, 72.0 × 90.0 cm. Amsterdam: Van Gogh Museum.

perspective frame he used, however, was not the standard grid of horizontal and vertical wires through which the artist looked. Rather, he used one of his own design, as we learn from a sketch he made for his brother, Theo. The frame was an open rectangular golden section frame with nothing more than two diagonals, a single horizontal horizon line, and a single vertical line through the center. The purpose of using the frame was, as he wrote, to capture the "true" form of things *as he saw them*. The forms he drew as a consequence shaped the spatial geometry of the motif differently. Van Gogh was persuaded that this was the viewer's natural—we would say culturally premodern—way of making visual sense of a room. I began then to think of visual space as having its possible origin not in rigid Euclidean measures, but in natural human measures. By "natural" I mean that they originate in the evolutionary biological development of human animal life rather than being assisted by rigid rulers or similar instruments. It is clear historically that the cultural space of Europe was neither infinite nor Euclidean before the age of modern science, and its model of space was influenced by Aristotle and Dante rather than by Galileo and Newton.

The insight I got from the study of Van Gogh's *Bedroom at Arles* turned out also to explain many curious everyday phenomena that are universally shared. For example, this insight explains why the driver of a car is tempted to visually misjudge the road curve ahead; why airline pilots are taught not to follow their eyes but to follow their instruments exclusively; and why certain so-called visual illusions occur, such as the absence of visual depth in the panorama of distant mountains seen on the horizon, and so on.[8] It seemed to me that the phenomenon of distorted visual space is a hermeneutical (interpretive) problem. It depends on how the body and the eye work together intentionally to make of the encompassing spatial environment a meaning suitable for local action, when assisted only by natural binocular vision and unassisted by modern ways of measurement. By "hermeneutical" I mean that the problem constructs the meaning or significance of the spatiality of the world for the active and engaged viewer. It would then be plausible to assume some variability in the curvature parameters of natural visual space better to accommodate the kind of hand-eye coordination for local action for a local task in a local world.

Ancient authorities support this view. Aristotle examines the finitude of space in his treatise *De caelo*. He writes that beyond the visual heaven (the visual sphere of the fixed stars) there is nothing, not even a void or empty space. "It is evident," he says, "that there is no place or void or time outside of the heaven"—where "the heaven" is the celestial sphere. But although Aristotle's visual imagination stops at the boundary of the heaven, the curiosity of his intellectual imagination does not, for he adds, "Whatever is there [beyond the heaven], it is of such a nature as not to occupy any place, nor does time age it."[9] Such is the notion of "pure intelligences"— *daimonic*, or divine—that has come down to us from Greek philosophy.

State University of New York at Stony Brook (1970–92)

In the fall of 1970 I was invited by John Toll, president of the State University of New York at Stony Brook, to become chair of the philosophy department at the new scientific research campus on Long Island, New York. My special task was to initiate a doctoral program in philosophy that would help bridge the natural sciences and the humanities. Having successfully set the doctoral program in motion, I was invited in 1975 to become vice president for liberal studies and the dean of arts and sciences.

John Marburger became president of the university in 1979. About that time I was asked to manage the identity crisis that was overtaking the humanities departments. Literary theory was challenging the study of the literary classics. The sciences of logic, sociology, and psychology were challenging the good and the beautiful as civilizational values. Old ethical and aesthetic boundaries were being broken by young faculty, and senior scholars were accusing younger scholars of indulging in the shocking, the bizarre, and the outrageous. It seemed to senior faculty that the ambient society was losing its cultural moorings. It was at this time that I began to reflect deeply on the limits of the empirical sciences of physical nature and the need for a new kind of scientific and philosophical discourse about the way we humans, embodied in physical nature, nevertheless transcend our physical nature to make meaning, to communicate meaning, and to act from meaning.

Conversion 5: Space-Perception and the Philosophy of Science (1982)

On the research and intellectual levels I gained further insight about the substantive role of intentionality (making of meaning) in shaping the geometries we use both in science and in everyday life. I had come to understand that perception is a function of the embodied person structured, in large part unconsciously, from habits gained by practical engagement with the world. Physical engagement can be natural—unassisted by instruments—or instrumentally embodied—structured by the use of measuring technologies. Natural human vision is guided by the natural inclination to adapt the role of vision to the best accomplishment of local hand-eye tasks we perform in the world. Such task-oriented visual spaces may present the world as projected only locally in a Euclidean way but projected distantly as an all-surrounding, curved but depthless backdrop that is nevertheless boundless, like the visual heavens above. When engagement with the world is mediated by the use of measuring instruments and other familiar technologies, such as rigid rulers or light rays, the instruments extend the embodied subject, and the perceived object then gets its space-time structure from the rulers and clocks that outline its space-time presence to the instrumented observer.

An object made present to human experience in consciousness, such as a perceived object, is not simply a mirror image of what Lonergan calls the "already out there now real," that is, an object specified independent of viewers and their subjectivity.[10] What is perceived is what is given as present and real to the perceiver, by the world so lived by the perceiver and so received. What is so given and so received is controlled by principles of meaning-making: principles that depend both on the neurologically controlled practices coordinated internally by the memory function of the brain, and on the cultural practices externally coordinated by the local historical, dialogical, and linguistic culture. What drives the human embodied system is the central role of symbolic communication between the symbols and the meanings they carry, insofar as a symbol and its meaning are linked by the transcendental processes of the hermeneutical circle. These processes are exemplified dialogically, socially, historically, and religiously. What characterizes each phase of the hermeneutical circle is something that looks very like what the quantum physicist Niels Bohr called "complementarity": here, complementarity between a symbol and its meaning, both of which function only in the domain of human consciousness. This domain is called "phenomenological" after the works of Edmund Husserl and Maurice Merleau-Ponty; and it is called "hermeneutical" after the works of Heidegger and Hans-Georg Gadamer. Husserl, Merleau-Ponty, Heidegger, and Gadamer are the continental counterparts of Bernard Lonergan and his commentaries on Aquinas.

I have found it very useful to connect Lonergan's lucid English writings with the more difficult European works of Husserl, Merleau-Ponty, Heidegger, and Gadamer. These German and French writers make up the core of the continental school of hermeneutical phenomenology. And for those who want to extend their familiarity with European philosophy and theology, truth is revealed to *dasein* (Heidegger's self-aware subject-living-in-the-world) in the mode of *aletheia* (representation as a response to questioning). Recognizing the symbolic representation is not intentionally (with respect to meaning-making) the same as or compatible with recognizing the meaning symbolized by the representation. Each involves a different subjective, embodied self-awareness as well as a different environmental framing of the perceptual process. Nevertheless, though objectively different, they belong together in human life and consciousness and cannot be separated in human practice. One might say they are complementary to one another, in much the same way as that term, "complementary," is used in quantum physics. These problems are addressed in my book *Space-Perception and the Philosophy of Science.*[11]

One way of approaching this problem of symbol vs. symbolized, or representation vs. meaning, is to consider them as analogues of the structure of quantum physics following Wigner's interpretation of quantum physics. Wigner held that quantum physics is about the perceiver's practical experience of the quantum object in laboratory measurements, as contrasted with the claim of classical physics that physics is about the way things are, independent of anyone's act of measuring. The perception of a quantum object describes for Wigner the richness and ambiguity of the conscious life of persons, embodied in a typically human consciousness.[12] The possibility of learning more about nature in the existential order, or about human nature as being-in-the-world, has of course implications for religion and culture.

Space-Perception and the Philosophy of Science uses vision as a starting point and as a helpful illustration of the principles and topics laid out above. The book addresses science and technology from the standpoint of an embodied, hermeneutical, and phenomenological philosophy, and it does so within the context of Lonergan's transcendental method. That things are localized in places and times within a finite cosmos was accepted by Plato, Aristotle, and nearly all of the ancient philosophers, and by most people in the West until the end of the fourteenth century. However, new technologies of perspective, mapping, navigation, and timekeeping changed all of this and made it possible for the cultural elite to entertain belief in a single—terrestrial and heavenly—unique, objective, and universal space and time. This banished the colorful and intimate feeling about the heavenly court: that it was up there above, in that single unique, objective, and universal space and time, beyond Aristotle's heaven or Dante's *Paradiso*—that God roams space and time, sometimes moving closer to human society and sometimes more distant from it. He is beyond our always finite natural vision, but nevertheless he is always present and all-seeing, ready to intervene in worldly affairs, as piously believed by Christians and many other religious people. My book *Space-Perception and the Philosophy of Science* then is a reflection on the unease of modern culture with this ancient mystical and mythic sense of God's presence and power as being present everywhere but especially in wild or natural places. But there are no such places or functions in the scientific cosmos.

Final Reflection

The world is knowable and known through the narratives we humans provide of natural history. We are a part of the world of nature that produced us, and only we can tell its unique story. Our human goal is to know what is . . . and what is, is *dasein*, being-in-the-world. Within that context there is no separation of subject and object; at the highest level of being, each is part of the other and so defined. The world writ large in its history is also the cosmos out of which come we and our narratives. We might think of the world or cosmos as independent of us, and perhaps even alien or hostile to us. But it makes no sense to say so within this context, for to be hostile to the world is to be hostile to humanity, because we are responsible for the history of the world and have guided its development by our practical skills.

We say that the narratives of cosmological history are the story of God's intentions. But in real life it is we who compose them, and they exist only in the human, and not divine, consciousness. We who possess the narratives also possess the world, and to that extent we also possess God-in-the-world. The world whose narrative we tell is not alien to us, because it is in a sense the product of our creation for which we accept responsibility. Science alone does not give us the *unique world of reality*; rather, the real world is shaped by the way we choose to relate to the environments that we create and sustain. The same is true of the space and time of our experience. We have found that the geometry of space is shaped by how we choose to relate spatially to things other than ourselves. Likewise, time flows quickly or slowly according to the age or interest of the timesetter, who measures time by moons, stars, or mechanical clocks. We are being-in-the-world, that is, human consciousness aware of the world we live in. We are not just people who come and go in the external world; we are what exists, and what exists is being-in-the-world, namely, human consciousness. There would be no world, no shaped cultures, no wild places, without us. What earth and cosmos were like before we humans came to be is a mystery. Until we came to be, there was not a world, because no world exists without he or she whose consciousness gives it an intelligible form, a purpose, and a history.

But was not God there first? God was neither first nor last, for God does not exist in time. But did not God give the cosmos its form and purpose and direct its history? Some think so and blame God for world and cosmic history. I think God is present in history; God is a helper to the being-in-the-world whose history is being shaped by and within human consciousness. Only by becoming aware of God's presence in the world in which we live can we find and pursue the purposes of God's creation. Human civilization and its evolution depends on our discovery within the being-in-the-world that is human consciousness, the presence of God-for-us-and-for-our-world—a timely, spacious, world-loving, and people-loving God-for-us!

But can we find such a God? If "he" is a God-for-us, he must be findable by us in human consciousness of self and world. God must be there! How then do we find him there? We learn to live rightly by following those who live rightly in the religious community. Religious communities have traditions as to how divine communications work within us—by prayer and spiritual reflection, by attention to the kind of peace, joy, and sorrow experienced within prayer but also in times of work or play or rest. Divine communications work in experiences that inspire our self-respect, our courage to make sacrifices for others, even for strangers, that give us a peace that fills the soul and the urge toward creative new tasks for human consciousness. Clearly this is the voice of the God who seeks human life, society, and the world to change, to innovate, and to grow. The voice within us is the divine within us, God as the Holy Spirit.

The divine voice within us speaks to us. Can we hear it? Yes! In the societies of religious peoples these skills are to be found. These skills are often learned during retreats; I have learned them during retreats in the spirit of the Spiritual Exercises of Saint Ignatius. He gave these skills rules: He called them "Rules for the Discernment of Spirits" in prayer and in everyday life.

Notes

1. My reflection is in the spirit of Pierre Hadot, *Philosophy as a Way of Life* (New York: Blackwells, 1995).

2. By "spiritual" and "transcendent" I mean that which is related to the highest good of humanity, generally taken to be the divine purpose of human life. Bernard Lonergan calls the habitual pursuit of this goal "authenticity" and defines it in religious terms. Lonergan, *Method in Theology* (London: Darton, Longmans, and Todd, 1972), chap. 4.

3. Bernard F. Lonergan, *Insight: A Study of Human Understanding* (London: Longmans, Green, 1957).

4. These notes later became Lonergan's book *Method in Theology*.

5. Ontology is about what exists, what is real. According to Martin Heidegger, it is

dasein (being-in-the-world); see Heidegger, *Being and Time* (London: SCM Press, 1962), 67–77. Eugene Wigner sustains this view and takes reality to be the subject and object conjoined within human consciousness; see Wigner, *Symmetries and Reflections* (Bloomington, IN: Indiana University Press, 1967), 171–84.

6. Eugene Wigner, quoted in Andrew Szanton, *Recollections of Eugene P. Wigner as Told to Andrew Szanton* (New York: Plenum Press, 1992), 309.

7. Patrick A. Heelan, *Quantum Mechanics and Objectivity: A Study of the Physical Philosophy of Werner Heisenberg* (The Hague: Nijhoff, 1965).

8. The well-known Cornell psychologist James J. Gibson, who trained young pilots during World War II, realized that he had to train pilots not to follow what their eyes told them, because he found that people are not naturally equipped to make reliable spatial judgments from the air. Instead they were to follow signs laid out on the ground, signs that are now standardized and adopted by international agreement for use at all airports of the world.

9. Aristotle, *De caelo* (*On the Heaven*), 279a.

10. See Lonergan, *Insight*.

11. Patrick Heelan, *Space-Perception and the Philosophy of Science* (Berkeley, CA: University of California Press, 1983).

12. See the meaning of "conscious life" as spiritual life or philosophy as a way of life, as discussed in Hadot, *Philosophy*.

CHAPTER 10

Toward a Catholic Christianity
A Personal Narrative

Michael McCarthy

> Unity without multiplicity is tyranny. Multiplicity without unity is
> confusion. —Blaise Pascal, *Pensées*, no. 510

> The incomplete and inadequate becomes mistaken insofar as it tends
> to be exclusive, as it tends to narrow down, to become fixed and static,
> instead of growing and developing and becoming whole.
>   —Bernard Lonergan, *Philosophical and Theological Papers 1958–1964*

Aggiornamento

Angelo Roncalli became Pope John XXIII when I was sixteen. After eight years of parochial school and three years in a Jesuit high school, I thought I knew what it meant to be Catholic. And in one sense I did. I knew the liturgy of the Mass, the biblical stories, the seven sacraments, the Apostles' Creed, a partial history of the Church, the importance of love and forgiveness. This early formation begun at home has never deserted me. Still, the unexpected selection of Pope John XXIII began a process of personal transformation that continues to this day. Søren Kierkegaard says that the great human calling is to *become* a Christian. He also says that it is very difficult to rise to this calling if one is born in Christendom, in a culture where *being* a Christian is taken for granted.[1] I was educated in primary and secondary schools where being a Catholic was taken for granted. Following the theme of this volume, I seek to explore in my narrative what it has meant for me to become more fully Christian by becoming more genuinely catholic.

Jesus commanded his disciples to bring the Gospel, the good news of redemption, to all the world. Their mission was universal, for "all the world" meant Jew and gentile, male and female, slave and free, tax collector and Pharisee. And it still does, though today we have a broader range of categories to articulate the awesome scope of his universal imperative. From the beginning the Christian mission was to become *katholou*, catholic, to integrate into a living community of faith the full diversity and pluralism of the human race, with all its concreteness and heterogeneity, in the radical equality achieved through Christ's redemptive work.

The complex history of Christianity reveals how difficult it has been to fulfill this mission. Although the dynamic thrust of the Gospel is unrestricted and all-inclusive, it is hard for Christians, for Catholics, to rise consistently to its demands. It is extraordinarily hard for us as individuals to do this; it is even harder for traditional Christian communities, especially when they feel themselves under attack. Perfect love, it is said, drives out fear; but human love is always imperfect, and fear tends to stifle love when danger is perceived on every side.

The Church that John XXIII was called to lead seems to me, in retrospect, a striking blend of love and fear: love for its traditions and its history, fear of so much that lay outside it. I am speaking, of course, in general terms. I am trying to capture a spiritual atmosphere created over several centuries in which the Roman Catholic Church struggled to respond to the defining events of modernity: the northern Italian Renaissance; the Protestant Reformation; the imperial colonization of Asia, Africa, and the Americas; the critical revolutions in natural science and historiography; the rise of democracy and industrial capitalism; the secular ideologies of liberalism and Marxism; the horrors of Hiroshima and Auschwitz; the global insistence on full equality and liberty for women.

There were important exceptions, of course, but by and large the leadership of the Church set itself in opposition to the emerging world that these events and movements had created. The Church saw itself as standing apart from that world, critical of its sins and excesses, and suspicious of its guiding principles: critical reason and autonomous freedom. Important movements within the Church that tried to reverse this oppositional stance were either repressed or condemned as "modernist."

John XXIII dramatically changed the tone and atmosphere within the Church. He led by personal example. He exuded goodwill to all, Christian and non-Christian alike. He was open to dialogue; he did not pontificate. His encyclical messages were ecumenical in spirit and focused on contemporary problems. And most importantly, he summoned the whole Church to *aggiornamento*, to a deep and comprehensive process of renewal.

When John XXIII spoke of *aggiornamento*, he used images of freshness. He called for opening the windows of the Church to allow fresh air and brisk wind to enter. Spring is the season of renewal when abundant life returns to the earth. That which was dead comes to life again; that which was dormant reawakens. A critical part of *aggiornamento* was the ecumenical council that John called into being, the Second Vatican Council. The purpose of this pastoral council, as he described it, was to bring Christ's saving message to the world with a new vitality of purpose and new forms of expression. John XXIII, unlike so many of his predecessors, used papal leadership to engage the modern world rather than condemn it.

Since John XXIII's death in 1963, after the first year of the council, the meaning and scope of *aggiornamento* have been intensely debated. How bold and far-reaching was the renewal John intended? How deep must it go in order to be effective? How discerning must it be to preserve the enduring legacy of the past while critically appropriating the genuine achievements of modernity? And if authentic renewal must be critical, comprehensive, and deep, what does this require of individual Christians and of the Church as a living pluralistic community?

We can't know for certain what Pope John himself intended, but in retrospect we can see what critical and comprehensive renewal requires: a spirit of honesty, humility, and mutual respect; a willingness to examine critically both the history of the Church and the history of the modern world in order to understand how they became estranged and how each side bears responsibility for their unwelcome separation. Genuine renewal begins with repentance and culminates in wise and constructive reforms. Authentic dialogue requires mutual understanding, candid acknowledgment of tensions and disagreements, a sustained and heroic effort to meet the profound challenges created by five hundred years of suspicion and distrust.

It is also clearer in retrospect what should be avoided if renewal and ecumenical openness are to bear enduring fruit. Superficiality must be avoided. Multiple ways of describing modernity and Catholic Christianity fail to address the heart of the matter. But the alternative to shallowness is deep understanding, which takes time, persistence, and a strong dose of learned ignorance. Pride, impatience, and a flawed sense of history preclude understanding in depth.

Anger, recrimination, and toxic and partisan criticism all make constructive dialogue impossible. This pointed caution applies to dialogues within the Church as well as conversations with others. Conservatives are bound to fear the loss of the old, liberals the disparagement of the new. But as Bernard Lonergan predicted, "What will count is a critical center, big enough to be at home in the old and the new, painstaking enough to work out one by one the transitions to be made, strong enough to refuse half-measures and insist on complete solutions even though it has to wait."[2]

The Second Vatican Council

The Second Vatican Council began in 1962 and ended in 1965. It opened under the leadership of John XXIII and closed during the papacy of Paul VI. While it unfolded, I graduated from Notre Dame, served in the army, and began graduate studies in philosophy at Yale. Although I knew the council was important, my immediate attention was often directed to other concerns. It was only later when I studied Catholic history since the Council of

Trent, especially the Catholic response to the French Revolution and to the nineteenth-century developments in critical history and hermeneutics, that I understood how momentous an event Vatican II really was.

It signaled a new beginning in the Church's relation to the modern world. Modern Europe and North America had largely developed without dependence on Catholicism. This was true of modern science, the political movement toward democracy, the rise of industrialism, the liberalization of popular culture and society, the demographic shift to urban patterns of living, the symbiotic connection between modern theory and practice. Though these formative trends developed over several centuries, the Church remained more comfortable with a model of society fashioned in medieval Christendom. Its basic tendency was to view modernity as a deviation from the medieval model and to judge modern history in a negative light.

The reappraisal of modernity initiated during Vatican II was long overdue. The good news of the Gospel should not be identified with specifically medieval patterns of thinking and living. The Gospel is intended for every society and every culture; the Church's obligation to become *katholou* means that it must understand and communicate respectfully with the modern world as fully as it did with its classical predecessors. But because the process of respectful dialogue, of reciprocal teaching and learning, had been long neglected, this dialogue with the world would not be easy.

For many Catholics Vatican II precipitated a crisis in self-understanding. I agree with Lonergan that, initially, this was a crisis not of faith but of culture.[3] For those who had been socialized to view medieval culture as normative, the new openness to modernity; the new imperative to understand modern intellectual, cultural, and political developments; and the new ecumenical spirit toward other Christians and nonbelievers were deeply unsettling.

This immense undertaking, too long delayed, was only begun by the Second Vatican Council. But a new pastoral agenda had been set, a new tone of candor and civility had been adopted, and the Church had recognized that authentic *aggiornamento* begins with personal and collective repentance for past sins and mistakes and with reform of historically embedded practices.

I want to comment briefly on two conciliar documents, *Lumen gentium*, the dogmatic constitution on the Church, and *Gaudium et spes*, the pastoral constitution on the Church in the modern world. How did the teachings in these documents help to shape a more catholic understanding of Christianity, the living community of faith that traces its origin to Jesus of Nazareth? *Lumen gentium* describes the Church as the pilgrim people of God in history. It is a spirit-driven covenant community that carries forward the mission of the Jews, to be a light unto the nations. It is a free and responsible community governed by the twofold law of Christ: wholehearted love of God and neighbor. All of its members are called to holiness; all are called to participate in the redemptive work Jesus entrusted to his followers. These traditional biblical images express an understanding of the Church that is less hierarchical, less juridical, less centralized, less clerically focused than many Catholics were prepared for. The leadership roles of pope, bishops, and priests are by no means rejected in *Lumen gentium*, but there is a new emphasis on collegiality, on collaborative governance, on the complementary charisms of the spirit, and on universal participation in the Church's redemptive mission. The Church's striving for unity is recognized and is carefully emphasized in this document, but true unity is achieved in and through the respectful interplay of differences. The Church is one body with Christ at its head, but its many living members are unique and individual.

How the pilgrim people of God can best serve the modern world to which they presently belong is the defining question of *Gaudium et spes*. Its opening lines affirm the Church's explicit solidarity with its contemporaries. The world's joys and hopes, its sorrows and concerns, are the joys and concerns of the entire Church. In this pastoral document the council makes a genuine effort to understand the dynamic aspirations of the modern world; to recognize the principles of freedom and responsibility that animate it; to explore the challenges it faces in bringing social, economic, political, and cultural life into accord with its declared ideals; and to distinguish carefully between its real achievements and its important limitations. The contradictions of modernity are also acknowledged, as well as the prevailing biases that make their resolution intractable.

If the tridentine Church unduly lamented the excesses of modernity, *Gaudium et spes* may have overcompensated in articulating its merits. The dangers confronting a global civilization driven by science, technology, unregulated capital, electoral democracy, and popular culture need more careful attention than they received. But correctly understanding those dangers and effectively addressing them require the collaborative dialogue that *Gaudium et spes* sets in motion. The council recognized that we cannot fairly appraise what we do not understand and appreciate, and it tacitly treated the earlier one-sided rejection of the modern world as a less than catholic response to its needs.

The institutional and cultural changes recommended by the council were bound to face resistance under the most favorable conditions. But after John XXIII died, Pope Paul VI often appeared to waver in his leadership, and the Church was immediately confronted by the anti-authoritarian spirit of the late sixties. All forms of authority came under attack. The counterculture was sweeping in its negations and uncritical in its enthusiasms. Many needed reforms were implemented unwisely. It became easy for conservative critics to conflate the essential reforms of the council with the excesses of the counterculture. In 1968 the promulgation of *Humanae vitae* occasioned a divisive split in the Church.[4] In the ensuing decades Catholics tended to divide into progressive and conservative factions, particularly on issues concerning gender and sexuality. The inherent difficulties of *aggiornamento* are heightened by these internal divisions and the rancorous passions they tend to evoke. Nearly fifty years after the council we still await the harvest it promised.

Notre Dame

I entered Note Dame in 1959 and graduated in 1963. It was there, on the plains of northern Indiana, that I discovered the joy and excitement of learning and committed myself to pursuing the life of the mind.

At the heart of my college experience was the great books seminar. I joined Notre Dame's great books program at the end of my freshman year, and it served as my intellectual home while I was there. My teachers were powerful examples of intellect and faith. My peers were young Catholic men from throughout the United States. We met twice a week for two-hour discussions of the critical texts that shaped the West.

Our teachers did not lecture but asked exploratory questions. There were no limits to what could be thought or said. The spirited discussions were, of course, uneven in quality, but they continued long after class had ended. We often met in a bar off campus to pursue unfinished lines of inquiry, among other things.

I learned the importance of intellectual freedom in that seminar. I began to think independently and critically. The discussions were so unlike the arguments I had at home. We could disagree passionately without being disrespectful. We could leave an important argument unfinished; no one had the last word. No arbitrary power determined what was true and acceptable.

These open, unrestricted, unfinished dialogues deepened my faith. I learned from my teachers and my friends a new way of being Catholic, a way rooted in inquiry, discussion, and the honest exploration of differences. I particularly remember an observation by Mary Lavin, an Irish writer, in a CBS interview: "Catholics are most alive when they are questioning." Not complaining, but questioning. This personal and intellectual stance became and remains an invaluable second nature that I share with my friends.

I also learned at Notre Dame the communal nature of inquiry. The thoughts that come to us in solitude need to be publicly shared and tested. What light they bring is best determined by the concrete test of experience and the critical scrutiny of peers. There is no better place to think than in an intellectual and spiritual community fully committed to the life of inquiry and the quest for truth. To create and sustain such inclusive communities of learning, in my judgment, is the central purpose of the Catholic college.

I want to recognize two other sources of my Catholic education. The first was extracurricular. As much as I learned from reading and discussing books, I learned even more from male and female friends, and from theater, music, art, film, athletics, the contemplation of nature, personal prayer, the liturgical and sacramental life. Once the mind is intensely alive, nearly everything in existence can be a source of insight.

But there is no substitute for human teachers whose power of example outlasts the memory of their words. I had many extraordinary teachers at Notre Dame whom I remember with gratitude. Given the specific purpose of this narrative, I limit myself to one in particular: John Dunne, a professor of theology. He had a remarkable spirit: open, exploratory, peaceful, sympathetic. For Dunne, no human achievement, however strange, should be set aside as devoid of insight. He showed us how to open ourselves to the light, whatever its source. But Dunne emphasized that we are likely to resist this Catholic precept as long as we are committed to the quest for certainty. To enlarge and deepen our minds, he taught us to surrender the ideal of certainty and to adopt the more human quest for deeper understanding.

Through his classes and his books Dunne revealed the importance of passing over and coming back. When certainty is our goal, otherness, difference, a plurality of perspectives make us uneasy. They seem to threaten the loss of what we prize. But Dunne insisted that our individual perspective on reality is always finite and relative. We have more to learn than we have to fear from engaging the other sympathetically, whether it be other lives, religions, cultures, or ways of responding to the prospect of death.

Dunne did not simply assert this principle; he lived it with a spirit of adventure and humility that was infectious. We learned from Dunne that Catholic theology is not a closed system but a dynamic, historical quest rooted in learned ignorance and the passion for greater understanding. At a critical period in our lives, he calmed our spirits while heightening our eros for whatever is good.

Philosophy at Yale

I entered Yale University in September 1964. I came to Yale from Fort Polk, Louisiana, after completing six months of infantry training for the National Guard. Fort Polk is isolated, humid, and snake-infested. My fellow soldiers were nearly all from the deep South: Mississippi, Alabama, Louisiana, Texas, and Arkansas. The summer of 1964 was a critical period in the struggle for equal rights, when three civil rights workers—James Chaney, Andrew Goodman, and Michael Schwerner—were murdered in Mississippi.

The divisive passions evoked by the movement for racial equality were palpable at Fort Polk. I was seen as a Yankee, an outsider, because my support for civil rights was explicit and clear. Several young Southerners whom I respected and liked were venomous on the subject of black equality. Christian loyalty cut both ways, as the Bible was cited for and against the "Negro cause." I learned, to my dismay, that the Christian faith is an uncertain guide on matters of justice. Given the Church's historical involvement in slavery, imperialism, and anti-Semitism, I should already have known what I learned firsthand that Freedom Summer of 1964.

It's a long way from Leesburg, Louisiana, the home of Fort Polk, to New Haven, Connecticut, even longer than the intellectual path from Notre Dame to Yale. Prior to Yale I had always studied in Catholic settings. Catholics were a clear minority at Yale, though their Newman Center, at Thomas More Parish, was vibrant and brilliantly led. To my mind, the important similarities outweighed the differences. Both Notre Dame and Yale were intellectual communities dedicated to the life of the mind. Both had excellent students and teachers committed to high standards and academic integrity. Both honored the liberal arts and a common set of intellectual virtues and values.

Notre Dame was warmer than Yale, more welcoming and communal. But graduate school is driven by disciplinary exigencies and professional expectations that are impersonal and often severe. Yale was reasonably humane, as graduate schools go, and I am grateful for the philosophical education I received there.

What I missed at Yale was the integration of the intellectual and spiritual life. At Notre Dame I had witnessed Christian humanism at its best, particularly in the teachers I most admired. Humanism was honored at Yale, but the intellectual and spiritual spheres tended to be separate— not hostile, in my experience, but segregated and deprived of reciprocal interaction. Though faith and reason are distinct, I believe they complement each other, as grace complements nature, and mercy complements justice. As a student learning to think philosophically, I benefited in some respects from this clear separation, but personally I missed the complementarity.

I met my wife, Barbara, at Yale. She was a graduate student in French who shared my faith and love of learning. We married at the end of our second year and later started a family with the birth of our daughter, Sarah. Marital and parental love (we now have three daughters) profoundly deepened my Catholic education. When two become one and then three, the meaning of interdependence and shared responsibility becomes fully concrete. Jesus's parables of love, forgiveness, and trust assume new relevance. I slowly began to understand the more abundant life Christ promised.

Bernard Lonergan

Before I left Notre Dame, John Dunne introduced me to the name of Bernard Lonergan and to the title of his groundbreaking work *Insight*.[5] This was the smallest of seeds, to be sure. Later at Yale I found a copy of *Insight* in the library and began to read Lonergan on my own. Over the next forty years I studied his work carefully while pursuing my philosophical and personal education. In my judgment Lonergan is one of the great minds of the twentieth century and one of the great thinkers in the history of the Church.

My intellectual debts to Lonergan are immense and incalculable. His rhetoric and personal example encouraged me to pursue the life of inquiry with unrestricted ardor. In the middle to late sixties when so much was in flux—in the Church, in the academy, in the United States—I relied on Lonergan to point the way to sanity, balance, and critical discernment.

Let me explain. The history of the modern world is marked by dynamic change: intellectual, cultural, and practical. From the Counter-Reformation to the papacy of Pope John XXIII, the Catholic Church largely resisted or remained aloof from this historic transformation. The Church prided itself on its permanent possession of essential truth.

In Lonergan's judgment John XXIII's call for reform and renewal was long overdue. Because Christianity is a historical religion, Christians must continually rise to the level of their times in both thought and practice. Yet for several centuries most Catholics had failed to do this. Momentous developments in science, scholarship, and human self-understanding had occurred since the Renaissance, creating equally momentous challenges for the Church. Although Lonergan welcomed *aggiornamento*, he believed the Church was unprepared for its radical demands. Unless the dynamic forces shaping modernity were carefully understood and critically appraised, the comprehensive renewal Pope John envisaged was likely to be superficial and ineffective.

Since Lonergan was a philosopher and a theologian, he naturally emphasized the renewal of Catholic philosophy and theology. It is in these fields that he made his greatest intellectual contributions.

For Lonergan, what does critical and enduring *aggiornamento* require? It requires a genuine assimilation of what is new in modern science, scholarship, philosophy, and theology. It requires the careful preservation of what is still valid in the older traditions. And most importantly it requires critical discernment in order to distinguish the authentic from the inauthentic in both our classical and modern legacies.

How are these requirements to be met? To understand modern science is to comprehend its methodical canons, its complementary heuristic structures, and its firm insistence on empirically verified truth claims. To understand modern scholarship is to grasp its specialized methods of research, interpretation, critical history, and normative dialectic. To understand modern philosophy is to deepen the historic shift to intentional subjectivity by exploiting its full range of epistemic and moral implications. Finally, to strengthen and renew modern theology is to articulate its methodological dependence on eight interrelated functional specialties that mediate an ancient religion for a culturally diverse and constantly changing world. Each of these epistemic tasks is easy to proclaim but extraordinarily hard to execute.

You may have noticed the recurrent emphasis on method. For Lonergan the deep way to understand modernity is through strategically grasping its defining methods of inquiry and conduct. These methods account for the distinctive dynamism of modern life by providing normative frameworks of collaborative creativity. In classical and medieval culture, where the results of science were thought to be permanently true, logic was the basis of epistemic and ontological integration. But the provisional results of modern science, scholarship, and practical activity are subject to continual revision and amendment. These distinctively modern practices locate invariance not at the level of propositional or practical outcomes, but rather at the level of method, a normatively patterned set of intentional operations yielding progressive and cumulative results.

As the human mind develops, it creates new methods for understanding and transforming reality. To rise to the level of one's time is gradually to master these methods and to honor their exigent norms and procedures. Lonergan's original reconstruction of philosophy is based on the intentional analysis of these evolving specialized methods and of the generalized empirical method that, he believes, underlies and unites them all.

His is a strikingly catholic philosophy in the deepest sense of the term. It is open, dynamic, comprehensive, historically minded, pluralistic, integrative, and critical. Lonergan takes his stand on human beings as they are, concrete existential subjects with a mature commitment to self-knowledge and self-appropriation.

All adult persons are invited to intellectual and moral conversion, in which they discover in themselves the de facto invariants of their conscious subjectivity. These invariant principles provide the critical ground for distinguishing human development from decline. To honor these normative principles faithfully, as persons and communities, is to achieve authenticity. To dishonor them is to lapse into alienation and sin. To justify such lapses from authenticity is the purpose of ideology, the rationalizing project by which all individuals and institutions are tempted.

I discovered in Lonergan's wake three foundational principles that partly constitute our common humanity:

1. The first principle is the unrestricted desire to know (the eros of mind) and the equally unrestricted desire for good (the eros for all that is truly worthwhile). These powerful, unrestricted desires make human inquiry and practice dynamic and open-ended; they explain the intrinsic restlessness of the human spirit.
2. Human consciousness is also subject to immanent norms that require us to be actively attentive, intelligent, reasonable, responsible, and open to grace in our personal and collective inquiry and existence. Lonergan

articulates these normative exigencies in the transcendental precepts, his contemporary analogue to the traditional natural law.

3. Because human existence throughout history is a tangled knot of greatness and wretchedness, we must also recognize the several forms of bias—dramatic, egoistic, group, and general—that compromise our fidelity to these fundamental principles and precepts. Bias invariably obstructs human development and makes us vulnerable to alienation and decline. The justification of bias and its aberrant effects is the root of ideology, the most significant personal and cultural barrier to repentance and reform.

Just as the foundational principles are universal and invariant, so is our vulnerability to bias and sin. This humbling caution applies to every human being and to every historical community, including the Church. It applies as well to the process of *aggiornamento*, for even renewal and reform can go awry. Since divine grace perfects nature and heals the violence of sin, Lonergan's principles are Catholic in another sense as well. They enable us to preserve whatever is genuine and good in both classical and modern history; they enable us to criticize whatever is compromised by bias, sin, and ideology. The gift of grace respects the integrity of human achievement while enabling us to transcend its de facto limitations and weaknesses.

Lonergan's methodological renewal of philosophy and theology has explicit historical analogues. He attempted to do for the twentieth century what Thomas Aquinas achieved in the thirteenth. The relevant analogy is one of proportion, for we no longer live in a medieval world. Aquinas rose to the cultural challenge of his time by integrating Aristotelian and Augustinian insights into a scripturally grounded theology. Lonergan responded to the challenge of modernity by identifying and articulating its intentional sources, methods, and norms; by distinguishing its enduring achievements from its limitations; and by encouraging the creation of collaborative communities actively committed to *aggiornamento* in depth.

Teaching and Learning at Vassar

Barbara, Sarah, and I moved to Poughkeepsie, New York, in the summer of 1968. I had accepted an offer to teach at Vassar, a pathbreaking women's college that had just decided to become coeducational. Radical change was in the air, politically, culturally, and intellectually. American cities were burning, American soldiers were dying, American campuses were swept by fierce winds of dissent.

Vassar's decision to admit men was a sign of the times. Old institutional patterns were dissolving as a participatory ethos emerged in the academy, the

Church, and the nation at large. It was an exciting and troubling time, a time of innovation, unrest, and upheaval.

Political and religious conservatives have severely criticized the late sixties for their excesses. And excesses there were. But the grievances that evoked them were real: racial discrimination, deteriorating cities, an unwise and unjust war, serious environmental neglect, restricted opportunities for women, a compliant academy too closely tied to the national government, a curial bureaucracy reluctant to implement the basic reforms of Vatican II. In my opinion we sorely need a dispassionate and balanced appraisal of this turbulent and seminal period.

My family and I have lived at Vassar for more than forty years; it has been our home. Originally nondenominational, Vassar is now effectively secular, though there are appointed chaplains for the major religious groups on campus. There is a small number of Catholics on the faculty, but a larger contingent in the student body. Vassar has a strong and vibrant feminist tradition; it is passionately committed to the liberty and equality of women. Vassar is liberal in its politics, philosophy, and culture; its impressive curriculum is remarkably diverse and flexible. You can study nearly everything except theology, though there is an active department of religion. Robert Bellah and colleagues have identified four distinct cultural traditions in the history of the United States: biblical, civic republican, utilitarian, and expressive individualist.[6] Expressive individualism is the dominant tradition at Vassar today.

I have deep respect for my Vassar colleagues. I admire their integrity, their exceptional personal gifts, their wholehearted commitment to teaching and scholarship. I have immense affection for our students. They are intelligent, critical, and adventurous: open to new ideas, bravely responsive to challenge. It has been an honor to teach and learn from them.

I have no doubt that my work at Vassar has been a form of Christian service. For me the classroom is holy ground, and the hours of teaching holy hours. What can this mean, since Vassar is a secular institution, and the integrity of the classroom precludes all forms of worship? It means seeking knowledge together, respecting the demands of truth, refusing no questions and appraising all answers, building a passionate community of learning, and obeying the normative precepts Lonergan outlined. In these shared activities I believe we are doing God's work. The great majority of our students don't see it that way, but I do. Our eros of mind is a gift from God; our eros for the good is a clear sign of God's presence within us. When human beings respond to these powerful desires with integrity and make them the operative center of their lives, they honor God and profoundly enrich human existence. All forms of service are holy: parenting, teaching, healing, creating, governing, feeding, cleaning, fighting for justice.

I've learned at Vassar many things I might not have learned as well if I had stayed at Notre Dame. I have learned to respect and admire colleagues with whom I profoundly disagree; to learn from students of every race, religion, ethnicity, and sexual orientation; to recognize the blatant and subtle prejudices that deny women full equality. I have also learned that we humans can fulfill God's will without acknowledging God's presence: that we should love this world with all its diversity, disorder, and strangeness and welcome signs of grace wherever they appear.

Vassar has been an essential part of my catholic education.

Charles Taylor

Next to Lonergan, the most important contemporary influence on my thinking has been his fellow Canadian, Charles Taylor. Lonergan was a Jesuit who studied and taught in Catholic institutions. Taylor is a lay Catholic educated in Canada and England who has taught at Oxford, McGill, and Northwestern universities. Lonergan was a philosophical theologian; Taylor is a remarkably capacious thinker whose principal audience consists of secular intellectuals. Although they lived and moved in different intellectual circles, their ways of thinking are fundamentally catholic, open to the whole of reality in its full complexity. Two central themes in Taylor's recent work, pluralism and unbelief, serve to illuminate his profound catholicity.

Taylor reminds me of John Dunne in his effort to understand rather than condemn views he does not share. This trait is apparent in all his works, especially *A Secular Age*, *Sources of the Self*, the *Ethics of Authenticity*, *A Catholic Modernity?*, and his recent lectures on William James.[7] Taylor is acutely aware of modern pluralism: moral pluralism in *Sources of the Self*, the different forms of individualism in *Ethics of Authenticity*, the multiple Catholic responses to modernity, contrasting genealogies of modern belief and unbelief in *Secular Age*. He thinks we oversimplify complex cultural traditions, frequently dividing them into narrow and polarizing contrasts. This bifurcation makes critical appraisal easier than it should be, for neither the advocates of modern pluralism nor its numerous critics really understand its complexity. Taylor's subtle genealogies are intended to reveal the multiple branchings that occur within a common tradition, like secular humanism or the normative ideal of authenticity.

Not surprisingly, he believes there are multiple Catholic responses to modernity as well. Catholics can openly embrace the moral insights and aspirations of their secular contemporaries without endorsing the restrictive ontologies of naturalism or historicism that are sometimes correlated with them. The authentic goods acknowledged in modernity—like human rights, the affirmation of ordinary life, universal benevolence, and the passionate struggle against suffering and injustice—are fully consonant with the imperatives of the Christian Gospel. The critical task facing Catholics and their secular peers is to distinguish genuine from counterfeit forms of these diverse modern goods and to determine the ontological commitments that are needed to motivate and justify their courageous pursuit.

Like Lonergan, Taylor believes that human beings have a natural orientation to discover and actualize the good. But our contemporaries tend to stifle or deny the deep implications of this profound moral thrust. Both scientific materialists and the numerous proponents of the hermeneutics of suspicion are openly skeptical of moral ontologies inconsistent with their secular prejudices. We are culturally constricted by an ethics of unbelief that treats doubt as more authentic than assent, and redemption as less credible than personal despair. Taylor does not condemn these powerful prejudices. While recognizing their spiritual grip on our contemporaries, he seeks to understand their cultural origins and the historical basis of their continuing appeal. Paradoxically, these reductive treatments of morality are often grounded in unacknowledged moral aspirations. Recognizing these aspirations leads to a fascinating reversal of Friedrich Nietzsche's genealogy of morals.[8] Nietzsche claimed to find envy, resentment, and weakness at the root of Christian ethics. Taylor reveals how the passion for justice and the devotion to personal freedom motivate ethical theories that explicitly deny the force of these critical moral concerns. The genealogical critics of morality are actually driven by implicit but unacknowledged moral passions themselves.

We humans are self-interpreting animals. Part of who we are is who we take ourselves to be. We seriously constrict our freedom to think and act by misunderstanding our past, oversimplifying our present, and unduly narrowing our future. Relying on this hermeneutic principle, Taylor insists that the dominant construals of modernity are one-sided and inadequate, particularly the stories we tell of modern unbelief.

According to the "mainline story" favored by the secular academy, it was the rise and advance of science and critical thinking that weakened Christianity in the West. In this account the empirical and critical spirit of modernity is incompatible with the requirements of authentic faith. In his persuasive rebuttal Taylor argues that the principal obstacles to religious allegiance in modernity are moral and spiritual, not epistemic. The modern scientific revolution was accompanied by a moral and cultural rejection of traditional hierarchies and Christian otherworldliness. The modern affirmation of ordinary life gave a new dignity to lay vocations. The insistence on individual rights, on freedom of inquiry and expression, on religious liberty and the primacy of conscience all made traditional forms of social control appear repressive.

The Church's entanglement in the *ancien régime* of pre-revolutionary France alienated the friends of democracy. Its passive acceptance of the injustices of capitalism alienated the working class and its allies. In our time the halfhearted acceptance of women's rights and the restriction of their religious ministries and leadership are a major barrier to the Church's credibility and effectiveness.

The critical insights of Lonergan and Taylor are complementary. Lonergan emphasizes the Church's epistemic failure to understand and appropriate the new forms of learning. Taylor emphasizes its belated commitment to modernity's moral aspirations. In both cases the Church concentrated on the excesses and aberrations of the new. It was also driven by legitimate fears of losing what was valid in the old. But a defensive, naysaying Christianity has limited attractive power for the young, for the creative advocates of innovation and change, and for all who suffer from the systemic injustices of the past.

Lonergan and Taylor show us a very different way. Without ceasing to be critical of the new, they emphasize the affirmative: the insights and achievements of modernity, its commitment to human freedom and responsibility, the goodness of this life that coexists with our hope for life eternal.

A Catholic Christianity

> Genuine Christian humility excludes the resentment that belittles the
> learning one does not possess.
> —Bernard Lonergan, *Philosophical and Theological Papers 1965–1980*

The renewal of Catholic Christianity should begin with a comprehensive and critical realism. We need to understand the dramatic decline of the Church: especially in Europe, but also in the United States, where many former and present Catholics feel deeply estranged. There are several reasons for this decline, not all attributable to the Church's failures. But all genuine renewal begins with repentance, with acceptance of responsibility for past errors and sins. In my judgment defensive apologetics will not be helpful.

I want to focus on three influential criticisms of Christianity whose polemical force still carries weight. These criticisms come from Marx, Nietzsche, and Freud, three seminal thinkers whom Paul Ricoeur has called "the masters of suspicion."[9] Ricoeur's thoughtful and balanced interpretation of Freud exemplifies the best way to address these critical assaults.

Marx rejected Christianity as "the opium of the people."[10] He thought its causal emphasis on God demeaned human agency; he thought its moral emphasis on heaven weakened opposition to injustice on earth. Nietzsche claimed that the affective sources of Christian ethics were suspect, that the Gospel of love was actually rooted in resentment and envy. And Freud believed that the religious mentality is infantile and regressive, that religious accounts of reality are unscientific, that religious ethics are unduly restrictive, and that religious hopes are illusory and vain.

All three of these thinkers confidently assumed that a mature and healthy society would reject religion as an obstacle to human development and freedom. In my judgment this influential belief is mistaken. It confuses aberrant forms of religion with the genuine article. But the aberrations are real, even if they are often exaggerated by the masters of suspicion. The rhetorical force of their criticisms resonates with everyone, believer and nonbeliever alike, who thinks that God is the enemy of human maturity, that the Church is complicit in systemic injustice, that it belittles achievements it does not understand, and that it fosters immature ways of thinking and feeling. When I say "the Church," I mean us, all of the pilgrim people of God. It is we who are vulnerable to these failings, who commit these sins, who dishonor God by the images of the divine we project and defend. We are called to be the salt of the earth and the light of the world. But is that what we really are? Is that how our contemporaries experience our presence among them? The most powerful witnesses, for or against the Gospel, are the lives that we actually lead.

What would a Catholic Christianity faithful to the message of the Gospel and Christ's mission of redemption be like?

1. Our thought and speech would be realistic and critical. We would be as truthful as we can in understanding ourselves, our past, and the complexity of the world that we are called to serve.
2. Genuinely repentant, we would not justify past failures, conceal present weaknesses, or shrink from the challenge of conversion and change.
3. Our understanding of the Church and the world would be deeply historical. The redemptive message of the Gospel is constant, but it has to be proclaimed with fresh credibility to each culture and people in history.
4. An ecumenical Church would treat everyone with dignity and respect. Without glossing over differences, its internal and external dialogues would seek mutual understanding and, where possible, consensus in judgment. It would be a continually learning and teaching Church, conscious of its limits as well as its strengths.
5. The Church would abandon all the baggage of patriarchy. Women and men are equally created in God's image, equally redeemed by Christ's sacrifice, equally inspired by the Spirit, and equally called to the service of God in the world. All the ministries of the Church would be fully open to women.
6. The principles of collegial governance and meaningful lay participation proclaimed in the Second Vatican Council would be fully implemented. The unifying role of the pope is fully consistent with a far less centralized, bureaucratic, and secretive manner of conducting the Church's affairs. The Church's internal practice must become a model of freedom and justice if its prophetic ministry to the world is to be taken seriously.
7. If we, the community of faith, become credible agents of redemption and reconciliation, if we reveal by our language and practice that we truly are the living people of God, we will find, I believe, a troubled world

hungry for our presence and ministry. For our world needs the insight, wisdom, and compassion of Christianity as much as any period in history. A humble and merciful Church, a joyful and honest Church, a genuinely catholic Church can be a light unto the nations by authentically searching for truth, overcoming evil with good, and charitably resolving the painful divisions within our own ranks. The continuous challenge of *aggiornamento* is ours.

Notes

1. Søren Kierkegaard, *Kierkegaard's Attack upon Christendom, 1854–1855* (Princeton, NJ: Princeton University Press, 1944).

2. Bernard Lonergan, *Collection*, ed. Frederick E. Crowe and Robert M. Doran, Collected Works of Bernard Lonergan 4 (Toronto: University of Toronto Press, 1998), 244–45.

3. Ibid., 244.

4. Paul VI, *Humanae vitae*, www.vatican.va/holy_father/paul_vi/encyclicals/docu ments/hf_p-vi_enc_25071968_humanae-vitae_en.html.

5. Bernard Lonergan, *Insight: A Study of Human Understanding*, ed. Frederick E. Crowe and Robert M. Doran, Collected Works of Bernard Lonergan 3 (Toronto: University of Toronto Press, 1992).

6. Robert Bellah et al., *Habits of the Heart* (New York: Harper and Row, 1985), 27–54.

7. Charles Taylor, *A Secular Age* (Cambridge: Harvard University Press, 2007); Taylor, *Sources of the Self* (Cambridge: Harvard University Press, 1989); Taylor, *The Ethics of Authenticity* (Cambridge: Harvard University Press, 1991); Taylor, *A Catholic Modernity?*, ed. James Heft (New York: Oxford University Press, 1999). Taylor's lectures on William James have been published in *Varieties of Religion Today: William James Revisited* (Cambridge: Harvard University Press, 2002).

8. Friedrich Nietzsche, *The Genealogy of Morals: A Polemic* (New York: Russell and Russell, 1964).

9. Paul Ricoeur, *Freud and Philosophy: An Essay in Interpretation* (New Haven, CT: Yale University Press, 1970), 32.

10. Karl Marx, *Introduction to the Critique of Hegel's Philosophy of Rights*.

CHAPTER II

The Hunting and the Haunting

Peter Steele

I have written well over a hundred poems that are to one degree or another after works of art—usually paintings. When I was asked recently about the attraction of such a topic, it occurred to me that the attraction lies in part in the fact that those works are finished things: whether or not they sport actual frames, they are all in some sense framed. Another way of saying this is that they are the polar opposite of the chaotic; and for reasons in part instinctive and in part educational, I do love the manifestly coherent—a brick wall can cheer me up any day. And out of the vast repertoire of Catholic Christianity, one thing I find appealing is its propensity for divining or discerning coherences, its stress on the way in which this answers to that, within this world and between this and another world.

I recognize of course that precisely this side of Catholicism can be distasteful to those of a different temperament, as it is to those who see in it principally a temptation toward exaction and domination: I understand what it is like to put one's money on Dionysus, so to speak, rather than on Apollo. But one is as one is, and must hope to make the best, not of a bad job, but of a partial one—which is to say, in the end, of a creaturely one.

At the end of his preface to *The Portrait of a Lady*, Henry James says, "There is really too much to say."[1] These words might appropriately conclude any exercise in self-delineation, because it is quite impossible to record all the events of a single day, let alone of many years. Then again, in retrospect the bulk of a lifetime may, without violence, be able to be summed up in two or three sentences, as is true in my own case. But between these extremes, a poet at least may hope to find in a little of his work something of the kind mentioned by the Australian Vincent Buckley, who speaks of "the few poems / that are the holy spaces of my life."[2] Accordingly I shall adopt the strategy of speaking of several of my own poems as foci of the ways in which much that matters to me does so.

Another Australian, the artist Justin O'Brien, has a small, finely wrought painting of the Madonna and Child, who are attended by short files of saintly or angelic figures. My own poem "Madonna and Child" salutes that work:

> He might have just come from the barber, unless
> She keeps razor and scissors bright in a jar
> To smarten him up on Fridays. There's finesse
> In the gowns' fall, the boy's bearing, the scar

That pinks each hand and foot, the woman's gaze
Towards you and beyond, the nailed-up throne
To house the poet's "soul in paraphrase,"
The haunting grown the stranger, being shown.
And here's the thing: among those out to see,
Young as they are, what he and she can tell
Of all time's blessings and its piracy,
The tolling or the spiring of a bell,
Guess as they do at the soured wine and the lance,
The feet are poised forever towards a dance.[3]

My "Madonna and Child" is cast as a sonnet: in part because I wanted to applaud the tradition out of which so many of hundreds of thousands, if not millions, of sonnets have emerged; and in part because I was betting that that form could once again work not as encasement of thought and feeling but as the equivalent of a skeletal structure in collaboration with our muscular and nervous systems.

The poem's first words, "He might," flag, I now see, something of central importance in all of the arts, namely the role of the conjecturing mind, its devotion to Saint Perhaps. A brick wall may, after all, enclose anything from a garden to a warren to a midden: Formality can be strangely compendious, and within its terms the sky can be the limit. In O'Brien's little painting, the Christ-child in his mother's lap has particularly neat, even sleek hair, which reminded me of the times, now more than sixty years ago, when my own mother would cut my hair of a Saturday for Sunday's events. Jesus, a good Jewish lad, might have been smartened up from time to time, for the Sabbath, and scissors had been invented in the Middle East well before he came on the scene, as had the razor.

Do I know or care whether that was so? Of course not, though I might if I were a barber. But the fact is that, to a degree that we rarely acknowledge, even our waking consciousness is a tissue of affirmation, denial, and conjecture. We have it in us to be powerful daydreamers, and art is among other things an embracing of the daydreams and, at once, an enhancing and a disciplining of them. So in "Madonna and Child" I salute some of the ways in which O'Brien has imagined with precision a scene that, if addressed with faith, might well be said to blow the mind. "Finesse," which in my poem rhymes with "unless," looks to the painting's exact orderliness, but I hope that it also carries a charge of admiration at O'Brien's having brought off a little coup of warranted imagination in, say, the small wounds with which the child's body are "pinked," as by a duelist who, scarring, is also adorning.

My poem is shadowed by its army of predecessors, its own "cloud of witnesses" (Heb. 12:1), and is accordingly vulnerable to being put in its place by them. I am glad to have written it, but I know that it is small potatoes compared with many by-now classic works. But then Catholics at least are accustomed to seeing themselves as small potatoes by comparison with the Sainted Ones: If they invoke those gone before them, it is from a position of solidarity mingled with inferiority. This is most particularly true when the two principal figures in O'Brien's painting are concerned; but this quasi-iconic work would probably not have been made if the whole vast matrix of Christian prayer had not existed. That it does exist is something alluded to, and rejoiced in, in the words "soul in paraphrase," which I have borrowed, as neighbors might, from George Herbert's own great sonnet, "Prayer" (I).[4]

His poem does not have a principal verb, and as Marianne Moore writes of a selection of her works, "Omissions are not accidents."[5] It is as if Herbert's poem is a reverie, something conducted in the presence of a reality that, for all the precision of his utterance, simply overwhelms him. In a genially intended piece of cant, many in the United States claim that this or that is "awesome." But for Herbert, prayer, and the subject of prayer, truly are awesome. An elementary honesty requires me to acknowledge how inept and inconstant I myself am in the enterprise of prayer, but it has still dawned on me that the merest twitch upon some rosary beads, the merest murmuring of a psalm's fragments, can take one into a country of the mind and of the heart that is spacious beyond conceiving and blessed beyond desiring. And I suppose that it was out of that assumption that "the haunting grown the stranger, being shown" emerged.

It is certainly true that for most of my life I have sensed that to be a Christian, and the more so to be a priest, may appropriately be described as being both God-haunted and a God-hunter. This haunting, like some others, may take different forms. One of them is via the palpable, something that is acknowledged and, as far as may be, furthered in Catholicism's embrace of the sacramental. The supreme instance of this is the Mass or the Eucharist, of which more later; but the ensemble includes not only the other six "certified" sacraments, or the use of crucifixes or blessed water or venerated images, but a whole propensity to find the world to be enchanted, even while it is acknowledged to be, in dreadful ways, wounded and defiled. Gerard Manley Hopkins, in more than one poem, attests to both the enchantment and the defiling, and God knows what he would have said of our inheritance from the twentieth century. But we have every reason to believe that he would have cast his characterization in much the same terms as those he already used—and perhaps he still does. And certainly, unless I have gotten the story quite wrong, Hopkins's principal allegiance, namely to celebration, remains an enduring challenge.

The dictum—standard among Jesuits and among others influenced by Ignatius of Loyola's writings—that one should seek to "find God in all things" works under twin assumptions. The first is that God has many presences and no absences; and the second is that he has to be sought again and again—that is, that one is indeed both haunted and a hunter. The God-hunting proper to our species, which lives in time and in its contradictions and afflictions, will always have to include elements of the labyrinthine. "Where was God in Auschwitz?" ask many voices, and "Where was God in the Tsunami?" ask many others. We do as little or as much as we can in reply, but in any case each of us has his or her personal version of the questions. In "Madonna and Child," the last word is given to "a dance," something benign, shared, and exultant, and very possibly a tiny miming of the trinitarian perichoresis, that supreme dance of being in and as which Christian thinkers have envisaged the life of God. But "the soured wine and the lance" are only a line away, as indeed our own version of them remains for us all, lifelong.

The reader will have noticed a bespeckling of these pages with a number of names. Their presence vouches for something that is true of us all: namely that unless we have been exceedingly unfortunate, we have gone through life befriended in a variety of ways. The Society of Jesus aspires to be a body of friends in the Lord and often, in my experience, succeeds in exactly that venture; and in varying degrees, one has an array of other friends, living and dead, close or casual. Among these, even if it is a one-way affair, are the many writers who have been friends to me, though they never knew it. But there are also those who have been flesh-and-blood fellow teachers, fellow essayists, fellow poets, and it has been natural to celebrate them from time to time. Accordingly, here is a poem, called "Love and Death at Papa Gino's," which is dedicated to an old and close friend, the poet, essayist, and teacher Chris Wallace-Crabbe. Papa Gino's is a pizza joint close to The University of Melbourne; Chris and I have been habitués there for several decades.

Telling the years as the chroniclers do—as, "the Vikings
    arrived again," or "a bumper crop
of cumquats has left us delirious," or alas,
    "desire is crowned in our cherished Leader"—
may be, after a fashion, comme il faut,
    but sells short the personal fervours.

And for them, braced like beasts invited by Noah,
    you could swan into Papa Gino's, aglow
not yet with ebullient red but the sheer prospect
    of high talk, of low esteem
for those wizened in dignity, of the laughter
    that warrants oddly the human estate.

True, it's a break. Even austere Augustine
    could deem the *patria* "endless vacation":
and a world, to improve on amateur nights in Dixie,
    needs a dash of the festive, as surely

as Adam needs Eve or the feathery angels a lift.
   Which is why, although in the mounting decades

we've been commensals we've been attended by ghosts
   and seen a dear one leave our table
for the long silence, back we come with pleasure
   to this cabin for comrades, arush with its aprons,
with lofted dough and glasses, where the bright posters
   hale water from Italian marble.[6]

Like most of my contemporaries, I joined the Jesuits straight from high school. After two years' novitiate and three years' seclusive study of philosophy, off most of us went to The University of Melbourne in 1962. I have been associated with that institution ever since, maintaining the contact and some employment even during the years when I was the provincial superior of the Jesuits in Australia. The place has changed enormously in that time; these days it has about forty thousand students and faculty. It is institutionally boastful, like most of its fellows; and although this is sometimes a comical spectacle and sometimes a sad one, the place does harbor many excellences. It has certainly treated me very generously, and I regard it as a blessing that I should have spent so much of my life in its secular milieu.

Part of the blessing is, again, friendship. The befriending has been with men and women but has also been, at their hands, a continued befriending of the life of the mind, especially as that is to be known in literature's often mysterious enterprise. I was a congenital scribbler before I arrived at the university, but in its environment I became increasingly intent on trying to further the relationship between what one might, over-grandly perhaps, call "the words and the Word." On occasion that relationship can be a patent one, as indicated very simply if one turns to the back of a volume of the Liturgy of the Hours, and finds, say, John Donne's "Hymn to God my God, in my Sickness," a state of affairs that I welcome. But insofar as one senses that, whether in poetry or in prose, language is capable of majesty as well as vulnerable to ignominy, one knows it to be indeed, more generally, an emblem of that condition of which it is also a product, namely the human. For someone steeped in an Ignatian humanism, it is no surprise that the character of particular words in particular relationships should warrant a lifetime's reflection.

Paradoxically, those relationships are often potential rather than already realized. Joseph Brodsky, when praised for poems he wrote, would say that they were all already there in the Russian language. Well, yes and no, but the twinned notions of potency and latency that his claim implies point to part of poetry's mystery: certainly in the old sense of an adept's mastery, and sometimes in the sense of something very hard to fathom and eminently worth the fathoming, when this can be done. Most poets worth their salt would acknowledge that, even if a poet is called in more than one language a "maker," it is still in large degree something to be sought out rather than something to be rigged up.

The Chris Wallace-Crabbe of my poem's dedication is agnostic as to things divine, which has never impeded an enormous amount of fellow-feeling between us as to things human, and most particularly poetry. I mention this because it is a reminder that some kinds of knowledge do have what might be called a coloration of the companionable. Truth, often portrayed as an icy absolute, may in fact come home to us as part of friendship's burden or blossoming. Theologically speaking, this is not so much a surprise as an axiom, if it is agreed that the one called "Truth" is indeed the one who is supremely the Friend; but of course it takes a great deal of steady application, and a greater degree of spiritual fidelity, for that to continue to seem obvious.

At all events, as the poem proclaims, a particular, largely unremarkable, restaurant can house wonders, year in and year out. Tip O'Neill's statement that "all politics is local" may or may not be true. But all worldliness, all being in this, our only experienced world, is local, as is recognized in Shakespeare's "local habitation and a name" given to what would otherwise be the airy nothings of a slothful imagination.[7] This is how incarnation goes; when in "Annunciation" Donne refers to "Immensity, cloister'd in thy dear womb," he is offering the paradigm of every divine, and every divinely sponsored, incarnateness.[8] So I find it natural that in "Love and Death at Papa Gino's" the Vikings and cumquats, aprons and pizza dough, should be lodged with Noah and Augustine, with Adam and Eve. It is, after all, a cabbages-and-kings cosmos. I am glad to know both that Jesus probably ate a lot of chickpeas, and that Cicero's name means "Mr. Chickpea." Weirdly, but certainly, they are part of the same team, the one that plays with a big *H* on its sweaters, and any poetry that gets too far away from that state of affairs is by definition beyond my ken.

The poem "Love and Death at Papa Gino's" alludes to death as well as to love. Not only have the two of us often lunched there with friends, some of whom are now dead, but on one occasion, of the several who were present, one gave a wordless sigh, closed his eyes, and died. Paramedics worked on him on the floor, his wife and his daughter came, but it was all over. The occasion is unforgettable of course, and it has its own sacredness; but to someone for whom the eucharistic meal is both a daily commemoration and a wellspring of the imagination, it is blended with that meal in memory and in construal. I do not know whether the upper room of the Last Supper happens to have had a public name, but if it did the evangelists' account of it might have been subtitled "Love and Death at So-and-So's."

Yet laugh we still do, not without help from the "ebullient red," and I for one certainly hope that there was laughter as well as gravity in the upper room. It is not a good idea to become pompous about laughter, but I have a good deal of sympathy with those who see in it not only a simple marker of our species—"the laughing animal"—but also a coding of our creatureliness. Laughter, like other exercises of the mind and heart, can be turned to questionable ends, as no student of satire will need to be reminded. But my longstanding and deep-seated admiration for G. K. Chesterton inclines me to see in laughter an impulsive, if tacit, acknowledgment that we are, first, last, and always, contingent, and that this is not necessarily bad news.

The word *patria* sticks out on the page in its little italicizing coat, though I defer for a moment something about having the heavenly on one's mind. I want though, before deserting this poem, to make the simple point that the poem is indeed a shaped thing. Auden begins his poem 'Whitsunday in Kirchstetten' with the words "'Komm Schöpfer Geist!' I bellow," and for me God is indeed "the Shaping Spirit," whose making-for-shapeliness is something I salute, if only to myself, when moving among forms, in poetry as to a degree in prose.[9]

I was born the day before the Nazi-Soviet Pact was signed in August 1939, a week before the ascribed beginning of World War II. I understood very little about that war, though I was keenly aware that my father spent a good deal of it in New Guinea as part of an army intent on keeping Japanese soldiers from visiting Australia without invitation. But one of the consequences of growing up at such a time was that one could, with the rest of the world, witness first the deployment of powerful military rockets and eventually human arrival on the moon.

For a very long time we earthlings have been moon-minded. Witness the calendars that have hitched their wagons to that large celestial rock, and witness too the frequency with which the supposedly too moon-minded have been mocked for it, as in words like "lunacy" and also like "moonrakers," said of dolts allegedly attempting to rake the moon's reflection from village ponds. In 1532 Ludovico Ariosto's *Orlando Furioso* mooted the notion that things lost from the Earth could be found on the moon; and thinking once of various odds and ends of information about that interesting body, I found that fantasy swimming into collocation with graver matters. At the time, I was writing many of the art-dependent poems mentioned above, and I came across a color image of the full moon that was taken by the Galileo spacecraft in 1990. Hence the next poem, called "Full Moon, Good Friday":

Once more a bomber's moon, and the planners know it,
 coffee to hand in the green-lit bunkers.
Up there, a spider's web spun in a cavern
 could hang untouched for millions of years,
the dust mounting in craters we've made our own—
 Autolycus, Lichtenberg, Sheepshanks, Hell.
The magma floods are still now, their basalt
 good for a world of tombs: the Bay

of Dew, the Marsh of Sleep, the Sea of Nectar.
  And little enough to drink at the Place
of the Skull, apart from the Legions' vinegar swig,
  a man's ration for the long march.
They have put him away in his own darkness as though
  to dream hard of all the losings
found again on the moon's shining meadows:
  tears grown fruitful, wrecked desire
come into port, time a dancing measure,
  and the worst night a cradle for dawn.[10]

The titles of poems often repay attention, and in this case a moment's reflection will show that both the natural and the historical are being evoked. And there we are, the lot of us. On the one hand and at every instant, we are the products of, and presumably the temporary participants in, nature's processes and panoply—in there with quasar and asteroid, caribou and jackrabbit. On the other hand, we go on putting our signature in the calcite layers of Lascaux, in Bach's Mass in B minor, in the hutments of Treblinka, in whirligig and pencil sharpener and steak diane.

I am fascinated by the fact that we are so biform; and I suspect that, whether in my teaching as a professor of literature, in my prose writings secular or sacred, or in my poetry, that fascination shows itself. Every hour of every day, waking or sleeping, we go on internalizing the universe of which we are a part: It is called breathing. And for many hours at least, simultaneously we stand out from all the other veteran creatures as the wild cards of thought, the namers and blamers and framers and tamers. It is all very familiar, and it is all very strange.

I am not claiming that it is better to be aware, occasionally or frequently, of something strange about our very constitution. I am only saying that it is the way things go for me. But I should also acknowledge that my belief in God as both the maker and the sustainer of the whole affair is no doubt colored by this particular keying of my attention. I do understand, however haltingly, the proneness of first Jewish and then Christian thinkers to voice, as it were in the one breath, both a sense that God is naturally the fountain of all—the air we breathe, the absolute mother, the fatherland indeed—and a sense that he or she or it is the stranger beyond strangeness. Such mystical talk can turn rhapsodic all too quickly, shedding plausibility as it goes; but the impulse to let such speech have its due seems to me not gratuitous but modestly dutiful to experience.

Out of some such bent of the mind, "Full Moon, Good Friday" emerged. I had the image off the web, courtesy of NASA. I had as a potential matrix that daily celebration of the Eucharist, whether in company or alone, in which nightmare is rehearsed: that being a feeble word for betrayal, desertion, torture, judicial murder, and execution—and the continuance of such things all over the earth until this day. I also had, as something testified to and proclaimed in the same Thanksgiving, the astounding story of resurrection, that "upstanding" of Christ like that, in time, of all who are finally bonded with him. Theologically speaking, there are a number of ways of characterizing the Mass, all of them orthodox, some more compendious than others. Among them is that way which sees it as the enacted epic of the cosmos, in which Christ the Word of all, scarred for time and eternity, rises for and among his siblings. Increasingly I have come to see the Mass in such terms—the splendor and the humiliation fused in a way that may defy naming, in spite of the torrent of words that spill forth about it all. My poem is a spoonful amidst the torrent.

Poets are not magicians, any more than are preachers or teachers or priests. But all are given to the enterprise of naming things well, however diversely they may be empowered to do just that. I have said in the past that theology is a matter of "watching one's language in God's presence," and also that theology might be called "Christian Wit." They both still seem to me to be sensible propositions. And although I should not be altogether easy about my poems' being called "theological," since I am the merest amateur in that high affair, those two phrasings might perhaps be applied to a number of my poems, including this one.

"Autolycus, Lichtenberg, Sheepshanks, Hell": They are indeed all craters on the moon. On the one hand, naming the craters at all makes them familiar to a degree, as when we name a canyon Grand or a volcano Vesuvius. On the other hand, the Autolycus of Greek legend and of the *Winter's Tale*; the Lichtenberg who was a German physicist, aphorist, and wit; the Sheepshanks who was an English astronomer's sister; the Hell who was a Hungarian Jesuit—all of them are, as the literary theorists like to say, "made strange" in their new locales. So it goes too with those lunar territories named by analogy with the resources of our own watery planet: the Bay, the Marsh, the Sea. They haunt me, for one, in their otherness. And after they are named, precisely halfway through the poem, we have another "othering," that in which a "Friday's child"—"loving and giving" in the old nursery chant—is ejected first to a place of sterility and then from earth itself.

Every army on earth, like every prison, is a scandalous thing, in the sense that it is a reminder of human dysfunction. In that sour sense it is appropriate that Christ, briefly a jailbird, should have been executed by the Roman army—the army whose very rationale was to extend an imperium that had no more legitimacy than that of any other bunch of warlords, however finely the roads were built, and however finely Virgil could write about the crushing of proud resisters. The Christ who spent his whole life, if not in an occupied country, at least in a manipulated one, stood in his conversation with Pilate for a liberation of such a depth and scope as would show the *Pax Romana* for the ramshackle parody of freedom and justice that it was—and that every analogous regime is.

"Ill met by moonlight, proud Titania," Shakespeare's Oberon says to his disaffected queen; all the encounters, or exposures, under a bomber's moon are "ill met."[11] But the moon has also presided over such coups of imaginative calm as, say, Ben Jonson's "Queen and Huntress." The moon has been envisaged as a stilling presence and as a witness of vindicated aspiration. I take it for such in the final stanza of "Full Moon, Good Friday." In a curious way, the cardinal words there are "as though," because in poetry, as in much other verbal, visible, and audible art, the whole affair hinges on the recipient's readiness to be open to revision and reversal when it comes to estimation. Michael Frayn says, "Think of the distance between your hand and your eye, between your hand and Alpha Centauri, between your hand and the bottom right hinge on the West Door of York Minster."[12] Frayn's injunction implies and encourages a readiness in the reader to entertain the surprising, and to entertain it as something that paradoxically is also part of our country. The supposedly dreaming Christ at the end of the poem is among other things the savior of surprise.

The final poem examined here concerns a painting by John Linnell, the nineteenth-century English painter. The painting, called *Wheat*, was done in 1860 and portrays the getting-in of a harvest. The poem has the same name.

> If he were able, Hopkins might have been here—
>   the stooks achieving their "barbarous beauty,"
> the main of sky possessed by a riot of clouds,
>   trees and wheat consorting in life:
>
> and would, in his native mode of excess, have told us
>   of the great medieval yellows borrowed
> from ochre and saffron, buckthorn and weld,
>   while gold smouldered behind them all,
>
> awaiting the burnisher's touch with a tooth borrowed
>   at best from lion or wolf, but accepted
> from dog or cat, the whole set off, as here,
>   by the fierce wash of ultramarine.
>
> "And it is common for the sea looked down upon,
>   where the sheety spread is well seen
> but the depth and mass unfelt, to sway and follow
>   the wind like the tumbled canvas of a sail"—
>
> of course it is, but the saying's a form of caring,
>   like the seeing itself: like the getting of black

from peachstone or galled oak, or gold again
    from tortoise bile, or vermilion hunted

out of its ruddled lair to a lad's cap,
    him with his bundle of brimming grain,
bent like the others on hauling it home for its trial,
    the tillage done and the waving carriage,

the world being, as Dante saw from a vantage
    in the blinding vast of his lone journey,
a little threshing floor that maddens us,
    with no mouthful the worse for that.[13]

One of the reasons for choosing this poem for this chapter is that it sounds teacherly, in part like a lesson being given by Hopkins. I have made my living largely on the understanding, chiefly in one university but also on occasion in others, that I am a teacher. Randall Jarrell said once that writing poetry well is only occasionally difficult—usually it is impossible. I am not sure that the same is not true of teaching. To a degree of course it depends on where one is pitching the bar; there is a marvelous moment in Robert Burton's *Anatomy of Melancholy* where he says that "every schoolboy has the famous testament of Grunius Corocotta Porcellus at his fingers' ends."[14] This has not proved to be so in my experience. Geoffrey Madan refers in a notebook to the "warm lagoon of indolence and irreligion which seems to be the proper habitat of youth"; and yes, I know that lagoon, though from time to time I take comfort from the fact that out of the most famous lagoon in the world Venice arose, and indeed gave us the word itself.[15]

As things turned out, I have often enough felt myself to be in, rather than of, the dark wood of contemporary literary studies, as they are still occasionally styled. Part of the problem for me has been the rampantly antihumanistic ethos of their atmosphere, and part has been patois evoked when Jarrell writes of an imagined sculptor speaking of her work: "Some of what she said was technical, and you would have had to be a welder to appreciate it; the rest was aesthetic or generally philosophic, and to appreciate it you would have had to be an imbecile."[16] Jarrell's sculptor is, I am sorry to say, fictional but not fictitious: I know her and her siblings well.

Still, it would be absurd to lose one's pedagogical nerve in the face of quasi-intellectual buffoonery. It is all the more absurd given a keenness to celebrate the aspirations and the practice of great mentors and teachers, of whose endeavors we are the beneficiaries every time we pick up some work that, by virtue of Samuel Johnson's "length of duration and continuance of esteem," has earned the status of a classic.[17] My poem "Wheat" is nothing of the kind, but it does aspire to applaud some of that imaginative plenitude that is the first and the final attraction of memorable art.

One writes a poem in part to see what will happen, and I did not know until almost the end that Hopkins and Dante would be tutelary presences. In various legal processes a responsible adult is required to be at hand. It has often seemed to me that the invocation of saints is analogous with this, if only in that our prayers, like much else in our lives, are often infantile in character. Similarly, and without any doubt as to the disparity of talents, various heroic writers or indeed other artists may properly be invited into the atelier when poems are being made, they being in part sponsors of the imagination and in part chasteners of one's excesses. This potential "cloud of witnesses" may in effect testify to excellence, but the witnesses may as readily fortify the case against the cranky, the lazy, the outright crass. They may also, from time to time, just come along for the ride.

When in "Hurrahing in Harvest" Hopkins wrote, "Now, barbarous in beauty, the stooks arise," he would have been well aware of the paradox in "barbarous beauty," playing as he was on the Greek sense of "barbarous" as "babblement" and the Latin word for a beard—as in the "bearded" wheat.[18] Again and again in his poetry runs a relationship, often elatedly, between "the raw and the cooked."[19] The Duke of Wellington was opposed to letting soldiers cheer, this being in his view too near to expressing an opinion; Hopkins is a great one for cheering when he can, that being an expression of his desired relationship, whether with the world or with God. He was an unhappy and I should guess rather inept performer in his classroom in Dublin, but he is a full-blooded teacher of elation in his poems' schoolroom.

Dante makes no bones about the fact that, in the *Divine Comedy* at least, he is out, might and main, to teach. His project is the more telling in that the figure cut by his namesake in that work often makes his way, even when well tutored, via blunder and ricochet. This epic, beyond the book of Exodus and beyond Homer's *Odyssey*, is the "big trip" book of Western culture, and its force is fed partly by the gradual transformation of the traveler. I saw once a notice in the Butterfly House in Perth Zoo, in Western Australia, which said, "Quiet please: metamorphosis is taking place." This might have been an injunction from Dante as his poem proceeded. Taken seriously, it could mark something of a change in the reader as well.

Of course in a poem like "Wheat," a double metamorphosis is taking place. There is Linnell's construal of his harvest scene—wonderfully like and unlike Brueghel's rendering of the same spectacle—and there is the poem's construal of Linnell, with Hopkins as attendant magus and eventually with Dante as confirmer, at least so I hope. Metamorphosis is work, sometimes hard work, and so is teaching, at least when it aspires to a metamorphic pitch. It too has its "largesse and its own restraint"; and to get the two into an appropriate concert is, at least in my experience, a demanding enough affair. Elementary common sense reminds me that the "work" of teaching or of making poems is leisure itself compared with the task of literal reaping, but so it goes with life and art.

The fourth stanza of "Wheat" is originally a piece of Hopkins's prose, which I have docked of a word for the rhythm's sake. I mention this because it is to me a reminder of language's versatility, in the right hands. Hopkins knew, nobody better, that poetry demands its own distinctive cast or cachet; his work would not have encountered so much misgiving had he not been almost obsessed by that fact. At the same time, it is as if he finds in the linguistic as such a potency well beyond that commonly attributed to it. He honors workaday pursuits (the smith, the soldier), and as far as he can he celebrates them; but it would be hard to convince him that there is such a thing as purely workaday language. In his heart of hearts he believes that there is a sleeping glory within it.

All art is alchemy, playing back and forth between likes and unlikes. And so is teaching, riddled though it be with ineptitudes and gaucheries, the teacher's as well as the students'. And most of all, God knows, so it does go with the daily haunting and the daily hunting, grace having a strangeness beyond description but a nearness beyond denying. A long time ago I was fascinated by a description of the traditional Irish bards' seven to eleven years' training in their art. When it worked, the standard mode of composition was for them to lie down, cloak over head, in beehive stone huts and compose additions to the classic repertoire. As I said in a poem, "It all came out of the dark and the cold."[20]

A lot of the best things, for a priest or a poet or a teacher, can be expected to come out of the dark and the cold. And by the same token, the first sound in my life that I distinctly remember was that of crows calling harshly over wheat fields in the height of a Western Australian summer. Their cry is inscribed deeply in me, and so is the silence that followed it. Perhaps, in the affairs of the spirit, the role of the sounds is to give a shape to the silences.

Notes

1. Henry James, *The Portrait of a Lady* (Middlesex, England: Penguin, 1963), xviii.

2. Vincent Buckley, *Golden Builders and Other Poems* (Melbourne, Australia: Angus and Robertson, 1976), 16.

3. Peter Steele, "Madonna and Child," in *White Knight with Beebox: New and Selected Poems* (Elwood, Australia: John Leonard Press, 2008), 66.

4. George Herbert, "Prayer," in *Herbert: Poems Selected by W. H. Auden* (New York: Viking Penguin, 1973), 54.

5. Marianne Moore, *Complete Poems* (New York: Macmillan/Penguin, 1967), vii.

6. Peter Steele, "Love and Death at Papa Gino's," in *White Knight*, 42.

7. Shakespeare, *A Midsummer Night's Dream*, 5.2.17, in *Complete Works*, ed. Stanley Wells and Gary Taylor (Oxford: Clarendon Press, 1988).

8. John Donne, "Annunciation," in Donne, *The Complete Poetry and Selected Prose*, ed. Charles M. Coffin (New York: Random House, 1952), 231.

9. W. H. Auden, "Whitsunday in Kirchstetten," in *Collected Poems*, ed. Edward Mendelson (London: Faber and Faber, 1976), 559.

10. Peter Steele, "Full Moon, Good Friday," in *White Knight*, 93.

11. Shakespeare, *A Midsummer Night's Dream*, 2.2.60.

12. Michael Frayn, *Constructions* (London: Wildwood House, 1974), sect. 180.

13. Peter Steele, "Wheat," in *White Knight*, 124.

14. Robert Burton, *The Anatomy of Melancholy*, pt. 3, sect. I, mem. I, subs. I, quoted in *Geoffrey Madan's Notebooks: A Selection*, ed. J. A. Gere and John Sparrow (Oxford: Oxford University Press, 1981), 7.

15. *Geoffrey Madan's Notebooks*, 66.

16. Randall Jarrell, *Pictures from an Institution* (New York: Knopf, 1955), 230.

17. Samuel Johnson, *Preface to Shakespeare*, in *Rasselas, Poems, and Selected Prose*, ed. Bertrand H. Bronson (New York: Holt Rinehart and Winston, 1958), 262.

18. Gerard Manley Hopkins, "Hurrahing in Harvest," in *Gerard Manley Hopkins*, ed. Catherine Phillips (Oxford: Oxford University Press, 1986), 134.

19. This phrase comes from Claude Lévi-Strauss, *The Raw and the Cooked* (Chicago: University of Chicago Press, 1983).

20. Peter Steele, *Word from Lilliput: Poems* (Melbourne, Australia: Hawthorn Press, 1973), 43.

CHAPTER 12

Attaining Harmony with the Earth

Cristina Vanin

I teach at St. Jerome's University, a small Catholic liberal arts university in southwestern Ontario. When I returned to work after an eight-month parental leave following the adoption of our two daughters from Ecuador, I indicated to close friends that on the day that I first met Sofia and Daniela, I felt as if I had been dropped off a very, very high cliff—from the life of work and relationship that I had known and had been living for a long time, into the incredible life of parenting two little girls in another country and culture, in another language, in an apartment in the capital city, Quito. It was exciting and overwhelming. For the next two months in Ecuador and then eight more months in Canada, my husband and I totally focused on the girls: helping them navigate a new country, culture, and language; learning to be parents; becoming a family; setting up routines and structures for survival; and starting school, to name just a small fraction of what awaited us.

The time came to decide when I would return to work. I realized that I was ready to go, ready to integrate my new life as a mother with my life as a teacher and academic. It seemed so long since I had written an article or essay, so long since I had read articles or books that stimulated my intellectual desire, that I was excited by the invitation and opportunity to write this chapter.

A number of years ago Jim Profit, director of the Ignatian Jesuit Centre of Guelph, Ontario, asked me to join an advisory group that he was setting up to help undertake the work of the Loyola Retreat House Ecology Project. I was delighted. The advisory group developed into a small Ignatian community made up of quite a diverse group of people (spiritual directors, arborist, addiction counselor, naturopathic doctor), all of whom are committed to attending to issues regarding ecology, spirituality, and justice. Over the years we have learned together, prayed together, and worked together on ecology retreats, parish missions, workshops, and the writing of a book.

The advisory group runs eight-day Ignatian ecology retreats every two years. They take place at the Loyola House. The retreat, which we call Mysticism of the Earth, begins on the morning of the first full day with a talk that is focused on the grace "to have a deep confidence in God's love for the universe, the community of life of which I am an integral part; to know that we are loved creatures in the same way that each and every other living and non-living being in this universe is deeply loved and held by God."[1] (as said on the prayer sheet provided to the retreatants). When I deliver that talk, I begin with "Canticle of Brother Sun, Sister Moon," a piece of music from the *Missa Gaia*, a Mass of the Earth composed by Paul Winter. This music, based on the text of Saint Francis of Assisi, invites the listener to "ask all the beasts and they shall teach you. . . . Ask all the trees and they shall teach you." What might beasts, trees, star, river, grain of sand, mountain, ocean, flower have to teach us?

Since we need to learn that we are intimately related to every other being—living and nonliving; present, past, or future—that is part of our universe, we need to ask the other members of creation for insight and understanding because we have forgotten who we are. To help retreatants contemplate their participation in the community of life, I offer a slide presentation of photos and images and read a text that integrates the insights of the biblical stories of creation with our contemporary scientific understanding of the evolution of the universe. This unique telling of the unfolding of the universe encourages us to experience and understand that the story of the universe is also our own story: that as a human being I truly am part of an amazing, sacred, and God-given universe story.

Day two of the retreat is based on the first week of the Spiritual Exercises of Saint Ignatius of Loyola. It therefore focuses on our participation in ecological sin, with the awareness that, as always, we are loved sinners. Days three and four reflect the second week of the Spiritual Exercises, when the focus shifts to the presence of God within creation. On day five we move into the third week of the Exercises and enter into the passion and suffering of the Earth, experiencing and understanding that God is intimately present in that suffering.

Day six provides us with the opportunity to reflect and pray on the resurrection, on the experience of hope in the face of destruction. On day six we ask for the following grace: "to have a growing and intense sorrow and tears for my contribution to the passion of the Earth, the passion of Jesus; for a deep-felt knowledge and awareness of my role and complicity in the crisis of the Earth; tears and deep grief because of the great affliction that Christ endures for me." I invite retreatants, through photographs of a series of stained glass windows depicting the universe story, to reflect on the fact that we have found ourselves in a period of history wherein humans are devastating the health of the Earth. Given the grace of the day, we strive to hear the cries of the Earth as it suffers because of our actions.

Day seven introduces retreatants to ecological aspects of the *contemplatio* of the Spiritual Exercises. As Ignatius suggests, we each pray for "a deep-felt knowledge of the great gifts I have received that, filled with such gratitude, I may be able to respond with total love and service." On the last day of the retreat we help retreatants to appropriate the gifts and the insights that they have received during the retreat and to focus on the actions they will undertake as they leave the retreat.

Throughout the retreat I present insights that I have learned from Thomas Berry—Passionist priest, cultural historian, and longstanding writer on ecological issues—about what is needed today in our relationship as humans with the natural world. Berry's invitation and challenge for me to think about who I am as a human being, how my human life is related to the life of the rest of creation, what might be the meaning and purpose of all of life, and how I should live in the world have struck a chord with me since I was first introduced to him more than twenty-five years ago.

Entering into the Thought of Thomas Berry

While I was working on a master of divinity at the University of St. Michael's College in Toronto, Ontario, I took a course titled "Personal Integration." In this course we reflected on all that we were studying, reading, and thinking about, and we began to integrate and appropriate those insights into our own understanding. Interestingly the writings of Bernard Lonergan and Thomas Berry were both part of that course; both thinkers are significant in my own development as a theologian. Yet at that time it was the writing of Thomas Berry that seemed to pull together different pieces of my life. And I wanted to enter into that thought as deeply and fully as I could. The opportunity arose when I spent five months at the Holy Cross Centre for Ecology and Spirituality learning about adult retreat work, as part of the pastoral training for my degree.

I became a longstanding associate of Holy Cross Centre after those five months. Holy Cross was a retreat center run by the Passionist community of Canada, situated on the shores of Lake Erie, near the town of Port Burwell, Ontario. Passionist spirituality is focused on the way of the cross and the Passion of Jesus, the suffering that Jesus underwent on the way to his death.[2] In Catholic churches one finds fourteen Stations of the Cross, each depicting a significant moment in the story of Jesus's Passion. The Stations of the Cross form a well-developed prayer, probably most often used during the season of Lent, when Christians prepare to celebrate the central feast of the Christian tradition, Easter. The Stations of the Cross are also often an integral part of Good Friday prayer.

In the 1970s the Passionist community began to integrate Passionist spirituality with the story of the universe presented by the natural sciences. One of the ways in which the center incorporated this new, deeper, and broader spirituality was through building a pilgrimage walk on the property called "Stations of the Cosmic Earth."[3] This pilgrimage takes one into the story of the universe: both the joys and beauty of its ongoing emergence, and the increasing suffering of the Earth. Berry describes the importance of such experiences: "We need to establish rituals for celebrating these transformation moments that have enabled the universe and the planet Earth to develop over these past many years. . . . To celebrate these occasions would renew our sense of the sacred character of the universe and planet Earth."[4]

For many years I heard both Berry and the staff at Holy Cross talk about the Passion of Christ as the passion of the Earth. Through many celebrations of the Easter Triduum at Holy Cross, I came to appreciate that the way of the cross means not only taking the steps with Jesus on his journey to the cross more than two thousand years ago, but also walking with Jesus as he suffers with and in the Earth, with all members of the community of life who are suffering today because of the sin of ecological devastation. At the entrance to the stations Holy Cross placed a very large cross, lying down. Since we usually see crosses standing in an upright position, this cross unsettles us and immediately invites us to shift perspective, to see the Earth differently. We are invited to enter the story of the Earth, of the Earth's way of the cross.

In one of his last books, *The Great Work: Our Way into the Future*, Berry talks about the great works that peoples have undertaken throughout human history. By "great work" Berry means significant movements in history when human beings took the time to articulate their sense of what it means to be human and how humanity fits into the larger reality of the planet and the universe. Such occasions help humanity give shape and meaning to life. One example Berry provides is the great work undertaken by the classical Greek world with regard to our understanding of the human mind, a work that made possible the development of the Western humanist tradition.[5]

In line with the great works of past human communities, Berry suggests that "the Great Work now, as we move into a new millennium, is to carry out the transition from a period of human devastation of the Earth to a period when humans would be present to the planet in a mutually beneficial manner."[6] In other words this is another moment in the evolution of the planet when human beings need to articulate a new and more adequate understanding of our relationship with this planet.

Stating that there is a great work to be done in our own time suggests that something is wrong with the current relationship between humanity and the natural world, such that once again we need to give shape and meaning to our human life by relating who we are to the story of the universe. Berry writes, "Our sense of who we are and what our role is must begin where the universe begins. Not only does our physical shaping and our spiritual perception begin with the origin of the universe, so too does the formation of every being in the universe."[7] In Berry's thinking, we should consider this as a moment of grace, that is, another privileged moment when great transformations can occur. This "cosmological moment of grace" points to the fact that, for the first time, human beings have a new experience and understanding of the deepest mysteries of the universe and the planet.[8] The universe and planet that we have understood primarily in terms of the cycles of seasons is now known also as an emerging, evolving universe that continues to proceed through a sequence of irreversible changes. This moment is also, however, a historical and religious moment of grace. For Berry this means that we need to understand the scientific story of the universe as a sacred story, one providing us with a cosmology that can help us to truly know our place in the emerging and evolving universe. It can help us to know where we came from and what our responsibility is.

How did Berry develop this understanding and conviction about the universe and the planet Earth? What influences directed the evolution of his thinking?

Thomas Berry's Personal History

In *The Great Work*, Berry talks about his experience of growing up in North Carolina in the early part of the twentieth century and the impact on the orientation of his life.[9] He recalls an experience from when he was eleven years old, a time when his family moved to the edge of town, where their new house was being built. The house was situated on an incline that led to a little creek; across the creek was a meadow.

> It was an early afternoon in late May when I first wandered down the incline, crossed the creek, and looked out over the scene. The field was covered with white lilies rising above the thick grass. A magic moment, this experience gave to my life something that seems to explain my thinking at a more profound level than almost any other experience I can remember. . . . It was not something conscious that happened just then. . . . As the years pass this moment returns to me, and whenever I think about my basic life attitude and the whole trend of my mind and the causes to which I have given my efforts, I seem to come back to this moment and the impact it has had on my feeling for what is real and worthwhile in life. This early experience, it seems, has become normative for me throughout the entire range of my thinking. Whatever preserves and enhances this meadow in the natural cycles of its transformation is good; whatever opposes this meadow or negates it is not good. My life orientation is that simple. It is also that pervasive. It applies in economics and political orientation as well as in education and religion.[10]

A concern that is the focus of so much of Berry's writing is that human beings no longer have these kinds of experiences that help them to know the magnificence of life as a celebration; consequently, we lack an attitude of gratitude as our response toward the gift of life. Human beings have arrived at a point of being so distant, so disengaged, from relationship with the Earth. Such distance needs to be overcome with profound presence. Berry writes, "Our world of human meaning is no longer coordinated with the meaning of our surroundings. We have disengaged from that profound interaction with our environment that is inherent in our nature. Our children no longer learn how to read the great Book of Nature from their own direct experience or how to interact creatively with the seasonal transformations of the planet. They seldom learn where their water comes from or where it goes."[11]

In the appendix to his book *Befriending the Earth: A Theology of Reconciliation between Humans and the Earth*, Berry again reflects on his life story, especially the factors and experiences that led to his engagement with ecological concerns. He begins this account by indicating that as a young child he was always on the margins, keeping a certain distance from what was officially happening. He talks about being independent and about being a brooder, a ponderer. He tells the story that, when the time came to decide where he was going to go as a young adult, he saw two places he could go to think about things: the army and the monastery. He chose the monastery.

> I began to study the Asian world, learned the Chinese language, and learned Sanskrit. I studied history and philosophy to find out and to test out how people found meaning. I wanted to go back through the whole human tradition and test the whole process, because it was obvious from the beginning, going into religious life, that the process was not working. Just like now, our modern world is not working. Christianity, in this sense, is not working. Particularly, there is the inability of the Christian world to respond in any effective way to the destruction of the planet. . . . There is this terrible lack of concern for biocide or geocide. We have no moral principles to deal with them. . . . Somehow, when I was quite young, I saw the beginning of biocide and geocide.[12]

Thomas Berry's Intellectual History

In order to understand the context for the emergence of Berry's central ideas about the Earth, it is important to see the breadth and depth of his intellectual life as a historian first of human cultures and then of the Earth. This understanding begins with his study of Eastern traditions.

Study of Eastern Traditions

In 1948 Berry set out for China, intending to study language and Chinese philosophy in Beijing. Because of Mao Tse-tung's communist victory, Berry had to return to the United States in 1949. But during that time in China, Berry met and worked with William Theodore de Bary, a premier scholar in Asian studies. Together they founded the Asian thought and religion seminar at Columbia University. Over fifty years of friendship, de Bary and Berry collaborated on projects regarding Asian thought. Berry himself later taught

Asian religions at Seton Hall University (1956–61) and at St. John's University (1961–65). He moved to Fordham University, where he taught from 1966 until 1979 and developed a graduate program in the history of religions. During these years Berry published two books, *Buddhism* and *Religions of India*.[13]

Berry's approach to these religions is to discuss their history but also to talk about their spiritual dynamics and their significance for contemporary society. In a booklet published in 1968 titled *Five Oriental Philosophies*, Berry presents the phenomenological core and historical development of Hinduism, Buddhism, Confucianism, Taoism, and Zen Buddhism, and he speaks to the value of multiculturalism: "Diversity is no longer something that we tolerate. It is something that we esteem as a necessary condition for a livable universe, as the source of Earth's highest perfection. . . . To demand an undifferentiated unity would bring human thought and history itself to an end. The splendor of our multicultural world would be destroyed."[14]

Berry spent several decades studying Western and Asian intellectual history before developing his own comprehensive vision of the universe story. Indeed, at the Riverdale Center for Religious Research, which he founded in New York City, he collected an immense library of more than ten thousand books: from the Latin texts of the Church fathers, to the Sanskrit texts of Hinduism and Buddhism, to the Chinese classics of Confucianism and Taoism. From all of this study, as Mary Evelyn Tucker says, "[Berry] has been able to discern what spiritual resources we need for creating a multicultural perspective within the Earth community. . . . For Berry, human diversity and biological diversity are of a continuous piece."[15]

Tucker argues that Confucianism has been most significant in Berry's thinking because "it emphasizes the cosmological dynamics of the universe, in which heaven, Earth, and humans form an interconnected triad."[16] Berry speaks of the Chinese regard for the human as the "understanding heart" (*hsin*) of the universe. He appreciates Confucianism's positive view of human nature, a fundamentally good nature that can be improved through education. Confucian cosmological concerns are evident in Berry's own cosmology, as he explains: "According to Confucian teaching, a mutual attraction of things for each other functions at all levels of reality as the interior binding force of the cosmic, social, and personal life. More than most traditions, Confucianism saw the interplay of cosmic forces as a single set of intercommunicating and mutually compenetrating realities."[17]

Influence of Giambattista Vico

Before he went to China, Berry had studied Western intellectual history as a doctoral student at the Catholic University of America, studies that he continued upon his return to the United States in 1949. His 1951 doctoral thesis dealt with Giambattista Vico's philosophy of history, looking especially at

Vico's *Principi di Scienza Nuova d'intorno alla Comune Natura delle Nazioni* (New science of the nature of the nations), first published in 1725. Vico wanted to develop a science for the study of human institutions that was comparable to the scientific study of nature. He also wanted to show divine providence at work in both sacred and profane history. Vico was convinced that pattern and order were operating in history and that humans could discern them.

In *Principi di Scienza Nuova* Vico identifies three stages in human history: the age of the gods, the age of the heroes, and the age of humans. Each age has had its own customs, laws, languages, arts, economies, and cultures. In each Vico suggests that a different human faculty is the focus: sensation, imagination, and then intellect, respectively. Vico argues that, along with rationalization, natural or poetic wisdom and intuition have also been important for the development of an age. He sees history moving through periods of disintegration and dissolution, periods of the "barbarism of reflection," as Tucker says. As we move through such periods, she says, new periods with a "creative barbarism of sense" can emerge.[18]

Tucker states that Vico was seminal for Berry in various ways. First, Berry provides his own sweeping periodization of history, four major ages that he names the tribal-shamanic, the traditional civilizational, the scientific-technological, and the ecological or Ecozoic. In this last period there is a new, mutually enhancing understanding of the relationship between humans and the Earth. But this period is not yet fully upon us. Berry refers to the present time as characterized by a "severe cultural pathology" that supports our blind but sophisticated assault on the Earth—this is similar to Vico's idea of historical periods of disintegration.[19]

Influence of Pierre Teilhard de Chardin

From Pierre Teilhard de Chardin Berry draws his appreciation for time as developmental. This understanding relates to Berry's persistent statement that we now know a universe or cosmos that is unfolding, that is cosmogenetic rather than static. This understanding must be integrated into all of our cultural and religious traditions. Teilhard suggests that evolution changes our understanding of ourselves within the universe: "For our age to have become conscious of evolution means something very different from and much more than having discovered one further fact. . . . It means (as happens with a child when he acquires the sense of perspective) that we have become alive to a new dimension. The idea of evolution is not, as sometimes said, a mere hypothesis, but a condition of all experience."[20]

Berry also draws from Teilhard the idea that the universe has both a psychic and a physical character. The implication is that if there is human consciousness, and if humans have evolved from the Earth, then some kind of consciousness has been present in the process of evolution from the beginning.

Matter is not dead or inert; it is a numinous reality, a reality with both physical and spiritual dimensions. Consciousness is intrinsic to life-forms and links life-forms to each other. There are various forms of consciousness; in the human, consciousness is reflective.

From Teilhard, Berry acquired the idea that evolution moves from simpler to more complex organisms. With increasing complexity comes increased consciousness. Humans have a special role in the evolutionary process as a highly complex species with the capacity for reflection.

Because of Teilhard, Berry can talk about the evolution of the universe as the most comprehensive context for understanding who human beings are in relation to other forms of life. Berry suggests that we are to think of ourselves as a species among other species. Furthermore, because of our capacity for reflection, we have a particular responsibility for the way in which the evolutionary process moves forward, especially on this planet.

Berry does critique Teilhard's optimistic view of progress and his lack of concern for the ways in which industrialization devastates ecosystems. He suggests that Teilhard inherited the view that human beings could control the natural world, especially through science and technology, without considering the possible negative consequences of that effort to control.

Appreciation of Indigenous Traditions

Berry also has a deep appreciation for indigenous religious traditions. He talks about the ways in which native traditions have a particular feeling for the sacredness of land, seasons, animals, birds, fish, and so on. He knows that their respect for creation stems from their honoring of the Creator and from their reverence for life as a gift. Native traditions also speak about the dependency of humans on nature for their own lives.

For Berry it is not a matter of romanticizing Eastern and indigenous traditions. He clearly states that people in all traditions have abused the Earth. But he insists that we can learn from these traditions as we try to move toward a viable future for all.

The Emergence of the "New Story"

From these early experiences of childhood; through his experiences in the time of worldwide war, depression, recovery, and growth; and finally through his education, Thomas Berry's ideas on a "New Story" begin to emerge in the early 1970s.[21] This brooding and pondering historian of culture was thinking deeply about the magnitude of the social, political, and economic problems humankind was facing. It is this magnitude that makes our present time so unique and so devastating for the planet. He began to articulate the need for a new human orientation because he was so concerned about the destructive path we were traveling, destructive to the Earth and to each other. This need for a new story or a new orientation was not an abstract idea; it was rooted deeply in Berry's recognition of the need to respond adequately to the immense suffering of human beings and nonhuman life. He saw human beings as thinking of themselves—consciously or not—as being deeply alienated from the Earth. This alienation, along with the West's commitment to increased industrialization and commercialization, has gradually spread across the planet.

In the spirit of Vico's understanding that historical development requires not just reason but poetic wisdom, Berry's development of the New Story, a new story of the Earth, was intended to remedy the disillusionment, despair, and alienation he saw in the world. His essay *The New Story: Comments on the Origin, Identification, and Transmission of Values* was first published in 1978 to inaugurate the Teilhard Studies series.[22] Berry's hope was that the New Story would provide human beings with a new orientation and perspective that can be the basis for appropriate moral action. Through it Berry is seeking to provide a comprehensive basis to nurture a new intimate relationship between humans and the Earth. As a functional cosmology this story can, for our time, help us to understand how things came to be as they are, where we are now, our human role in the story, and how our future can be meaningful.

The sense of developmental time is significant in the New Story. Through the Copernican revolution, the entire sense of our spatial orientation in the universe was changed. Then the Darwinian revolution altered our sense of time. We have arrived at a point in human history when we can no longer disregard the irreversible developmental sequence of time.

Furthermore, as we come to recognize this reality of developmental time, we also realize that humans are in communion with the Earth. Berry says: "The human emerges not only as an earthling, but also as a worldling. We bear the universe in our beings as the universe bears us in its being. The two have a total presence to each other and to that deeper mystery out of which both the universe and ourselves have emerged."[23] This idea of the subjective presence of things to one another is drawn from Teilhard de Chardin, who writes about the interior attraction of things: "In the Divine Milieu all the elements of the universe touch each other by that which is most inward and ultimate in them."[24] To communicate values within this new understanding of the story of the Earth, Berry identifies three fundamental principles of the universe process: (1) differentiation, variety, or distinctiveness; (2) subjectivity, or the interior numinous component; and (3) communion, or the ability to relate to all beings. For Berry these principles can function as the basis for a comprehensive social and ecological ethics, an ethics that thinks of the human as intimately related to the larger Earth community. Without this comprehensive perspective, neither humans nor the Earth as we know it will survive.

The Influence of a Cultural Historian on a Theologian

When I teach, write, or give presentations on ecological issues, it is often in relationship to the Catholic Church's teachings on justice. Presently a good number of theologians approach ecological issues from the context of Catholic social teaching and argue that the principles of that teaching need to be extended to include the Earth.[25] The Canadian Conference of Catholic Bishops, in two pastoral letters (2003 and 2008), state, "The cry of the earth and the cry of the poor are one." Or again: "The preferential option for the poor can be extended to include a preferential option for the earth, made poorer by human abuse."[26] The bishops quote John Paul II's 2001 statement that "the ecological crisis is a moral issue" and is "the responsibility of everyone": "Care for the environment is not an option. In the Christian perspective, it is an integral part of our personal life and of life in society. Not to care for the environment is to ignore the Creator's plan for all of creation and results in an alienation of the human person."[27] Questions arise: How are we to understand this connection between human and ecological justice, and the bishops' imperative to respond? Why should we care about the health and well-being of the planet Earth? Is our care for the planet the same as our care for humans? How do we compare the value of human beings to the value of a spotted owl or a codfish or a polar bear? Is it possible to answer such a question? Is this the only way to pose this question about the relationship between human beings and other beings? Does the question itself reflect a problem?

I recently heard part of a news piece on CBC radio about the probable death of a species of ducks in New Zealand because the last female in captivity had died of old age, leaving only two males alive. The interviewer asked the person responsible for the ducks about the feelings associated with this loss, suggesting that he must be feeling some sadness. Indeed he was. Yet is sadness all that we should feel?

Berry invites me to ask myself: Why am I, why are we, not profoundly disturbed by what we are doing to this planet—disturbed enough to respond as adequately and quickly as possible to the devastation? Why do we not respond to the cries of the Earth in the same way in which we would spontaneously respond if we suddenly heard the cries of a child? Should we not mourn the death of a species with the intensity and sorrow with which we would mourn the death of our child? Does God not mourn the death of a duck, the death of a species, in the same way, to the same degree, in which we readily feel that God must mourn the loss of one of God's human children?

Again I find myself facing a question that Berry continually asks: What is it about the way in which we understand ourselves that makes us wreak such havoc on the planet without seeming to be very affected by the consequences of our actions? I am challenged to see that there are problems with the way in which I understand myself, and the way in which I understand the nature, purpose, and responsibility of the human species. I am challenged to continue to shift my understanding of myself as a human being. Over many years I have slowly awakened to understanding myself as part of an amazing universe story.

I regard this as a profound shift because it is not simply a matter of deepening my appreciation for nature, especially its beauty. This appreciation is something that I have always had. I was raised in a family that grew much of our own food in our backyard. My Italian immigrant parents brought with them their love of growing, making, and preserving their own food. I have many fond memories of helping my father till the garden around lettuce, corn, herbs, radishes, tomatoes, and zucchini; taking food scraps to the back corner of the garden, where we had our low-tech compost pile; sneaking down to the basement to watch my father make various salamis and sausages; and helping my mother clean and preserve fruit, fish, and vegetables. To this day I wait in eager anticipation for spring and the chance, once again, to dig my hands into my back vegetable garden and front flower garden. I know this to be a crucial way in which my spiritual life is fed.

The shift in understanding the nature and role of human beings requires us to do more than appreciate nature if, in the meantime, we still think and understand ourselves as quite distinct from it, even quite separate from it. Instead Berry talks about entering deeply into the dynamics of creation and the story of the universe. It is about beginning to know that this story is also my own story. It is about learning that each moment of the story is a graced moment. I think about my own struggles in shifting from appreciating nature as something "out there"—something I look at, camp in, take photographs of, enjoy—to coming to understand that I am *in* this Earth community, that I live *with* this Earth, not simply *on* it.

I remember a moment from writing my doctoral dissertation. I realized why it was that I had to write a dissertation on Thomas Berry's ideas about the nature of the universe. It was because of my own sense of alienation from the universe, from this phenomenal thirteen-billion-year reality. It was about coming to know myself as welcomed by and into this universe. It was about learning that I belong, intimately and deeply, with this universe. This invitation to conversion continues to be, for me, a matter of really living what I know, that is, living as though I am with the universe, that I am part of its emerging story. This living is so difficult for me or any of us to do. Berry writes: "Everyone lives in a universe; but seldom do we have any real sense of living in a world of sunshine by day and under the stars at night. Seldom do we listen to the wind or feel the refreshing rain except as inconveniences to escape from as quickly as possible."[28]

As indicated above, Berry suggests that the universe is characterized by three basic principles, each of which our present human way of living on the

Earth is violating. The first principle is differentiation, regarded as the basic direction of the evolutionary process. Yet our modern world is much more inclined toward the development of monocultures. For example, industries push for standardization, a process of multiplying the production of things that ensures invariance. But this push means we are losing diversity, such as diversity in our food and even in our human cultures. Berry's second principle of the universe is subjectivity. Not only is each individual being different from every other being in the universe, as the first principle points out, but each individual being also has its own unique spontaneities, what Berry calls "the sacred depth of the individual." "Each being in its subjective depths carries that numinous mystery whence the universe emerges into being."[29] Berry's third principle is communion. This speaks to the fact that there is a unity to the universe, a way in which the presence of each individual is felt throughout the whole of the universe. For Berry this capacity for bonding makes it possible for such a vast variety of beings to come into existence and exist in unity.

Unfortunately, at least since the rise of modern science, we have begun to think of the universe "as a collection of objects rather than a communion of subjects"—probably one of Berry's best-known phrases.[30] The world has become an "it" that we can use as we see fit, rather than something we can relate to as a "thou." We no longer truly relate to and hear the voices of the rivers, the mountains, the seas. We do not regard the trees and meadows as intimate ways in which the Spirit of God is present to us.

We are not conscious of the cost to our souls, to our sense of ourselves, of being deprived of an intimate relationship with the universe. Berry writes frequently about the deep alienation that human beings live in relation to the universe; he even describes it as a kind of autism or a deep cultural pathology. We live in the world and yet are so separate from it that we do not even recognize how alienated we truly are. For many of us, contact with the natural world is limited to photographs and television programs. Berry often reminds people of Saint Augustine's remark that a picture of food cannot nourish us. The irony is that we have more knowledge of the universe than any people has ever had, but it is not the type of knowledge that leads us to have an intimate presence to other creatures, one that makes it possible to live in a world that we regard as truly meaningful in itself.

Although such intimacy is still experienced by some, it is no longer as extensive as it once was. We need only think about the culture of consumerism in which each of us lives, a culture that has shifted ancient holy days into holiday shopping days. Early Christian liturgies corresponded to the movements of the sun. Feasts were celebrated in relationship to the seasons so that, for example, it is no accident that in the northern hemisphere we celebrate the feast of Christmas around the time of the winter solstice or the feast of Easter in the heart of spring. But now our social order is governed not by the rhythms of the natural world, but by the rhythms of commerce, of industry, of consumption.

The industrial civilization that has emerged over the last few centuries has developed the power to devastate the Earth in profound ways. We have the capacity to affect the Earth's geological structure, its chemical constitution, the health and well-being of all of its living forms. We are losing more than twenty-five billion tons of topsoil each year and do not really know what the consequences will be for our future food supply. Some of the most abundant species of marine life on the planet have become extinct because of overexploitation by factory fishing vessels and the use of extremely large drift nets. We are using our rivers for waste disposal. We are polluting our atmosphere and changing our climate patterns with the burning of fossil fuels. By the end of the twentieth century we had cut down over 95 percent of the primordial forests in North America. The Canadian Conference of Catholic Bishops asks,

> How many of us remember a childhood spent playing under the sun, a beach we were once able to swim at, a river we were once able to drink from—but no more! The closing of the once overwhelmingly bountiful cod fishery in Quebec, Newfoundland and Labrador is a particularly painful example of this [ecological] crisis. Indeed, every region has been affected in some negative manner. Environmental health concerns are frequent, arising from the Sydney Tar Ponds in Nova Scotia to urban smog alerts in Toronto or Montreal, from contaminated mine sites in northern Saskatchewan and the Northwest Territories to the safety of food that every Canadian family will eat.[31]

The deepest cause of this kind and level of devastation is a certain consciousness that has developed in human beings. It is a consciousness that has established, Berry says, "a radical discontinuity between the human and other ways of being."[32] It is a consciousness that has given all rights to humans. It is a consciousness that regards other beings as having reality and value only when used by us. When this kind of consciousness is operating, we find it very easy to exploit what we regard as completely other from us. We learn to regard and treat certain human beings, like the poor, people of color, people with AIDS, people with disabilities, the elderly, and so on, as other, even less than us. We do the same with most other beings, and with the planet itself. The Canadian bishops write: "Since overconsumption and waste have become a way of life, conversion implies that we free ourselves collectively from our obsession to possess and consume. . . . Our humanity will gain in the process. It will then be easier for us to look at nature with new eyes. Instead of considering it primarily as a resource to be exploited, we will be more inclined to admire its beauty and grandeur. . . . To convert is also to regain a sense of limit. It means adjusting our lifestyle to available planetary resources."[33]

The Magnitude of the Situation

Berry emphasizes that what is taking place on the planet is not just another historical or cultural change, similar to such changes in the past.[34] It is an unparalleled change because the fundamental systems of life itself are threatened. We are seeing, experiencing, and hopefully understanding that we are extinguishing the amazing developments that have taken place over the past sixty-five million years.

The reality of this order of magnitude is profoundly changing all of our human ways of being: political, economic, social, religious. For more than twenty-five years, Berry did not see any of the world's religions, including Christianity, adequately responding to what was happening to the planet: "The traditional religions in themselves and out of their existing resources cannot deal with the problems that we have to deal with, but we cannot deal with these problems without the traditions."[35] Berry continually says that if we fail to take responsibility for the Earth, we fail in our responsibility to the divine and to other human beings. The more we damage the planet, the more our sense of the divine is degraded.[36] Here as elsewhere Berry reminds us that the loss of species, the loss of an intimate relationship with the community of life, is a profound revelatory loss and a soul loss; it deeply affects our sense of ourselves.

A New Revelatory Experience

A new revelatory experience is available to us as human beings through the new understanding of the universe as time development, as cosmogenesis.[37] For Berry this experience of the divine "has given us a new sense of the universe, a new sense of the planet earth, a new sense of life, of the human, even a new sense of being Christian. . . . The story has its imprint everywhere, and that is why it is so important to know the story. If you do not know the story, in a certain sense you do not know yourself; you do not know anything."[38]

The new understanding of the universe is a significant way in which the divine is being revealed to us today. This is why Berry regards the story of the universe as a sacred story. It is also our primary story, our primary community, our primary religious reality—primary not in the sense of first in the order of time, nor in the sense of first in importance or value. For Berry, rather, the universe is our primary sacred reality in the sense of most basic, most fundamental, that which is meant to first awaken us to the divine.

Relationship of Origin

Everything that exists in the universe is genetically related to everything else. Community is at the heart of the nature of existence, Berry says: "There is literally one family, one bonding, in the universe, because everything is descended from the same source. . . . On the planet earth . . . we are literally born as a community; the trees, the birds, and all living creatures are bonded together in a single community of life."[39] This assertion is related to Berry's insistence that we need to think of the universe as a community of subjects rather than a collection of objects. Indigenous peoples, Berry argues, can help us to learn to hear anew the voices of the trees, birds, polar bears, fish, mountains, rivers, children. Truly intimate relationship with the natural world overcomes our autism, our experience of being so locked up in ourselves as humans that we cannot be present to other beings.

Berry speaks of how remarkable it is that Christianity goes beyond the notion of the divine as pure simplicity, a notion common to other religions, to speak of the inner life of the divine as community. He offers the three-fold model of differentiation, inner articulation, and communion as a way to talk about the Trinity in the context of our present understanding of the universe.

Berry honors the theological work of Teilhard de Chardin, who, he suggests, "showed that the Christian story was identical to the universe story and that if we could only understand it in this light, then theological studies would become more integral. . . . From now on, there is going to be, in my estimation, no effective human relationship with the divine that is not integral with this story of the universe that we know at the present time."[40] Along with describing the universe as having a psychic-spiritual dimension and identifying the human story with the universe story, Teilhard talks about the importance of moving from overconcern for the process of redemption to greater emphasis on the process of creation, of appreciating "the self-organizing dimension of the universe."[41]

To talk about the phenomenal order, as Berry puts it, does not eliminate discussion of the numinous context, the question of the origin of this capacity for self-organization, of how it functions. We can talk about the universe in the context of the divine, but God does not run the universe as if it were a puppet show. The universe is its own reality, functioning from within its own spontaneity. "The divine enables the universe to function in this remarkable way. There is a capacity of self-articulation inherent in the universe, and the more we know about that, the more clear it is that we will gain a totally different sense of the universe than we had previously, and a different sense of how the divine functions in relation to the universe."[42]

The Work of Theology

In a 1990 colloquium at Holy Cross Centre, Berry suggested that Christianity had not yet fully accepted the scientific vision of the universe and is unable to see its religious value. Instead Christianity focuses only on its own resources. That is a lack, a problem, within Christianity itself. "If theology is not itself in a healthy situation, how can theology contribute to healing the larger culture in our present, disturbed situation? . . . The difficulty is that theology, in its fidelity to the past, has isolated itself from the larger community of life and existence in the presence. It was not always this way."[43]

Berry celebrates the significant creative work of Augustine in relating Christianity to the dominant philosophy of his day as in, for example, *City of God*. Berry has a high respect for what Thomas Aquinas accomplished in the writing of a comprehensive theology in relation to Aristotle. Berry honors the intimacy with the Earth that is found in the Christian mystical tradition as developed by those such as Hildegard of Bingen, Meister Eckhart, John of the Cross, Richard of Saint Victor. Berry argues that similar work needs to be done today to integrate theology with the insights of contemporary science.

Ecology and Theology: The Whole That I Seek for All the Children

So much of the impetus for Berry's work is his concern for the children, for all the children of the Earth. That concern resonates all the more deeply for me, now that I have two children of my own. In loving my daughters, I recognize them as gifts for which I am grateful to God. I regard them as something created by God; as the image of God; as persons who deserve to be able to grow into the fullness of who they are; as persons of dignity and worth; as persons who are significant, valuable and valued, lovable and loved. I understand them to be part of the whole community of life that is this Earth, part of the entire evolving and developing universe that God has created. In loving them I am accepting my daughters as my responsibility—which includes but is not limited to teaching them what I love and value, my sense of justice, my convictions of how we are to be and live in the world; being consistent between what I say or teach and how I live and act in the world; delighting in their wonder and their way of "running out into the world," as Jerome Miller says, a world with no parameters, an inexhaustible world with no horizons.[44] Part of what I want to teach them is the importance of having deep relationships of love and justice with the whole of the community of life, with other human beings, and with God, and of understanding how the three are inextricably linked.

Though Berry does not help me in a direct way to deal with the human relationship with God, in no small part because he is not a theologian, Berry does affect my work in attending to these three relationships or three loves as fully, completely, and authentically as I can and as much in relationship to each other as I can. In the last fifteen years Berry has been referred to often as a "geologian," one who speaks of the Earth. He says himself that his intention is to speak across cultures, religions, and traditions.[45] The work of developing Christian theology in the direction of integration with what we know now about the nature of the universe, and in the direction of enhancing mutual human-Earth relationships, he leaves to others. Part of that work entails understanding the universe and the Earth as the primary or fundamental way in which we experience God. I think here of Jerome Miller's comments on the child:

> And the world, as the child sees it, is such that to see it is to fall immediately in love with it. . . . The glory of the world itself is what provokes the child to throw open the door to her affections. Wonder is the hinge. Running is the headlong "yes!" . . . But if this is the case, then we must say that the child who is "full of life" *receives* this fullness of life *from* the world; and her running into the world is, as it were, only her way of giving it back. . . .
>
> Insofar as the affections of the child are moved to do this, childhood is sacramental—a response to what is experienced as sacred and worthy of unreserved expenditure. . . .
>
> The joy experienced then was no conundrum. It was the natural, spontaneous response to a world that was experienced as utterly lovable.[46]

Precisely because we are fulfilled through our relationship with the universe, Berry laments what has happened to human children: "For children to live only in contact with concrete and steel and wires and machines and computers and plastics, to seldom experience any primordial reality or even to see the stars at night, is a soul deprivation that diminishes the deepest of their human experiences."[47] It is also why he frequently talks about Maria Montessori and honors her insight into what children need in their education to be able to develop intimacy with the Earth. Berry writes:

> In speaking about the education of the six-year-old child, [Maria Montessori] notes in her book, *To Educate the Human Potential*, that only when the child is able to identify its own center with the center of the universe does education really begin. For the universe, she says, "is an imposing reality." It is "an answer to all questions." "We shall walk together on this path of life, for all things are part of the universe, and are connected with each other to form one whole unity." This comprehensive context enables "the mind of the child to become centered, to stop wandering in an aimless quest for knowledge."

She observes how this experience of the universe creates in children admiration and wonder, how this enables children to unify their thinking. In this manner children learn how all things are related and how the relationship of things to one another is so close that "no matter what we touch, an atom, or a cell, we cannot explain it without knowledge of the wide universe."[48]

When Thomas Berry first began to put together the elements of his ideas regarding the universe story, after years of pondering and brooding over the plight of the planet, after years of studying the great religions of East and West, there were no religious voices speaking with him. That situation has now changed. Now many religious voices, including many Christian voices, are contributing to the theological work of responding to the ecological crisis. With Berry I strive to keep in mind that we do our work because we are dedicated: "to the children, to all the children, to the children who swim beneath the waves of the sea, to those who live in the soils of the Earth, to the children of the flowers in the meadows and the trees in the forest, to all those children who roam over the land and the winged ones who fly with the winds, to the human children too, that all the children may go together into the future in the full diversity of their regional communities."[49]

Notes

1. Unless otherwise noted, quotations pertaining to the retreat are taken from prayer sheets handed out to retreatants.

2. The Passionist order was founded in 1720 by Paul of the Cross, "who saw in the Passion of Jesus 'the greatest work of divine Love' and the revelation of the power of the Resurrection to overcome the forces of evil." Passionists have "the task of announcing to their contemporaries the love of God for each and every person shown in the passion and death of Jesus who rose victorious on Easter day." For more on the Passionist spirituality and charism, see the Passionists, St. Paul of the Cross Province, "Passionist Spirituality and Charism," accessed July 15, 2009, www.thepassionists.org/Spirituality_%26_Charism.html.

3. In 2004 I had the opportunity to visit the Maryknoll Ecological Sanctuary in the Philippines. The Maryknollers have developed their own meditative walk on the universe story, one that was inspired by Thomas Berry's work and that integrated indigenous craft and images. In 2009 the Ignatian Jesuit Centre opened a similar set of stations called Stations of the Cross.

4. Thomas Berry, *Evening Thoughts: Reflecting on Earth as Sacred Community*, ed. Mary Evelyn Tucker (San Francisco: Sierra Club Books, 2006), 21.

5. Other great works mentioned by Berry include Israel's new articulation of human experience of the divine; Rome's work to develop an ordered relation among many different Western peoples; the work in the medieval period of shaping a Christian Western world; India's development of a unique way of expressing the mutual presence of time and eternity to each other; China's creation of an elegant, human civilization; the First People of North America and their establishment of an intimate relationship with the continent. See Thomas Berry, *The Great Work: Our Way into the Future* (New York: Bell Tower, 1999), chap. 1.

6. Ibid., 3.

7. Ibid., 162.

8. Ibid., 196.

9. Thomas Berry died on June 1, 2009.

10. Ibid., 12–13.

11. Ibid., 15.

12. Thomas Berry, *Befriending the Earth: A Theology of Reconciliation between Humans and the Earth*, ed. Stephen Dunn and Anne Lonergan (Mystic, CT: Twenty-Third Publications, 1991), 143–44.

13. This history is drawn from Mary Evelyn Tucker's "An Intellectual Biography of Thomas Berry," in Berry, *Evening Thoughts*, 151–71. See also Berry, *Buddhism* (New York: Columbia University Press, 1989); Berry, *Religions of India* (New York: Columbia University Press, 1992).

14. Thomas Berry, *Five Oriental Philosophies* (Albany, NY: Magi Books, 1968), 45–46, quoted in Berry, *Evening Thoughts*, 157.

15. Tucker, "Intellectual Biography," 159.

16. Ibid.

17. Thomas Berry, "Affectivity in Classical Confucian Tradition," in *Confucian Spirituality*, vol. 1, ed. Tu Weiming and Mary Evelyn Tucker (New York: Crossroad Publishing, 2003), 1–2, quoted in Berry, *Evening Thoughts*, 160.

18. Tucker, "Intellectual Biography," 154.

19. Thomas Berry, quoted in ibid.

20. Pierre Teilhard de Chardin, *Science and Christ* (New York: Harper and Row, 1968), 193, quoted in Berry, *Evening Thoughts*, 163.

21. See Tucker, "Intellectual Biography," 165–70.

22. Thomas Berry, *The New Story: Comments on the Origin, Identification, and Transmission of Values*, Teilhard Studies 1 (Chambersburg, PA: Anima Press, 1978). A slightly revised version was included in Berry's collection of essays titled *The Dream of the Earth* (San Francisco: Sierra Club Books, 1988).

23. Berry, *Dream of the Earth*, 132.

24. Pierre Teilhard de Chardin, *The Divine Milieu* (New York: Harper and Row, 1960), 92, quoted in Berry, *Evening Thoughts*, 168.

25. See, for example, Leonardo Boff, *Ecology and Liberation: A New Paradigm* (Maryknoll, NY: Orbis Books, 1995).

26. Canadian Conference of Catholic Bishops (CCCB), Commission for Social Affairs, "You Love All That Exists . . . All Things Are Yours, God, Lover of Life: A Pastoral Letter on the Christian Ecological Imperative," October 4, 2003, www.cccb.ca/site/Files/pastoralenvironment.html; CCCB Commission for Social Affairs, "Our Relationship with the Environment: The Need for Conversion," 2008, www.cccb.ca/site/images/stories/pdf/enviro_eng.pdf. The 2008 letter was issued for the United Nations International Year of Planet Earth.

27. John Paul II, general audience, January 17, 2001, no. 4, quoted in CCCB Commission for Social Affairs, "You Love All," 3.

28. Berry, *Great Work*, 54.

29. Ibid., 163.

30. For example: "The first condition for achieving this objective [establishing the conditions for entering into a future that attends to the well-being of the entire planet] is to realize that the universe is a communion of subjects, not a collection of objects. The devastation of the planet can be seen as a direct consequence of the loss of this

capacity for human presence to and reciprocity with the nonhuman world." Berry, *Evening Thoughts*, 17–18.

31. CCCB Commission for Social Affairs, "You Love All," 2.

32. Berry, *Great Work*, 4.

33. CCCB Commission for Social Affairs, "Relationship with the Environment," 4.

34. This subsection and those that follow are drawn from Berry, *Befriending the Earth*. This book is based on a colloquium that took place at the Holy Cross Centre for Ecology and Spirituality in 1990, in which Thomas Berry was in conversation with Thomas Clarke.

35. Ibid., 6–7.

36. Berry often points out that our sense of the divine is related to the fact that we live on this magnificent planet. If we lived on the moon, our sense of the divine would be meager.

37. "Revelation is the awakening in the depth of human psychic awareness of a sense of ultimate mystery and how ultimate mystery communicates itself." Ibid., 7.

38. Ibid., 7.

39. Ibid., 14–15.

40. Ibid., 23.

41. Pierre Teilhard de Chardin, quoted in Berry, *Befriending the Earth*, 24.

42. Ibid., 25.

43. Ibid., 27.

44. Jerome Miller, "Joy and Gravity: A Meditation on the Will to Live," *Second Opinion* 20, no. 1 (July): 57–69.

45. "I wish to address myself to people of any belief, so I try to use words that make sense to everybody. In my writings generally, I am concerned primarily with the larger society." Berry, *Befriending the Earth*, 10.

46. Miller, "Joy and Gravity," 59, 60. In an earlier period of human history, "whatever humans needed was supplied by the surrounding world. . . . This joyful fulfillment found expression in poetry and music and song and dance, a fulfillment that continues to find expression in our children running through the meadows, wading in the creeks, playing with animals, or simply sitting with utmost satisfaction in a backyard puddle experiencing the cooling delight of such an environment on a summer's day. Such is the beginning of education, of aesthetic experience, of physical vigor, of acquaintance with the universe. This is the awakening of both the senses and the mind. Ultimately it is the awakening of the universe to itself." Berry, *Evening Thoughts*, 118.

47. Berry, *Great Work*, 82.

48. Ibid., 16, quoting Maria Montessori, *To Educate the Human Potential* (Oxford, UK: Clio Press, 1948), 6. See also Berry, *Evening Thoughts*, 119–21.

49. Berry, *Great Work*, dedication.

Epilogue

These twelve essays have several things in common. For one, they are eminently original. The authors have plumbed their inimitable subjectivities in ways that make them accessible to the reader. This volume is a case of the multiplication of the loaves or, to mix metaphors, an instance of what can be produced when a haunting is moved by a hunting that can locate its catch with words. I read these authors through a theological lens and do so unapologetically. So I see their haunted hunting representing twelve unique cuts into the catholicity of the mind and its fecundity when it allows the elasticity of the spirit full play.

Rather than settling for simply being "true to the faith," all of these chapters forage beyond the initial faith their authors learned. Reason pushed them out in twelve different directions. Their forays could have had them evolve into being post-Christian or postmodern or just plain post wherever they were before they started. But they have made synthetic wholes of what would otherwise have been just an additional story built onto their individual habitats.

It is one thing to continually appropriate one's faith as one evolves and matures. It is another thing to break camp and go out into a no-man's-land to try to bring something back that contributes to the development of faith. Why is this a good? Because *Deus semper major*. God is always greater! Foraging can of course be egoistical or ignorant or needlessly restless. But some of foraging can be charismed. When this is the case, the foragers are graced to contribute to the "more" by trying to be true to what is distinctively given to them for others. "To each a manifestation of the Spirit is given for the common good" (1 Cor. 12:7).

Each generation, wittingly or unwittingly, hands on some version of its faiths to the next generation. This passing-on can be lazy, meaning the generation hands on the faith clothed in the same worn, tired clothing in which it was received. That kind of transmission does not do justice to a living faith. A better scenario would involve handing on what has been confected through the hard work of deconstruction and reconstruction.

There are syntheses here expecting, encouraging, and coaxing further syntheses out into the distant future. I see these chapters as forays in the Catholic intellectual tradition, as that phenomenon was described and analyzed in *Where Is Knowing Going?*[1] The thesis there was that the Catholic doctrinal tradition is continually freshened by developments within an intellectual tradition generated by an authentic subjectivity, as that moves in the direction of an objectivity in one's area of competence, whether that be academic or by self-appropriation.

Note

1. John C. Haughey, *Where Is Knowing Going? The Horizons of the Knowing Subject* (Washington, DC: Georgetown University Press, 2009).

Contributors

Michael Amaladoss is a Jesuit from south India whose PhD is from the Catholic Institute of Paris. He also has a degree in south Indian classical music and is a composer. He has served as director of the Institute for Dialogue with Cultures and Religions in Chennai, India; professor at Vidyajyoti College of Theology in Delhi; president of the International Association for Mission Studies; consultor to the Vatican and the World Council of Churches; and general assistant to the superior general of the Society of Jesus in Rome. He has taught theology in Delhi, Manila, Rome, Paris, Brussels, and Washington, DC. He has written twenty-five books, more than 370 articles, and numerous musical compositions. His latest books are *The Asian Jesus*; *Making Harmony: Living in a Pluralistic World*; *The Dancing Cosmos*; and *Beyond Dialogue: Pilgrims to the Absolute.*

Patrick H. Byrne has a bachelor's degree in physics, a master's degree in philosophy from Boston College, and a doctorate in philosophy from the State University of New York at Stony Brook. He is currently professor and chair of philosophy at Boston College. Recent books include *The Dialogue between Science and Religion: What We Have Learned from One Another* and *Analysis and Science in Aristotle*. Recent articles include "Lonergan, Evolutionary Science, and Intelligent Design," published in *Revista Portuguesa de Filosofia: Special Edition—Bernard Lonergan and Philosophy*; "Evolution, Randomness and Divine Purpose: A Reply to Cardinal Schönborn," published in *Theological Studies*; and "The Goodness of Being in Lonergan's *Insight*," published in *American Catholic Philosophical Quarterly*. He is currently working on a book about Bernard Lonergan's ethics.

Cynthia Crysdale has her bachelor's degree in psychology from York University in Toronto, Canada, and her master's and doctoral degrees in theology from St. Michael's College in the University of Toronto. After teaching for eighteen years at The Catholic University of America, she is now professor of Christian ethics and theology in the School of Theology at the University of the South, Sewanee, Tennessee. She specializes in foundational theology and ethics, with an expertise on the work of Bernard Lonergan. Dr. Crysdale has authored *Embracing Travail: Retrieving the Cross Today* and edited *Lonergan and Feminism*. She has also written numerous articles appearing in the *Journal of the Society of Christian Ethics*, *Theoforum*, *Cross Currents*, and *Theological Studies*.

Robert J. Deahl has his bachelor's degree in theology and philosophy from St. Francis Seminary College in Milwaukee, Wisconsin, and a licentiate and doctorate in sacred theology from the Pontifical Gregorian University in Rome. He has also studied and worked in Paris, Jerusalem, Calcutta, and Cape Town, South Africa. Dr. Deahl has been the dean of Marquette University's College of Professional Studies since its inception in 1994. His teaching focuses on the dynamics of leadership, ethics, and organizational systems. In addition, his academic and professional work focuses on adult learning pedagogy and programming.

Ilia Delio, a member of the Franciscan order, holds a doctorate in pharmacology from the University of Medicine and Dentistry of the New Jersey Graduate School of Biomedical Sciences, as well as a doctorate in historical theology from Fordham University. She has served as chair and professor in the Department of Spirituality Studies at the Washington Theological Union, and as director of the Franciscan Center at the Washington Theological Union. She was on the board of directors of Metanexus; on the advisory board of the Dialogue on Sciences, Ethics, and Religion of the American Association for the Advancement of Science; and on the editorial board of *New Theology Review*. In 2000 she received the Templeton Course Award in Science and Religion. She is a senior research fellow at the Woodstock Theological Center at Georgetown University in Washington, DC. Her latest books include *Christ in Evolution*; *Care for Creation: A Franciscan Spirituality of the Earth*; *Clare of Assisi: A Heart Full of Love*; and *Franciscan Prayer*.

William P. George received his PhD from the University of Chicago Divinity School, his MDiv from Weston School of Theology, and his MA and PhL from Gonzaga University. He is currently an associate professor of theology at Dominican University in River Forest, Illinois, where he also serves as director of the undergraduate core curriculum. His numerous articles and reviews in journals and magazines cover such topics as religion and international relations, gun violence, undergraduate education, global ethics, and concern for future generations. With particular reliance on the thought of Bernard Lonergan, his main research focus centers on the intersection between theology and international law.

Patrick A. Heelan, an Irish Jesuit, has a doctorate in philosophy from the University of Leuven in Belgium and a doctorate in geophysics from Saint Louis University. He taught for many years at the State University of New York at Stony Brook, where he also filled several major administrative positions. He moved to Georgetown University in 1992 as executive vice president for the main campus, and he became the William A. Gaston Professor of Philosophy in 1995. His major interest in philosophy lies in perception and quantum measurement and in the phenomenological, cultural, and religious dimensions of science. A member of the New York Academy of Sciences, he participates in many national and international conferences on the philosophy of modern physics, cognitive science, and embodied human consciousness.

Richard M. Liddy received his doctorate at Gregorian University in Rome. He is the director of the Center for Catholic Studies and the Bernard J. Lonergan Institute at Seton Hall University. At Seton Hall he has been a professor of religious studies, has served as acting chancellor, and was rector of the Immaculate Conception Seminary School of Theology. He also served as spiritual director of the North American College in Rome and senior fellow at the Woodstock Theological Center at Georgetown University in Washington, DC. In 1993 he published *Transforming Light: Intellectual Conversion in the Early Lonergan*; and in 2006 he published *Startling Strangeness: Reading Lonergan's Insight*, which focuses on his encounter with Bernard Lonergan as Lonergan's student in Rome in the 1960s.

Michael McCarthy received his AB from the University of Notre Dame and his master's degree and PhD from Yale. He taught philosophy for thirty-eight years at Vassar College before retiring from teaching in 2007. He has been a visiting fellow at the Woodstock Theological Center at Georgetown University and a Lonergan Fellow at Boston College. Dr. McCarthy has lectured broadly in the United States, Canada, Peru, and Rome on both Hannah Arendt and Bernard Lonergan. He has published three books, and his scholarly work has appeared in the *Review of Metaphysics, Soundings, Method,* and journals in Sweden and Peru. Since retiring from teaching, Dr. McCarthy is actively engaged as a thinker, writer, and scholar who also writes poetry as a form of prayer and interpersonal communication. He is currently working on a collection of critical essays titled *Objective Knowing and Authentic Living: The Enduring Achievement of Bernard Lonergan*.

J. Michael Stebbins received his BA in philosophy from Gonzaga University, his BSN from the University of Washington, and his PhD from Boston College, with areas of specialization in systematic theology and Christian ethics. He taught for several years at Boston College and was a visiting assistant professor at Gonzaga University. As a senior fellow at the Woodstock Theological Center, Dr. Stebbins directed the Arrupe Program in Social Ethics for Business and authored *Faith and Values at Work: A Seminar in Spiritual and Ethical Integration for Executives and Managers.* He was director of the Gonzaga Institute of Ethics at Gonzaga University and is currently president of inVia, Inc. He has published several scholarly papers and book reviews and facilitated many workshops and retreats throughout the United States and Canada.

Peter Steele is an Australian Jesuit who holds an MA and a PhD from the University of Melbourne, where he has taught for many years and holds a chair. He has been a visiting professor at the University of Alberta, Loyola University Chicago, Fordham University, and Georgetown University. For five years he was the provincial superior of the Jesuits in Australia. Along with having had broad administrative and educational responsibilities within Australia and in East Asia, he is widely published as a poet, with his religious insights forming the basis of his poetic, academic, and ethical imagination. His six poetry books include two that are prompted by works of art. He has also published a book of homilies and many articles on the secular and the sacred.

Cristina Vanin received her BA from St. Jerome's University, her MDiv from the University of St. Michael's College, and her PhD from Boston College. She is an associate professor of theology and ethics in the Department of Religious Studies, associate dean, and director of the Master of Catholic Thought program at St. Jerome's University in Waterloo, Ontario. Her areas of research include ecotheology, feminist theologies, and Christian ethics, as well as the thought of Thomas Berry and Bernard Lonergan. Her most recent publication is "Canadian Women's Religious Communities: Models of Contextual Ecological Justice," in *Feminist Theology with a Canadian Accent*, edited by M. A. Beavis with E. Guillemin and B. Pell (Montreal: Novalis, 2008).

Index